UTAH CONSTRUCTION
& MINING CO.

Utah International

A Biography of a Business

Utah International

A Biography of a Business

Gene A. Sessions

Sterling D. Sessions

A Commemorative Edition
published by
Weber State University
and the
Stewart Library

2002

To those who worked for Utah International

Printed by Publishers Printing in Salt Lake City, Utah.

Commemorative Edition published in 2002 by Weber State University and the Stewart Library, Ogden, Utah 84408.

All photographs and maps, unless otherwise credited, are part of the Utah Construction/Utah International Collection, Stewart Library Special Collections, Weber State University.

Book and cover design by Richard Firmage.

Includes bibliographical references and index.

First Edition ISBN 0-9722102-0-2

Front dust jacket and frontispiece photograph: This image of worker, machine, and mass was captured by a company photographer, circa 1975, at the Shirley Basin site of the Lucky Mc uranium mines in Wyoming.

Contents

Publisher's note: In 1900 The Utah Construction Company incorporated in Ogden, Utah. In 1959 the company changed its name to Utah Construction & Mining and, in 1971, to Utah International Incorporated. Capitalizing "The" gradually became passé and, in common parlance, the name "Utah" was most often used, meaning the company and not the state. For the ease of the reader, the company name is standardized throughout this text, reflecting the appropriate era. Other spelling and punctuation used in company records are also standardized except within direct quotations.

Preface

THIS MANUSCRIPT HAS ITS ROOTS in a talk I was asked to give in January 1976 before the Weber County (Utah) Historical Society on a prominent company that had been founded locally. Since I had recently joined the faculty at Weber State University (then Weber State College) as business school dean, I accepted the invitation and considered it an opportunity to become more familiar with the business community.

I selected Utah Construction Company, now Utah International, Inc., as my subject. Although this company had been founded in Ogden in early 1900, I found little about it except for a few articles in *Fortune* magazine, *Business Week,* and the *Wall Street Journal* along with a chapter in the book *The Earth Changers* by Neil C. Wilson and Frank J. Taylor. Coincidentally, a friend in San Francisco, Joseph K. Allen, was a vice president at Utah International. I called and asked for his help. Not long after, I visited him and returned with pages of notes, copies of reports, and other materials that gave me a glimpse into the international scope of this originally local company.

This modest research effort ended in a twenty-nine-page speech to the members of the historical society. Some time afterwards, I received a letter from Edmund Wattis Littlefield, president, CEO, and chairman of the board of Utah International, Inc., in San Francisco. He had received a copy of the talk and found it informative, particularly in revealing hitherto unpublished facts about the company; but the text contained some errors. As a result of our correspondence, I visited him in San Francisco in March 1976. Rather optimistically, I suggested that I write the company history (a type of project I had never undertaken before). He agreed and gave me access to every document in the company files, in addition to facilitating interviews with every senior officer still associated with the company. He also made himself completely available. His sole condition was one about which I had misgivings. He insisted on being the final arbiter on any material written for the general public. However, the only time he ever exercised this prerogative was in withholding a single page in the corporate board minutes. It contained a strategic statement for entering a particular country.

Given this mandate and support, I devoted several months to reading and digesting seventy-six years of monthly board meeting minutes and annual shareholder meeting minutes, information which would constitute the factual spine of the story. I was amused by the picturesqueness of the early minutes. For example, at one point the company's assets included a numerical count of its horse collars and spittoons. Similarly, unpopular personnel decisions were recorded with little heed to the litigious potential of such straight talk.

Once this foundational research was in place, I branched out. I conducted interviews with scores of founding family members, their friends, and retired employees. I spent a great deal of time with Ed Littlefield, who, representing the third generation of family leadership, held a phenomenal grasp of the company's history and evolution. During Utah's fifty years as a small firm, it engaged in such landmark engineering/construction projects of the twentieth century as Hoover Dam and the Alcan Highway. From there, it went on to become a multinational success story in mining and construction. Utah's people shared with me numerous historic and contemporary journals and correspondence, adding color and personal interest to what might otherwise have been an honest-but-dull, celebratory recitation of company facts and accomplishments. The goal was to create a one-volume record of the company's numerous projects that would be interesting for the casual reader, educational for the student of American business, and helpful in pointing more serious scholars toward deeper documentary resources.

I drafted a few chapters, which Littlefield approved; but the magnitude of the project, which I was doing in evenings and weekends, soon convinced me that a collaboration would be fruitful. I asked Gene Sessions (no relation), a professor of history at Weber State and the author or editor of several books, to join me. He agreed; and we made research trips to San Francisco delving into detailed project histories, internal publications, and other material from the firm's archives. Gene undertook the laborious task of constructing the history of the company, from its earliest days until 1976, when Utah International merged with General Electric, from the perspective of a professional historian. Next, Ed Littlefield, who remained devoted and indefatigable throughout this effort, James T. (Jim) Curry, former CEO of Utah Development, Co., and I went over this historical document to add a business perspective. Gene then performed the final polishing of the manuscript.

Finding a form to reflect the scope of Utah's activities was a major challenge. A chronological approach worked well when we described the company's early years; but its rapid diversification into a variety of fields and the major projects it generated—each of which had its own life cycle—was more difficult. Constructing the Hoover Dam was a comparatively brief project, but other major activities such as the Navajo Coal Mine (the nation's largest), mining iron ore in Peru, building up one of the world's largest fleets of transport ships, and developing its iron ore and coking coal mines in Australia spanned decades. A chronological approach would have yielded chapters resembling six-layer sandwiches, but a thematic approach meant repetition and recapitulation. After some experimentation, we settled on a combination of both chronological and thematic approaches. It was evident that Utah International's significant record, especially during the latter half of the twentieth century, reflected the expertise of a senior management team skilled in making decisions under uncertainty. Naturally, the firm stumbled from time to time, but even such "failures" are instructive for the student of business. As Arjay Miller, former vice chair of Ford Motor Company and a member of Utah's board of directors, commented, "No other firm, to my knowledge, has so successfully shifted from one major business [construction] to another [mining] so smoothly and with such an outpouring of net operating profits."

Utah International: A Biography of a Business tells about this transformation from horse collars to gigantic earth-moving machines. Like biographies of individuals, it does not cover everything the company did; that would fill volumes. Instead, it rehearses essential components of the story of building and maintaining an extremely profitable business enterprise, which served its employees, customers, and communities with care and concern, all the while scrupulously preserving an untarnished reputation for ethical and honest dealings. On all three of these counts, Utah was a rarity among the companies I've known.

Sterling D. Sessions

Acknowledgments

A pleasant challenge lies before us to acknowledge those many people who graciously provided information and encouragement over the course of twenty-five years. Fortunately, copies of thank you letters have been kept, which blunt the risks of being inaccurate. Where to begin in recognizing these people involves either an assembly by importance of person and contribution, or a chronological arrangement that skirts the possibility of offending someone without intending to. We've adopted the latter.

Once the in-depth research began on the history of the firm, many persons assisted with obtaining significant amounts of information including Joseph K. Allen of Utah International; Zeke R. Dumke; Donnell B. Stewart; Thomas D. (Tommy) Dee II, a grandson of Thomas Duncombe Dee and a Utah director; Lawrence T. Dee, father of Tommy and also a Utah director; Murray Moler of the *Ogden Standard Examiner*; Ernest C. Arbuckle, chairman of Wells Fargo Bank; and Arjay Miller, former dean of the Stanford Business School. Jim Curry, in particular, devoted several months to assure the accuracy of the account.

Bruce T. Mitchell, Utah's senior counsel and secretary, opened the board meeting and shareholder's meeting minutes, an account which provided an extraordinarily helpful amount of instruction and enlightenment in being able to understand why Utah was so successful. Utah's vice presidents, as sources, included Drew Leonard, who answered our every question on financial and accounting matters; Weston Bourret, who provided considerable insight on mineral explorations; and Johnny Horrigan and Charles Travers for their respective contributions in financial management and commercial land development matters. Deborah Haynes, editor of *Utah Report,* Mary L. Murphy, and Jerry McWilliams were most helpful in leading us through Utah's extensive archival holdings. Bonnie Predney, Ed Littlefield's executive secretary in recent years, always came through with requested information.

Finally, A. M. (Bud) Wilson, president of Utah following Littlefield, assembled a group of senior executives to discuss their careers with Utah International, including their comments on the firm's construction and mining projects over the years. We appreciate his courtesy in making this forum a vital source of facts and viewpoints.

Nedra Bachman of Weber State University transcribed all of the notes prepared from the board minutes and all of the tapes made from many oral interviews, a tedious task for which our sincere appreciation is extended. Dorothy Bowman Hetzel loaned many newspaper accounts about the Utah Construction Company and, in particular, about W. H. Wattis. Patricia McNamara shared documents and letters, which have become an integral part of the history, as did her sister, Helen Jarman. The family members of Mattie Wattis Harris have been instrumental in providing articles and photographs concerning Edmund Orson Wattis. Edna Wattis Dumke, with Barbara Browning's assistance, recounted a number of experiences from the days with her father, E. O. Wattis. Earl Corey, a grandson of Warren W. Corey, painted a vital and lively picture of the Corey family members from numerous diaries, newspaper accounts, and journals, for which he will not be forgotten.

Many people have been most encouraging and informative concerning book publishing and book merchandising, including Dr. Susan Sessions Rugh of Brigham Young University and Sam Weller of Sam Weller Bookstores. To Lavina Fielding Anderson goes our appreciation for her many years of editorial devotion to the story: she really made a difference.

The authors owe their deep appreciation to three exceptional scholars who joined the effort in its early stages by writing first drafts of three of the topical chapters. Dr. Rex J. Casillas, then of Penn State University–Behrend College, produced a groundbreaking version of the Marcona/Peru chapter that brought that complicated story into immediate focus. Similarly Dr. Richard Waters, at that time studying at the University of New Mexico, provided a wonderfully insightful account of the Navajo Mine that facilitated immeasurably work toward the final draft of that chapter. Written work on Australia began with the labors of Roger Kent Petersen, who did a marvelous job of sorting out all the research materials the authors provided him and drawing them into a single essay from which the final version of that chapter developed.

During the long course of the project, many wonderful people did so many "little things" that were really big things in the final analysis. Among those who lent able hands to such tasks were Cheryl Brown, Matt Schoss, Jack Valletta, Steve Starks, Kimberly Nielsen, Julie Jenkins, Shantal Hiatt, the late Jerry Bernstein, Shaunna Burbidge, LaRee Keller, Kay Brown, and Dorothy Draney. As with all projects of this magnitude, there were many others. In the end, however, the authors bear the full weight of responsibility for whatever weaknesses or inaccuracies this volume may possess.

The City of Ogden was a bustling metropolis and rail center by the time Utah became the forty-fifth state in January 1896. Pictured is the first Independence Day celebration after statehood.

Introduction

by Thomas G. Alexander

In a moment of insight, the noted Austrian economist Joseph Schumpeter called entrepreneurs "creative destroyers." That designation seems especially appropriate for officers of Utah International, whose principal business consisted of altering the land through such earth-gouging projects as grading railroad beds, building high dams, and stripping coal and iron. Employees of the company took landscapes—many virtually unmarred by previous human activity—and transformed them into built environments from which they supplied goods and services to customers throughout the world.

In this book, Gene Sessions and Sterling Sessions recount the story of Utah International's entrepreneurs and managers. Above all, this is the story of how two entrepreneurs, Edmund Wattis Littlefield and Marriner Stoddard Eccles, transformed the company incorporated in 1900 by Wattis brothers Edmund Orson, William Henry, and Warren Lafayette into the largest and most profitable mining company in the United States. The brothers founded the company to excavate and grade railroad beds, but by the 1970s, the company had abandoned the construction business entirely.

Since this book chronicles the work of entrepreneurs, with few exceptions it does not detail the daily life of the laborers who sweated over the picks, shovels, and scrapers of the early years or piloted the drag lines, dump trucks, and cement buckets of more recent times. The construction workers and miners will undoubtedly serve as subjects for other works. Fortunately, historians interested in these people will find ample grist for that mill in the collection of Utah International papers housed at the Stewart Library at Weber State University.

With the possible exception of Huntsman Corporation, First Security Bank, and Zions Bank, Utah International may be the most successful of those interstate companies organized, owned, and managed over a long period of time by Utahns. Like WordPerfect, ZCMI, and First Security, the last a company that descendants of the David Eccles family also managed, Utah International, for strategic and financial reasons, negotiated a merger with a larger multinational corporation.

Other companies organized by Utahns have taken different management directions. Unlike Utah International and First Security, a number of such companies have remained under Utah management. These include Zions Bank, Huntsman Corporation, and Evans and Sutherland. Some of these are, of course, public corporations with shares traded on national exchanges.

Other Utah companies have had diverse and often checkered histories. Many of the earliest of Utah's home-grown companies, such as the Brigham Young Express and Carrying Company, the Deseret Manufacturing (sugar) Company, and the Deseret Iron Company, failed shortly after their organization. Others like the Provo Woolen Mills, McCornick Bank, and Consolidated Wagon and Machine operated for decades then failed, apparently because their managers could not meet the demands of changing economic conditions. Some, including Utah Power and Light, Utah-Idaho Sugar, and Utah Copper, had their origins on Utah soil within a decade and a half of Utah International, but were rapidly acquired by outside owners, generally because of a need for sustained capital.

Although Utah International moved its headquarters from Ogden to San Francisco, it remained under the majority ownership of the descendants of the original incorporators until 1976 when the stockholders agreed to sell the company to General Electric. Prior to that sale, again as part of long-range strategic planning, in 1969 the company's management took the company public and offered its shares on the New York Stock Exchange.

The company has an extremely interesting background.

Descended from English converts to Mormonism, the Wattis brothers started working in construction in the late nineteenth century. At first the Wattis boys worked for Corey Brothers, a company owned by their uncles. In 1900, they purchased the assets of the uncles' business and incorporated as Utah Construction Company. Seeking additional capital, the Wattis brothers secured investments in the company from a number of Ogden entrepreneurs and bankers such as David Eccles, Thomas Dee, and James Pingree, all of whom were involved in the incorporation from the beginning. In fact, David Eccles, Marriner Eccles's father, was the company's largest single stockholder.

During the first decades of the twentieth century, although Utah Construction specialized in building railroads, the company also began constructing dams and other irrigation works. The officers negotiated contracts with railroads such as Denver and Rio Grande Western, Union Pacific, and Western Pacific, which at its completion in 1911 was probably the last of the transcontinental railways. In 1914 the company began to diversify by taking contracts to construct dams. Building railroads and dams took it throughout the states of the American West, and in 1923 it took its first international contract by building a railroad for Southern Pacific's Mexican subsidiary.

The Wattises planned and fulfilled these early contracts by rule-of-thumb figuring and fabrication. Not until 1920 did the company hire its first engineer. In building the railroads and structures, the company used human, horse, and steam power until 1927 when it began to employ machines powered by internal combustion engines.

Although Utah Construction had undertaken projects on joint agreements with companies such as Morrison Knudsen of Boise, in 1930 it launched a joint venture that hastened its rise to international prominence. In that year, W. H. Wattis put together a consortium called Six Companies to construct Hoover Dam, perhaps the largest public works project in the western United States to that time. In addition to Utah Construction, the consortium included such important western companies as Kaiser, Bechtel, Morrison Knudsen, Pacific Bridge, and McDonald & Kahn. The Six Companies' bid of $48.9 million was $5 million lower than the next lowest offer, and industry analysts predicted they would lose their shirts on the contract. In fact, through creative management and skilled workers, Six Companies realized a profit of $10.4 million or 21 percent of the bid price.

During the 1930–40s, Utah Construction entered into joint agreements with many of its Six Companies partners as well as with other companies in what was undoubtedly the most dynamic period of public works enterprises in the United States to that time. The company helped construct such works as the Oakland Bay Bridge, Bonneville Dam, Grand Coolee Dam, Parker Dam, the All American Canal, the Delaware Aqueduct, and dams for the Tennessee Valley Authority. After the outbreak of World War II, Utah Construction built ships, constructed bases, fabricated docks and storage facilities, and laid down highways throughout the American West and in the Pacific Theater of Operations.

Before the completion of Hoover Dam, E. O. and W. H. Wattis both died, and the company's leadership had passed to Marriner Eccles as president and Lester S. Corey as vice president and general manager. Corey had come up through the ranks of Utah Construction, while Eccles, who joined the company's board of directors in 1921, had engaged in a diverse range of businesses such as banking, sugar refining, and real estate development. After assuming the presidency and vice presidency in 1931, Corey became president and general manager in 1940 and Eccles became chairman of the board.

Corey is virtually unknown to students of American history, but Eccles may well be the most important Utah-born business leader of the twentieth century. After Eccles and his brother, George S. Eccles, saved the predecessor of First Security Bank from failure in the early years of the Great Depression, Marriner envisioned the role of the Federal Reserve System and the national government as prime movers during such times of economic crisis. By contrast, during the depression of the early 1890s, President Grover Cleveland anticipated no role for government in economic downturns except balancing the budget. He said that although the people should support the government, the government should not support the people. Moreover, in what in retrospect seem both counter-productive and destructive policy decisions, the Federal

Reserve Board actually stalled economic recovery during the depression of 1919–21 and the Great Depression by contracting the money supply. Federal Reserve Board members feared inflation!

Eccles, on the other hand, believed that the government should provide mechanisms for guaranteeing the stability of the banking and monetary systems and that the federal government should finance projects to compensate for the failure of the private sector to provide full employment. Although many economists credit John Maynard Keynes with originating the idea of compensatory governmental spending, Eccles came independently to the same conclusions, and he had a decisive influence on policy during the New Deal in spite of opposition to many of his ideas from Treasury Secretary Henry Morganthau. Eccles moved to Washington and helped to draft the Emergency Banking Act of 1933, the Federal Deposit Insurance Act of 1933, the Federal Housing Act of 1934, and the Federal Banking Act of 1935. These acts created the modern federal reserve and deposit insurance systems, and helped revive home construction. In recognition of Eccles's ability and service, President Franklin Roosevelt appointed him to the chairmanship of the board of governors of the Federal Reserve System, a position he held for seventeen years. Continuing in his efforts to promote compensatory government spending, Eccles convinced Roosevelt to help cushion the impact of the recession of 1937–38, and after World War II he helped organize the World Bank, the International Monetary Fund, and the Export-Import Bank.

As Eccles worked in saving the nation from economic disaster, he also exercised his extraordinary executive skills on behalf of Utah Construction. As often happens in closely owned companies, some family members thought that the business ought to provide them with jobs and management positions regardless of their level of business acumen. Recognizing this as an invitation to disaster, Eccles and his supporters resisted these efforts, and the resulting internal feud led members of the W. H. Wattis family to sell their stock. The Browning family and others secured stock at that time.

As chairman of the board, Eccles moved aggressively to hire and keep active and creative entrepreneurs in company leadership positions. In 1951 the board appointed Allen D. Christensen as executive vice president and general manager. Christensen moved

Utah Construction aggressively into mining ventures, a number of which the company had already undertaken during the 1940s. In 1951 the directors also hired Edmund Littlefield as financial vice president. Littlefield, though a young man, had already made a distinguished career for himself in the petroleum and milk processing businesses, and he joined Utah Construction only after the board agreed to grant him an independent hand in managing the company's financial affairs.

After Littlefield spent seven successful years in administering the company's finances, in 1958 the directors named him executive vice president and general manager. Littlefield managed the company quite differently from Christensen. Where Christensen tended to keep colleagues and the board in the dark about both plans and results, Littlefield insisted on openness with all of his associates.

In 1959, under Littlefield's direction, the company moved its corporate headquarters to San Francisco where it had operated a subsidiary office since early in the century. From its San Francisco offices, the company moved aggressively to construct and mine throughout the world, generally in collaboration with other firms. Construction projects included Minuteman silos in Wyoming, Colorado, and Nebraska and irrigation works in Bangladesh, India, and Australia. Mining operations included uranium oxide in Wyoming, iron in Peru and Australia, and coal on the Navajo Reservation.

Eventually, after finally tiring of the uncertainties associated with construction projects, Littlefield and the other company officers agreed to abandon that part of the business. Construction had always carried a heavy risk, but during the 1960s the company's construction profits shrank while its mining profits grew. After taking measures to revive the income from construction, Littlefield negotiated the sale of that part of the business to Fluor Utah Engineers & Constructors.

Still, the company continued to increase its mining activities. In 1976 the company, renamed Utah International in 1971, ranked first among United States mining companies in earnings and first in market value of its shares. In 1976 the company merged with General Electric.

What follows, then, is a story of creative destruction well told by Gene Sessions and Sterling Sessions.

Thomas G. Alexander
Brigham Young University

Utah International

A Biography of a Business

Section I

Utah Construction Company

The town of Uintah, west of Weber Canyon, was closely bypassed by track laid by the Union Pacific Railroad in 1869. (Photograph courtesy of W. Dee Halverson)

Chapter 1

Enterprising Young Men

WITH THE END of the Mexican War in 1848, the United States almost instantly acquired a vast new domain stretching from Texas on the east to the shores of the Pacific. By treaty with Mexico and Great Britain, the map of the great American West suddenly unrolled before an expansive nation. The curtain had opened on the most rambunctious conquest of undeveloped territory in the history of the world. Then, during that same year, news spread eastward of the discovery of gold in California. Over the next two years, some 100,000 adventurers flooded across the Great Plains in search of Eldorado. While the promise of easy riches eluded the large majority of them, they nevertheless formed a firm cornerstone in the building of the West. Among the first of these eager pilgrims was a twenty-one-year-old Englishman named Edmund Orson Wattis. Although he found only danger in the gold fields, his frontier journey marked the beginnings of one of the great stories in the annals of American enterprise.

Wattis was born in London on January 20, 1828, and died in Uintah, Utah, sixty-three years later, on April 2, 1891. When he was twelve years old, his family converted to the Church of Jesus Christ of Latter-day Saints through the efforts of Mormon apostle (and later church president) Wilford Woodruff. In November 1841 Edmund, his older brother John, and his parents, Edmund and Hannah Compton Wattis, left their comfortable home and considerable parcel of land in Alfrick, Worcestershire, boarded the ship *Chaos,* and sailed to New Orleans. From there they took a river boat up the Mississippi to Nauvoo, Illinois, the latest gathering place of the westering Mormons. In 1844 young Edmund's father fell victim to cholera and died. A year later, Hannah married Elam Cheney, twenty years her junior, to whom she soon bore a daughter. Shortly thereafter, the family joined the first wave of Mormon pioneers trekking one thousand miles across the Great Plains to their new Zion in the Great Salt Lake Valley.

Arriving in Utah in October 1847, Edmund spent two years helping to establish the new Mormon refuge at Salt Lake City. Family tradition maintains that Brigham Young called on him to join a party of two dozen men, headed by Amasa Lyman and Orrin Porter Rockwell, to collect the "tithes and offerings" of the gold field missionaries, whom Young had sent to California in hopes of bolstering the struggling Mormon economy. Edmund's errand to collect these tithes became the stuff of family legend:

> They had been dogged by Indians for over 400 miles. En route they were attacked several times, but were successful in repelling each skirmish. As the party approached the halfway point to Sutter's Fort, they came upon a white man being pursued by a small band of ferocious Indians. The man was severely wounded with arrows, but was able to outrun his pursuers. Later [the wounded man] told how three other men in his group were overtaken and scalped.

After a wealth of similar adventures, Wattis returned to Utah where his family had moved north to Uintah at the mouth of Weber Canyon near present-day Ogden. Joining them there, he applied himself to farming, successfully coaxing a living from the rocky ground despite an arid climate and harsh winters. Thus established, Edmund married seventeen-year-old Mary Jane Corey on June 27, 1852. Their union produced seven children, arriving at two-year intervals beginning in 1853. The firstborn was Mary Jane, followed by three boys, Edmund Orson, Jr. (born March 6, 1855), George Lyman, and William Henry (born August 14, 1859). Next came another daughter, Eunice Elvira, and two more boys, Frank Archie, who died in childhood, and Warren Lafayette.

Edmund quickly learned that he had married not only Mary Jane but also the gregarious and dynamic Corey family. Her brothers, George Lyman, Warren Wright, Charles Joseph, and Amos Bonesteel Corey were ambitious, iron-willed, and enterprising young men. Characterizing his grandfather Warren years later, Earl Corey would remember that the old man possessed "a pretty strong, stubborn character. If he fell in the river, you'd look for him upstream." As a frontier mother, Mary Jane also commonly displayed the indomitable Corey spirit. On one occasion, she captured and skinned a stray cat, then turned his hide into a pair of shoes for William Henry (W. H.)—his first foot coverings.

The rigors of the family farm provided the Wattis children with no luxuries and little free time, but their parents insisted on education. Itinerant teachers, who seldom spent as long as six months in town, favored the *McGuffey Readers* series and *Smith's New Grammar*. E. O., the eldest son, remembered the exceptional teaching skills of Louis Frederick Moench, who later helped found what would become Weber State University in Ogden. Farm chores, however, led to the development of more practical skills. By the age of eleven, E. O. could plow with a team of oxen as well as any grown

Edmund Orson Wattis and Mary Jane Corey, whose families settled in northern Utah, married in 1852. They are pictured here around 1860. (Courtesy of W. Dee Halverson)

man, but he also nurtured an enterprising spirit and dreamed of life beyond the farm. His chance came when the great transcontinental railroad passed virtually through the Wattis front yard.

The Union Pacific Railroad, on its way to a historic rendezvous with the Central Pacific at Promontory Summit, Utah, in May 1869, was laying track from South Pass, Wyoming, through Weber Canyon. Contractor William Miller from Provo, Utah, had secured a grading contract to help prepare the way for Irish spikers who were stringing rails from Granger down the tortuous canyon to Ogden. Though only twelve years of age, E. O. persuaded his parents to let him take his ox team and work for Miller for $15 per month and free lunches.

Too small to yoke and unyoke his team alone, E. O. nevertheless impressed his fellow workers and his boss. He successfully completed his work on the Miller contract and then drove a team of mules for another employer for $2.50 a day, plus meals. After several months, the youngster presented his mother with his total earnings of $225. He then set off in the fall of 1868 with his Corey uncles, Warren and Charles, and three other men freighting to mines in Nevada. During a three-week trip, E. O. drove a team of mules to Old Toana, west of Montello, Nevada, then hauled freight to Pioche for $85.

On their way home, the group stopped in Kelton, Utah, a booming railroad town on the northern end of the Great Salt Lake, where another uncle, Amos Bonesteel Corey, worked a truck farm supplying food for the railroaders. Although it was November with winter snow already on the ground, Amos managed to persuade the group to take a load of whiskey to Boise, Idaho. "A sleigh road had been broken," E. O. remembered, "but we were either too young or had not had enough experience to think of converting our wagon into a sleigh, so on we struggled as best we could." E. O. returned home with only 15 cents and a new supply of prudence. "I was the only one in the party who did not drink," he wrote later, "and also the only one who did not have some portion of my body frozen." That experience behind him, E. O. stayed on the farm until the spring of 1881.

Eventually, E. O. and W. H. rented the forty-acre family farm from their father, working it together and sharing the proceeds equally—a practice that endured until 1909, when the brothers agreed to divide their interests fifty-fifty. (It took less than an hour to work out the details.) Also during that period, E. O. married Martha Ann Bybee on June 25, 1879, a union that produced five daughters and three sons.

In the midst of their farming and family activities, the Wattis brothers regularly took time to socialize. On November 19, 1878, E. O. wrote with the rococo flourishes of the time to C. H. Bybee: "Yourself and ladies are respectfully invited to a social party to be given at the Uintah School House on Friday evening, November 22nd. Admission 50 cents. Yours respectfully, E. O. Wattis." At the bottom of the page, he drew two chickens with their heads upturned toward a whiskey bottle. "If you are buying chickens," he inscribed cryptically beneath the picture, "take these and fill the bottle."

Although they farmed successfully, the brothers remained alert for business opportunities. E. O.'s early experience on the Union Pacific had apparently kindled his appetite for railroad construction. During the spring of 1881, twenty-six-year-old E. O. and W. H., who was almost twenty-two, extended their partnership to contracting with railroaders. Their first project involved work on the Oregon Short Line Railroad ten miles east of Montpelier, Idaho. After completing that contract in the early fall of 1881, E. O. took their teams to work until Christmas with his uncles on the Portneuf River above McCammon, Idaho. With his father-in-law, Ira E. Spaulding, and his brothers George, Charles, and Amos, Warren Corey had organized the Corey Brothers Construction Company earlier that year. During the spring of 1882, W. H. took a turn with the Coreys on a project in Deer Lodge, Montana, while E. O. worked a second Uintah farm that he and W. H. had purchased.

The projects away from Uintah opened the brothers' eyes to the vast and numerous construction opportunities available in the West. They traded two forty-acre farms and borrowed $800 from their friend Charlie Middleton to purchase more teams and equipment, then set off for Calgary, Alberta, where they worked on the Canadian Pacific Railroad for Corey Brothers during the summer and fall of 1883. The following spring, they returned to Canada with thirty-two horses, twice the number of teams they had taken the year before. Harsh working conditions increased the

Edmund O. Wattis and Martha Ann Bybee married on June 25, 1879, and were photographed on their wedding day. Their family would consist of five daughters and three sons. (Courtesy of W. Dee Halverson)

brothers' sense of isolation during their eighteen months at the rustic construction site. Rarely did the Coreys or Wattises receive mail from home, and they had to haul all their feed and supplies 150 miles from the end of the track.

For E. O. and W. H., the Canadian Pacific project seemed an endless series of mishaps and disappointments. For instance, nearly two dozen horses fell victim to the ulcers and skin lesions of the disease glanders. Discouraged, the brothers sold their remaining nine horses and equipment to Canadian Pacific contractors for

$4,200 in supplies available from the commissary in Beaver, Alberta. To collect the supplies, E. O. slogged the twenty-two miles to Beaver through deep and still-falling snow. Unable to find a hotel in Mountain Creek, he bedded down on a billiard table in a saloon. Once he reached Beaver, he gathered the supplies and resold them to other contractors for the full $4,200.

Notwithstanding these hardships, the Wattis brothers joined in the formal organization of Corey Brothers, Inc., a railroad contracting firm, in the spring of 1886. The two sets of brothers capitalized the company for $6,000, with $3,000 coming from each family. The Corey uncles, however, received two-thirds of the equity while the Wattis nephews received one-third, presumably reflecting the men's proportionate experience in the construction business, or perhaps resulting merely from the numbers of participating brothers in each family.

On January 9, 1888, W. H. Wattis wed Anna Maria Dortia Sophia Hansen Stander, and they became the parents of three daughters and a son. Now that both E. O. and W. H. were married, they assumed their usual fifty-fifty partnership would prevail with their wives, and so the couples used a common checking account. Inevitably one or another of the four would dispense more funds than someone else, causing the checkbook to fall out of balance; and so, before long, the brothers separated their private incomes.

Over the next several years, the Wattis partnership with the Coreys evolved as several Corey brothers left and sons replaced them. Meanwhile, a number of contracts kept the principals busy well into the closing decade of the century. Major projects included construction on the Colorado Midland Railroad near Glenwood Springs, Colorado; a Union Pacific job on the North Platte River in Wyoming; the B. and M. Railroad in Cheyenne; the Bear River Canal in Utah's Box Elder County; two Denver & Rio Grande contracts in Colorado; and a Great Northern Railway job near Kalispell, Montana. These experiences led to an agreement in 1893 with John C. Sheehan, president of the Portland Astoria Railroad Company, to grade, place the ballast, and lay track on one hundred miles of railroad bed in Oregon between Portland and Astoria.

At the time, many believed that this project would boost Astoria into position as one of the world's outstanding cities. Colonel Pat

Donan of South Dakota, for example, predicted the city's future in *The Oregonian*, July 25, 1892. "The railroads must come to Astoria, and are coming," he wrote. "It will be but a few months at most till the ponderous iron steed, with hoofs [*sic*] of steel and lungs of fire, will thunder into the portals of Astoria, and shriek his flaming salutation to the ships along her docks and wharves." In a stirring vision of the future that never materialized, Donan saw "a mighty city" arising "at the mouth of the Hudson of the West, the Mississippi of the North." Because of its harbor and the coming of the railroad, he argued, "Astoria is the most promising spot in the New World today." Such was the common faith in the magic of railroads in the late nineteenth century.

Although Astoria did not become the New York City of the West as a result of their labors, the Wattis brothers added to their reputation as accomplished contractors and started a process that changed dramatically their relationship with the Coreys. The company's involvement in the project had begun when Amos Bonesteel Corey obtained the subcontract from Sheehan. Early in April 1892, a train loaded with grading equipment left Ravelli, Montana, for Portland. Another train, similarly loaded with teams, carts, and scrapers, followed a few days later. On April 11, 1892, a reporter from *Daily Talk* caught up with W. H. Wattis at the Occident Hotel regarding the scope of the grading project, which the Corey Brothers principal outlined in some detail. The equipment had been unloaded at Kalama, on the east bank of the Columbia River north of Portland. Wattis described his plan for reloading the equipment and shipping it to "the front" at Astoria.

That term "front" and its connotation of combat suggested the difficulties of the job. Not only did the builders face the elements and perform bone-jarring work, but financial battles also raged around them as some wondered about the motives of the project's "mysterious" backers. Ostensibly, the railroad line would serve Portland, which had a natural deep-water harbor and reasonable land transportation from Astoria. Nevertheless, many suspected that the line was more than a modest inter-city shuttle. Rather, it might connect with tracks laid hundreds of miles to the east, bypassing Portland completely. Indeed, Andrew B. Hammond, hoping to export the Northwest's timber through Astoria, had

William H. Wattis and Anna Maria Stander posed for this wedding photograph on January 9, 1889. They would rear three daughters and a son. (Courtesy of W. Dee Halverson)

attracted the interest of Collis Potter Huntington, representatives of the Mark Hopkins estate, and John Chaflin of New York in financing the new line.

This information, however, remained under wraps; but suspicions ran high. As one newspaperman editorialized, "The idea of building a railroad through the roughest country in the world for the mere purpose of running a line to Portland seems to a sensible man an absurdity." Otherwise, he wrote, the Corey Brothers, "the largest graders in the world, would not have moved all their supplies and working materials here on any jerk-water line without first being fully satisfied that they would be remunerated for their services and loss of time." (Quite likely Corey Brothers was not the world's largest grading firm, but the title must have cheered the friends and relatives the clipping might reach, to say nothing of reassuring officers of the First National Bank in Ogden, which had lent the firm $81,000 for the Astoria project.)

Despite such suspicions, the work went forward through the pleasant weather of mid-May 1892. Six camps accommodated two thousand workers as the clearing gang prepared ten miles of land for grading and wagon teams kept supplies flowing to the front. Railroad ties were expected by June 1, with tracks due to arrive in Astoria on seven ships by July 15. The contractors assured both backers and the press that the project would be completed in time to move that year's grain crop over the hundred-mile route between cities.

This optimism highlighted centennial festivities in Astoria on May 10–12, commemorating the discovery of the Columbia River by Captain Robert Gray, who sailed out of Boston on the ship *Columbia*. The celebration included receptions hosted by the

The Corey Brothers Construction Company built railways in several western states. This crew posed in Wyoming about 1882.

Oregon Pioneer Association, an excursion to Fort Stevens, street parades, a concert at the opera house, banquets, a torchlight procession of steamers and boats, and a literary exercise with a stirring oration by John Fiske of Cambridge, Massachusetts, a Harvard-educated philosopher, educator, and historian. Without similar fanfare, Corey continued laying track through 1892 and into 1893. Then, as the national financial Panic of 1893 hit, banks began to close and funds disappeared.

The Ogden bankers who were underwriting Corey Brothers organized an expedition to visit the Portland-Astoria site. David Eccles, president of First National Bank in Ogden, Thomas Duncombe Dee, board vice president, and Second District Judge Henry H. Rolapp arrived late one morning in 1893 to discover W. H. Wattis operating a horse-drawn slip plow. Dee later recalled how Wattis responded to the visitors' whistle by dropping the reins, wiping his forehead, and striding over, his worn shoes crunching in the bed of dirt and gravel. As the red-haired W. H. greeted the bankers, one handed him a cigar. "I wish it had been a 25-cent piece," he later quipped, "since I hadn't eaten food for a day and a half."

Corey Brothers' obligations had to be met, and the contract called for completing twenty miles of roadbed before payment came due. Corey completed the first twenty miles of blasting, grading, and track-laying, cleared the second twenty miles, and began tunnel work on the third twenty-mile stretch. The unusual payment terms included a financial subsidy from the City of Astoria but forced the Corey-Wattis partnership to pay all construction costs without any interim income from the railroad company. Due to bank failures, the firm could find no funding to fill that gap.

Predictably, building twenty miles of railroad and preparing another forty miles of track bed exhausted the fledgling company's resources. As a consequence, all of the Corey's outfit went on the auction block to meet local obligations. The company's plight worsened with the bankruptcy of the Gold Creek Mining Company near Elko, Nevada, where Corey Brothers was constructing irrigation canals and a dam. Corey had filed a lien on those Gold Creek assets related to its construction activities but not on the water rights, and consequently obtained nothing.

Ultimately, Corey Brothers filed for bankruptcy as a business, with attendant personal liabilities placed squarely upon the Corey and Wattis partners, according to the two-thirds/one-third agreement. Inasmuch as Corey Brothers had reached the bank's lending limit of $50,000 but still needed money, the bank forced the firm to reorganize. Receivers transferred the assets of the defunct Corey and Wattis partnership {about $7,000 in miscellaneous equipment) to a new company, incorporated as Corey Brothers Company, on November 6, 1895, with officers and shareholders as follows: President Thomas Duncombe Dee (10 percent), Vice President and General Manager W. H. Wattis (1 percent), Secretary and Treasurer James Pingree (10 percent), David Eccles (36 percent), Julia (Mrs. Warren W.) Corey (31 percent), Warren W. Corey (1 percent), Amos B. Corey (1 percent), and Joseph Clark (10 percent).

That momentous reorganization brought Ogden bankers and entrepreneurs Thomas D. Dee and David Eccles into direct partnership with the Wattis brothers for the first time. It would mark the beginning of a long and fruitful relationship among those men that would stretch across generations and into the next century. The new shareholders all represented the First National Bank of Ogden, the predecessor organization of First Security Corporation (recently merged with Wells Fargo). Eccles was president of the bank, Dee vice president of the board, James Pingree cashier, and Joseph Clark a director and member of the executive committee. A noted industrialist, Eccles had wanted to purchase a share of the Corey equity earlier, but apparently met resistance from Warren W. Corey, a rebuff that possibly heightened the banker's resolve to obtain stock in the company.

Dee was born in Llanelly, Carmarthenshire, South Wales, on November 10, 1844. His parents converted to Mormonism twelve years later and relocated to Ogden, Utah, in 1860 when Thomas was sixteen. His father was a prominent merchant; and Thomas, who had apprenticed in Wales as a carpenter, was soon constructing residences and commercial buildings. At age thirty-two, he joined with David Eccles, twenty-seven, Hiram H. Spencer, twenty-four, and others to start many businesses ranging from sugar and shoes to bricks and banking.

Thomas D. Dee was a longtime municipal judge and vice president of the National Bank of Ogden. In 1900, Dee became a stockholder and the first president of the Utah Construction Company.

Born near Glasgow, Scotland, on May 12, 1849, Eccles immigrated to Salt Lake City with his parents and six siblings in 1863, eventually settling in Ogden where he became the family's chief provider when his father lost his eyesight. Although he received no formal education before the age of twenty-one, he worked industriously to support the family and founded his own lumber company while still in his twenties. Eccles maintained that a company should remain free from long-term debt, possibly explaining why he insisted that First National take a more active role in the Corey-Wattis enterprise after the Portland-Astoria Railroad disappointment.

During the reorganization, a transition lasting many months, W. H. Wattis continued to work on the Portland-Astoria project, which finally concluded in 1898. By March 1896, W. H. had struck

David Eccles created twenty-seven corporations, including the predecessor of the First Security Bank. A founding stockholder of the Utah Construction Company, Eccles became its second president.

a deal with Warren W. Corey to share the net proceeds on an equal basis, inasmuch as some profit had slowly begun to develop. Writing from Astoria to E. O. in Ogden, W. H. reaffirmed his solid partnership with his brother: "Of course you are in with me." E. O. had remained at home untangling his business affairs, including a purchase for $3,000 of a herd of sheep that he sold eight months later for $9,200.

The financial impact of the Portland-Astoria disaster hit the Wattises and Coreys hard, leaving a deficit of $69,465.88 owed to First National, Citizen's Bank of Ogden, and Astoria First National Bank. The Wattises had to give up nearly two city blocks near downtown Ogden to First National Bank of Ogden, along with one hundred separate land parcels, to satisfy their obligations. Amos B. and Eva Corey lost their property on Van Buren Avenue between

Twenty-fifth and Twenty-Sixth streets in a sheriff's sale on November 28, 1894. United States Marshal Nat M. Bingham conducted the sale, which brought $20,000 from a single bidder representing the First National Bank.

As the end of the nineteenth century approached, the reorganized Corey Brothers Company, with the bankers aboard, continued to obtain construction contracts, although its net worth on December 8, 1898, was a paltry $10,000, about equal to its original capitalization some years earlier. Most of the Coreys eventually left the company, although Lester S. Corey, son of George Lyman Corey, would become general manager of the descendant company, Utah Construction, in 1931.

Ironically, the real estate that Amos Bonesteel Corey lost to the First National Bank became the site for a home E. O. Wattis built for his daughter Veda Ruth. Another daughter, Ethel Wattis Kimball, later occupied the house. Still later, Marriner Eccles and his first wife, May (Maisie) Campbell Eccles, owned the home from 1923–43. It still stands at 2454 Van Buren in Ogden as a reminder of the hopes and aspirations, both fulfilled and unfulfilled, of the Corey and Wattis brothers. Now, with the Dee and Eccles names connected to the fortunes of their enterprise, the hardscrabble days were over, and a new company would take them to places far beyond any of these families' individual or collective dreams.

Brothers Edmund O. Wattis (left), Warren L. Wattis, and William H. Wattis founded the Utah Construction Company to complete work undertaken by Corey Brothers, a freighting and railway company.

Chapter 2

Steeling the West

At the close of the nineteenth century, the conquest of the West had nearly run its course, yet many Americans remained in an expansionist mood. The United States had emerged as a world power after the Spanish-American War of 1898, and the world seemed open to Yankee industry and ingenuity. As a result, and despite financial losses during the Panic of 1893 and its aftermath, E. O. Wattis and W. H. Wattis decided to embark on a new venture. On January 8, 1900, they joined with their younger brother Warren L. Wattis in the incorporation of the Utah Construction Company, successor to the Corey Brothers firm. The brothers subscribed for eighty shares of stock, valued at $8,000. By the end of the nation's bicentennial in 1976, those original shares (after adjustments for stock splits and dividends) would multiply to nearly six million shares as the $8,000 investment soared to a value of nearly $478 million.

Exactly one month after the incorporation, February 8, 1900, the first meeting of the new firm's board of directors convened in Ogden at 8:50 p.m. Joining the Wattis brothers were the same four bankers who had participated in the reorganization of the Corey company in 1895: Thomas D. Dee, David Eccles, Joseph Clark, and James Pingree. The principal item of business was the confirmation of the subscription and payment of capital stock, amounting to $24,000.

Table 1
Apportionment of Stock, 1900

Investor	Shares	Sum
Thomas D. Dee	40	$4,000
W. H. Wattis	1	100
E. O. Wattis	1	100
W. L. Wattis	1	100
Marie Wattis	77	7,700
David Eccles	80	8,000
Joseph Clark	20	2,000
James Pingree	20	2,000

Continuing in the offices they had held in the Corey company, Dee became president of Utah Construction, with W. H. as vice president. (At age fifty-six, Dee was senior among the five officers, while W. H. was the youngest at only forty-one.) Eccles, Clark, and Pingree became directors. To avoid forfeiture in the event of Utah's bankruptcy, Marie Wattis held seventy-seven shares on behalf of her husband W. H. and his brothers. Thus the Wattis family collectively held the same number of shares as did David Eccles, already a major stockholder in several other companies ranging from lumber and milling to banking.

The board approved two other items of business that evening. W. H. moved that "the Company purchase the outfits, contracts, debts, credits, properties, grading outfit, and all and everything owned by the said Corey Brothers Company except their books and records for the sum of $24,000." The board approved the motion and authorized the treasurer to "pay the said Corey Bros. Co. $24,000 and receive the proper transfers and assignments therefore." Second, Eccles moved that W. H. Wattis be named general manager at a salary of $25 a month. With that, the Utah Construction Company opened for business.

The new company's first construction contract was a carryover from an earlier Corey Brothers project—grading a railroad bed between Idaho Falls and St. Anthony, Idaho, for E. H. Harriman's Oregon Short Line (OSL), a subsidiary of the Union Pacific. (Wattis cousin Lester S. Corey, who later served as company president, worked as a timekeeper on that project.) Completing this job in 1900, Utah accepted contracts for the Denver & Rio Grande Western's Park City branch line and the OSL's Blackfoot spur in Idaho that same year. OSL management also awarded Utah several smaller contracts, to change grades and curves on existing trackage.

These projects in 1900 gave the young company an encouraging start. By early 1901, Utah Construction's net worth had risen to $50,338, a 24 percent increase over the $40,485 Corey Brothers had posted a year before. At the board meeting on March 11, 1901, Eccles proposed "a dividend of 165 percent on the capital stock issued, declared payable on demand." The board ratified the proposal out of profits, with a paid dividend of $39,600. At the time, inventory amounted to $53,580, including three spittoons, a roll-top desk and chair, six bobsleds, 271 horse collars, 103 horse blankets, 147 slush scrapers, and thirty-three sets of chain plow harnesses.

A year later, net worth had increased to $161,207. But, at the end of 1903, Dee informed stockholders that business had "been reasonably successful but not as remunerative as during the previous year." He explained that the company simply had "not performed as much operations work nor received as much compensation, but we have done fairly well." The board consequently voted to award a comparatively modest stock dividend of 10 percent, but there were reasons for optimism. In addition to a number of small projects, Utah had acquired a major contract from the OSL for construction of a Nevada portion of the Oregon and Utah Northern Road. Also, the firm had hired Andrew H. Christensen, an experienced contractor who had worked with the Coreys, adding considerably to Utah's railroad construction savvy. Christensen concomitantly purchased approximately 10 percent of the company, partially in exchange for his outfit and the cancellation of some notes payable.

The Nevada project promised substantial profits for Utah, but no one foresaw the intrigue of the adventure ahead, due to a kind of giant chess game in the desert between E. H. Harriman and Senator William Andrews Clark of Montana, owner of the San Pedro, Los Angeles, and Salt Lake Railroad. Clark planned to link the Los Angeles area directly with Salt Lake City, thereby shortening the distance to Denver, Omaha, and points east by eliminating the necessity of going through San Francisco. (The senator was familiar with the mountains of Utah and Montana, having hauled goods by wagon from Salt Lake to Bannock, Montana, in his first entrepreneurial effort.) In league with Jay Gould, owner of the Denver & Rio Grande, Clark hoped to beat Harriman to the completion of another transcontinental line.

To counter Clark's scheme, the Harriman forces worked at breakneck speed, at times laying track parallel to the senator's road, where there was room to do so. Trouble came when both teams chose the same route through some rugged terrain near Caliente. In a narrow gorge called Meadow Wash Canyon, Utah crews, working for Harriman, encountered Clark's men, who had already completed more than 450 miles of railroad from Los Angeles. A tense standoff ensued, but fortunately good sense and humor dissolved the tension. As Les Corey remembered,

> The OSL was laying rails at the rate of a mile per day and reached a spot of disputed possession ahead of the Clark people, who had erected a barrier of wire fence threatening to shoot the first man who came across. The OSL chief engineer was with the crew at the time, so he had the cars backed up against the fence and personally pushed and dumped across the fence a small car of railroad cross ties. The riflemen were poised to shoot, but the chief, William Ashton, jumped to the ground across the fence to call the bluff. The riflemen shot all right, but they only had blank cartridges, so away went the race with a lot of laughing and kidding from both sides.

Taking such adventures in stride, the Utah Construction Company began to prosper, with a building reputation, plenty of contracts, and respectable profits. The partners in the enterprise had just settled in for a long and healthy business relationship when suddenly the unexpected death of the firm's president forced a reorganization at the top. On July 3, 1905, Thomas D. Dee slipped into water up to his waist while inspecting a site east of Huntsville for a possible reservoir for an irrigation and power company.

In the early 1900s the Utah Construction Company hired contractor Andrew H. Christensen, an experienced contractor who had worked with Corey Brothers.

Despite hot weather, Dee contracted pneumonia and died six days later. On August 7, 1905, W. H. Wattis called a meeting of the board of directors. After appropriate and heartfelt memorials, the board selected David Eccles to serve as Dee's successor. (Eccles would serve in that capacity until his sudden death of a heart attack on December 5, 1912, at the age of sixty-two.)

By the time the mantle passed to Eccles, Utah had accepted its most daunting contract yet, a project so challenging that it would establish the company's reputation as a premier builder of railroads. Late in 1904, the company won a bid to build a line over Western Pacific's Feather River route, stretching 942 miles between Salt Lake City and Oakland, California. Utah received $22.3 million for its share of the $60 million award. The job consumed more than five years, beginning with a ceremonial driving of the first spike at Oakland on January 2, 1906, and ending with the joining of the rails on July 1, 1911. The plan called for the company to construct a railroad through the High Sierras with a maximum grade of 1 percent and a maximum curvature of 20 degrees, a first for mountain railroads. Seventy-five miles stretched through the rugged Feather River Canyon, demanding forty tunnels ranging between forty and 7,500 feet in length for a total of 6.44 miles, as well as scores of bridges, trestles, cuts, and fills. But Utah persisted, focusing its attention on the heavy work while subcontractors performed lighter, specialized tasks.

The rugged features that make Feather River famous as a scenic route also made constructing a railroad there a technological nightmare. Tracing the twists and turns of a turbulent river, sometimes at the water's edge and sometimes hundreds of feet above the gorge, the western segment of the line presented one engineering difficulty after another. E. O. Wattis managed the California section of the construction, which demanded expertise in drilling, blasting, and clearing granite. As his daughter Edna Wattis Dumke recalled, "Some of the blasting occurred near our home in Oroville, where we lived in a two-story brown house between 1906

Between 1905–10, the rugged landscape along the Feather River route posed complex engineering and construction problems.

and 1908." One day her father took her "by the hand up the canyon where the blasting was being performed and we found a nugget of gold. There were a number of Hindu and Chinese workers. The Hindus frightened me nearly to death with their red turbans and black beards."

Many workers came from abroad, particularly from Europe—Swedes, Italians, Austrians, and Greeks—through an employment agency in Chicago. The immigrants readily abandoned one construction company for another if they heard of improved working conditions or pay. Thus Utah had every reason to treat its employees fairly in order to minimize turnover. W. H. Wattis, in particular, enjoyed a reputation for protecting his employees' jobs even during economic downturns.

The eastern portion of the route ran over desert and presented its own obstacles, such as few towns, minimal supplies, and scarce water. The four hundred arid miles between Salt Lake City and Hockstaff, north of Reno, involved desert and salt flats lying at low elevations. Since salt flats would not support conventionally laid tracks, laborers stacked wooden planks in trenches dug into the briny sand.

Utah employed as many as 7,772 men on the project, sometimes abandoning steam-driven shovels for picks, shovels, sledge hammers, and horse-drawn slip plows—with a Harris Track Layer aiding in the final stages. In places the steam shovels could not reach, mules hauled two-wheeled wagons from the canyons. Despite the large and mainly inexperienced work force, few casualties occurred. Five men died in an explosion at Beckwourth in the Sierra Valley of California, and a collapsed trestle injured a few men on Beckwourth Pass. Another death came during a gunfight over a woman.

Rough living conditions prevailed in the work camps, though the men did not consider these undue hardship. Bosses often managed to sleep on bunks, but their crews bedded down on hay mattresses. Tents provided shelter, with an occasional wooden shack covering a blacksmith shop or expensive equipment. Good food boosted morale in camps sometimes fortunate enough to harbor a fiddler or harmonica player. Card games and other forms of gambling filled leisure hours. "Rag saloons" sprouted near the camps to tap the workers' paychecks with cheap whiskey and easy women, though the company discouraged such establishments, sometimes with the help of local sheriffs. Foremen tended to be tough characters, skilled at keeping the men on the job and the project moving forward.

With so many people about, Utah Construction used a code to preserve the security of its telegrams. For instance, "outlaw poker" meant that work should continue. "Laconic princess beyond castle. Smash outpost. Dragon inhabits caldron," somehow meant, "E. L. Brown just returned from First National Bank, Reno, Nevada. Have resumed work, progressing slowly. Friday or Saturday, will be able to load minimum carload." Although such cryptography gradually disappeared from the company's operations, its code books tell their own story as they document a colorful legacy of tough jobs up against tougher men.

Despite such challenges, the Feather River project did not consume all the company's attention. Simultaneously, Utah accepted a contract with the Nevada Northern Railroad to construct its 150-mile line from Cobre south to Ely. Grading commenced at Cobre on September 11, 1905, under the direction of W. H. Wattis. Utah ordered rails from the Colorado Fuel and Iron Company while its crews began erecting 4,500 telegraph poles. Grading went well until a November blizzard halted work in Nevada and delayed the promised shipment of rails. Not content to spend a frustrating winter grading frozen ground, six crews of twenty-five men each moved to southern Nevada and then returned in the spring to complete the work. On September 29, 1906, as townspeople from Ogden and Salt Lake City came by reserved train to join the cheering crowd, Mark Requa, organizer of the White Pine Copper Company and general manager of Nevada Northern, drove the last spike, appropriately made of solid copper. "Not only had a railroad been completed," remarked railroad historian David Myrick, "but its actual cost had been decidedly less than estimated."

Understandably weary, Utah's management intended to return to Ogden after finishing the projects in Nevada. So many opportunities beckoned in California, however, that Utah Construction opened an office in the Flood Building in San

Utah Construction's impressive performance on the $22 million Feather River rail line from Oakland, California, to Salt Lake City, Utah, led to many other railroad contracts.

Francisco in 1908. From then on, E. O. Wattis (known as the "inside man") headed the San Francisco office, assisted by Henry J. (Hank) Lawler, John G. Tyler, and J. Q. Barlow. E. O. missed his home and extended family in Ogden. A year after the San Francisco office opened, he wrote to his sister in Utah:

> I am getting very tired of [railroad] work. I don't know whether I will ever tackle another job or not. It is very monotonous for me to always be away from home and I think I am needed at home about as bad as anybody[;] besides that I am 54 years old and have always worked very hard and I never had but very little pleasure in my life. I don't think I have had hardly my share. My young life was spent in poverty and hard work and I am not [in] the best of health and I don't think there is any real enjoyment for old people. The greatest pleasure that there is in store for me is to help to make my family and others happy and have my family grow up so they will be an honor to me when I am gone and so that I can be proud of them while I am alive and always have them love me as I love them.

Meanwhile, W. H. Wattis (the "outside man") remained a visible figure in Ogden, serving on a variety of corporate boards and running several times for public office. Like his brother, he also held family dear and enjoyed presiding over weekend dinners at the old Weber Club on Kiesel Avenue and joining his chauffeur in the front seat of his red Hupmobile. When his daughter Mary visited London in July 1914, W. H. urged her to consider visiting the company-owned ranch upon her return. "I believe you would enjoy it and perhaps some of your friends might like it," he wrote. "I don't mean the Lords and Dukes or even the Princes, just good friends such as Miss Castle ... who wouldn't be ashamed to be seen with Father and the balance of the cowboys."

When the company's work on the Feather River project approached a triumphant conclusion, E. O. Wattis and a large party of friends, relatives, and business associates honored W. H. Wattis for his able leadership. The menu at the May 31, 1910, banquet at the Weber Club memorialized the company's major adventures by listing the following delicacies:

Meadow Valley Wash in a cup
Sumpter Valley Hobo Trout
Oroville Olives served ala cement gravel
Western Pacific Roosters ala spring garden

Rio Grande Potatoes, bridge timber style
Spring Lamb ala Leamington Cutoff
Bridge Trestle Asparagus
Manilla Rope Cigars—Steam Shovel Brand
Bloomer Bar Coffee

During the next decade, while E. O. devoted his energies to the internal management of Utah Construction from the San Francisco office, W. H. began a strategic process of networking the firm with outside interests through his own associations with the officers of other western companies. The procedure developed from well-established local models. David Eccles was, or had been, president of seventeen different companies at the time of his death, and Thomas D. Dee had headed nine different enterprises. Not surprisingly, W. H.'s roster of outside activities included involvement in many of those same companies as a vice president or board member. He also held positions of responsibility in a number of civic and social organizations, all of which put him in contact with like-minded businessmen.

In May 1915, the Utah Construction Company began building an arched, reinforced concrete dam just downstream from an earthen structure built in 1896 to catch the flow of the East Canyon Creek and the Weber River.

In the meantime, a variety of small railroad and tunnel projects in western states bolstered the company's backlog. In 1908, for instance, the company completed the Natron-Oakridge line in Oregon for Southern Pacific under a $2.5 million contract. Then, with the end of the Western Pacific project in 1911, Utah undertook several more small-scale projects, including the Nampa (Idaho) Branch mainline for the OSL; the Sherwood-Arcata mainline in California for Northwestern Pacific; and a mainline from Helper to Soldier Summit, Utah, for the Denver & Rio Grande. Utah drilled more than thirty tunnels for these projects, amounting to some 20,000 linear feet. These three projects brought in nearly $10 million in contracts. Although railroad building continued to occupy most of its efforts, after 1915 the firm regularly undertook water projects. One of the first was the East Canyon Dam near Morgan, for the Utah Irrigation District, a concrete structure completed in 1916 at an approximate cost of $700,000.

When the United States entered the Great War in Europe in 1917, railroad construction in the West slowed considerably. Utah nevertheless managed to remain busy through the duration of the war with a $2.5 million contract for building the mainline from Coyote Wells to Jacumba, California, for the San Diego and Eastern Arizona Railroad Company. By the time of the armistice in 1919, Utah had completed this project. Anticipating a postwar construction boom, it employed its first engineer in 1920. Prior to that time, Utah officials had bid on projects by comparing the new job with a previous one. The firm's engineer, on the other hand, computed the quantities and types of material moved and determined costs with hard numbers.

Also in 1920, the Utah Railway Company, a subsidiary of the United States Smelting, Refining and Mining Company, employed Utah Construction to lay a main track with a $6 million contract. The next three years brought a series of small contracts—the Haig Branch extension in Nebraska for Union Pacific; a line extension between Santa Ana and Los Angeles and lines to Fillmore and Cedar City, Utah, for the Los Angeles and Salt Lake Railroad Company; and tunnel work for the Southern Pacific south of San Francisco. Although these jobs were relatively minor, they nevertheless brought more than a million dollars in contracts to the firm.

Starting in 1923, Southern Pacific initiated a series of contracts of a similar nature with Utah, including the construction of track between Montello and Valley Pass; between Wells and More, Nevada; and between Truckee and Andover, California; as well as a job near Mojave, California, involving tunnel work. Other work that came to the company during 1923 required minor railroad construction at Garfield, Utah; tunnel work for Utah Railway; betterment work on the entire OSL system; and numerous small contracts in Wyoming for Union Pacific.

After the Feather River operation, these relatively small jobs, as important as they were to the company, demanded only a fraction of its abilities in undertaking projects of major proportions. Then, in 1923, the Utah Construction Company reached a significant milestone with its first international agreement, a challenging $7,029,500 contract from Southern Pacific of Mexico to build a 110-mile railroad line through the rugged country between La Quemada and Tepic (near Guadalajara) in western Mexico. This time, the whole gamut of construction hurdles—terrain, weather, labor, the political environment, and logistics—would test Utah's mettle to its core.

The company's first foreign contract involved building a 110-mile railway for Southern Pacific in Mexico, completed in 1927.

Chapter 3

Companía Constructora Utah

After more than three decades of dictatorship, a social revolution erupted in Mexico in 1910, embroiling hundreds of thousands of Mexicans and billions of dollars in property in a civil war. By 1923 the fires of la revolución had burned down, but their embers continued to smolder for many years as Mexico struggled for stability in the modern world. La Companía Constructora Utah came into that volatile setting armed with a contract to build a 110-mile main line through the rugged *barranca* country between La Quemada and Tepic in the State of Nayarit. A fierce sectionalism that fed on the isolation of various regions of the country was among the many serious geopolitical problems that had plunged Mexico into civil war. Consequently, the purpose of the La Quemada–Tepic line was to connect the region north of Guadalajara with the country's more populated core around Mexico City.

The Mexican project provided Utah with its first international experience, and it could not have been more difficult. Furnace-hot temperatures, torrential rains, and high humidity burdened the already backbreaking labor of breaching the mountainous terrain. A lack of roads prevented the use of heavy equipment, forcing supplies onto the backs of pack animals and demanding hand labor in many areas. Primitive living conditions, dysentery, and malaria plagued the workmen. On top of all this, renegade bandits roamed the countryside at will, requiring the Mexican government to station troops along the route to protect the construction workers. Unwilling to trust its safety solely to the Mexican troops, Utah armed its managers with revolvers and established its own police force.

True stories of the ensuing adventure soon grew to legendary proportions in company lore—a paymaster with bags of silver pesos, hard-riding revolutionaries and banditos, gunfights, bustling camps where as many as five thousand laborers lived in banana-leaf huts, breathtaking scenery, hair-raising skirmishes with nature and the terrain, and strong-willed Americans determined to manage thousands of Mexican employees in a culture as remote as the common border was close. To wrangle with these dynamics, corporate officers sent to Mexico a fifty-four-year-old veteran manager named Henry J. (Hank) Lawler. Short in both stature and temper, the outspoken Lawler abstained from tobacco, alcohol, and nonsense of any kind. For example, an associate remembered him to be "as punctual a man as possible to be. If he had an appointment with anybody, regardless of their status, if they were late, he would leave."

Consistent with these characteristics was Lawler's quick pen, with which he readily described job conditions and routinely complained about every one of them. While the steady stream of his letters and telegrams constantly worried company leaders in Ogden and San Francisco, it also provided a colorful and prolix chronicle of the Mexican enterprise. Additionally, his correspondence with the Wattis brothers opened an intriguing window onto the management style of Utah's top leadership at the time.

Lawler had taken the position under somewhat strained conditions. E. O. Wattis planned to supervise the Mexican job himself. Plagued by ill health, he persuaded Lawler to take it although the stocky foreman subsequently expressed misgivings to company president W. H. Wattis on June 24, 1923, when the two met at the Weber Club in Ogden. When W. H. bristled that it did not matter to him one way or the other whether he accepted the post, Lawler sulked away, taking Wattis's response as a negative reflection on his worth to the company.

After brooding for four days, Lawler wrote W. H. saying he would either resign from the firm or take the Mexican assignment

The project's first superintendent, Henry J. (Hank) Lawler, was known for his diligence and competence, but he found it difficult to adjust to the Mexican culture and climate.

on the following conditions: an annual salary of $12,000 plus expenses for himself and his wife, and two months vacation each year. Probably he would not take all the allotted vacation time, Lawler wrote, but wanted it reserved. "Should anything happen to you in the meantime [I] don't think it unfair to have [a] thorough understanding, so the time will be mine if I care to take it." Promptly, W. H. agreed to Lawler's conditions. Although Utah had five other major contracts underway at the time, top management apparently considered the feisty Lawler and the daunting Mexican project a perfect match. Unfortunately, Lawler remained painfully unconvinced.

After establishing company offices in Tepic in July 1923, Lawler bypassed W. H. in Ogden and began flooding E. O.'s office in San Francisco with complaints about working conditions and his personal sacrifices. Although most of the equipment he needed to begin work had arrived, seasonal rains hampered the startup. In an odd twist to the old saying, it apparently seemed to Lawler that if he talked about the weather enough, perhaps E. O. would do something about it. Out of patience, W. H. wrote Lawler a stiff reprimand on August 18 for failing to observe the proper chain of command. The letter arrived in Tepic at an inopportune time. A broken part on a steam shovel had shut down operations until a replacement part could arrive from San Francisco. Lawler fired off a letter demanding an apology from W. H., or he would resign.

Still fuming and apparently unwilling to wait for a reply, Lawler wrote a formal letter of resignation. "Under no conditions will I work for the company any longer. I would [rather] work in a ditch with a pick and shovel and keep my self respect rather than to be President of the United States." After two more weeks of silence, Lawler wrote again to retract his resignation while still demanding that W. H. "square himself." No reply followed. W. H. simply took counsel with E. O., allowed Lawler time to cool down, and thus kept his superintendent. The brothers felt satisfied with Lawler's abilities to manage the job, noting that he had dealt well with many of its more difficult problems. As time passed into the fall, however, they nevertheless grew concerned about the schedule, realizing that it had been folly to begin fill work before the rainy season ended, usually by mid-October.

Finally, on November 2, 1923, W. H. sent his superintendent in Mexico a news-laden letter, concluding with an apology. "The letter I sent," wrote Wattis, "which you took such strong exception to, I had no thought of personal criticism ... I dictated it hurriedly just as I was leaving for Salt Lake and it never occurred to me that there was anything that would be taken so seriously." At this point, W. H. hoped to put off any further discussion of the matter, so the company could focus on more pressing issues relative to the floundering project. "It is my opinion that nothing special can be gained by much correspondence about this letter. I certainly hope you will forget about it—at least until such time as I can come down and discuss it with you in person. I feel certain that the explanation I can make to you will be entirely satisfactory."

This exchange highlights an important facet of W. H.'s management style. He clearly preferred to make major decisions and then let his subordinates come to terms with them without much discussion in the aftermath. He also refused to respond immediately to behavior he did not want to encourage. This allowed short-fused but valuable employees considerable room to fuss and fume without jeopardizing either the project at hand or their careers. While undoubtedly frustrating to people like Lawler, it kept them on the job as they waited in vain for some excuse to walk away.

In the meantime, as this one-sided feud fizzled, friction developed between Lawler and Chief Engineer E. B. Sloan, of El Ferrocarril Sud Pacifíco de México (SPM). Lawler wrote W. H. on January 8, 1924, calling Sloan "the tightest wad we ever worked for...." Lawler faulted Sloan, "who surrounded himself with a bunch of highway engineers," for haggling over approvals and slipped communications and for nagging Lawler with textbook issues on materials and engineering. Lawler ignored Sloan as much as possible while doing things Utah's way.

With Lawler squarely in the saddle and the rainy season ended, work on the line gradually accelerated. By early 1924, seven subcontractors employed hundreds of teams and filled several camps with workers. Unfortunately, the dry season encouraged die-hard revolutionaries to step up their activities, so the government assigned some three hundred federales to protect the camps. They

Here, Utah Construction workers prepare a load of blasting power. The company built thirty-five tunnels and thirty-three bridges in Mexico.

Due to political unrest, bandits roamed the countryside. Company officials carried pistols despite police protection from federales, shown here guarding the payroll.

lounged about company headquarters, used company equipment and animals, refused to send out pickets, and burned huge fires near the powder houses. Fearing that rebels could effectively kill everyone by blowing up the conveniently illuminated powder houses, Lawler complained to the Mexican general, who merely made a counter-demand that Utah's men surrender their guns. When Lawler promised that his men would fight to keep their weapons, the general backed down, but the strained relationship continued.

With the threat of marauding rebels vexing his every move, Lawler wrote W. H. Wattis in early January. "As you know I never tried to side-step a job or a fight either no matter how hard the going might be if I was sure I was right." He added, "We should stick, for it may not amount to anything more than a big scare." Still, Lawler knew many of his subcontractors felt intimidated. For example, he counted thirty-seven different warehousemen coming and going "like chickens." As a result, Utah's managers and the few Mexican workers they trusted took over most of the crucial work around headquarters.

By late January 1924, the situation grew so tense that executives in Ogden and San Francisco planned to meet with Lawler and other principals in Los Angeles. The Wattis brothers invited SPM to send

Sloan, President H. B. Titcomb from Tucson, and T. G. Wright, manager of the shipping terminal in Nogales, Arizona. In response, Titcomb wired E. O. Wattis on January 26 that he had received a wire from Sloan informing him that Lawler was "not satisfactory to military authorities. Believe you should consider quick change." Titcomb also assured E. O. that the rebels posed "no serious trouble and no cause for worry." In addition, on January 28, Lawler himself refused in a terse telegram to come: "Impossible leave at this time as I want to try to get forces organized again." Three days later, he sent another cable in which he sought to reassure the Wattises: "Situation greatly improved. All camps working between Tepic and Port Ozuelo."

Then, only days after Lawler's second telegram, a Mexican bystander was wounded in a gunfight with the rebels. Lawler refused to send a company rail car to pick up the wounded man, and he fired two Utah Construction employees who helped the federales take the injured man to Tepic. Titcomb sent the Wattis brothers a telegram on February 4, demanding that Lawler be replaced at once. The Wattises responded the next day: "We have wired Lawler instructions to put work in charge someone else and immediately come in for conference."

What happened next is not entirely clear. That same day, E. O. wrote his brother: "I am enclosing two telegrams that I have sent to Lawler. Seems to me that either one of them is plain enough so that he should come." E. O. suggested that Lawler bring his personal belongings, in case of a change in superintendents. He then tried to sweeten the message with an indication that rewarding opportunities awaited Lawler in the States. Amazingly, Lawler seemed to ignore both Wattis directives and remained at La Quemada for another month. On February 29, he wrote brusquely, "If we expect to finish anywhere near on time, we will have to quit posing, go to work and let somebody else do the wet nursing of Mexicans and quit chewing the fat as to who did or did not step on the dignity of some ex-Mexican peon." This was Lawler's last communication from Mexico. When he began receiving death threats, he left for the United States.

Despite Lawler's important efforts during the early phase, his inability to deal with SPM officials, the Mexican army, and local employees led to his removal from the job. As a result, his substantial contribution to the railroad's eventual completion became less important to top management than the lesson his behavior taught them about operating in international waters. The Wattis brothers replaced him with their affable cousin Lester S. Corey, who saw the La Quemada-Tepic line through to its last spike in 1927. The project's four arduous years included building thirty-five tunnels and thirty-three bridges and earned the company a profit of more than $1 million on the $7 million contract.

During the 1920s, Utah built several other railroad lines, including tunnels and bridges, in the western United States, under contracts totaling some $20.5 million. For Southern Pacific, Utah constructed the main line and summit tunnel through Donner Pass at close to $4 million; a line extension at Kirk, Oregon, at $2.5

W. H. Wattis (second from left) enjoyed golfing with ZCMI official Stephen Love (left); LDS Church President Heber J. Grant; Grant's counselor and businessman Charles W. Nibley; and United States Senator Reed Smoot. (Courtesy of the LDS Church Historical Department)

Lester S. Corey, a cousin to the Wattis brothers, replaced Lawler as superintendent on the Mexican railroad project. He later would serve as company president.

million; the Natron Cutoff from Weed, California, to Oakridge, Oregon, at $2.5 million; the Black Butte line at Grass Lake, California, at $2.4 million; a main-line improvement in northern Nevada at $1.8 million; and a new line from Klamath Falls, Oregon, to Alturas, California, at $932,000. Utah also worked on several Union Pacific jobs during this period, including a major branch line from Ashton, Idaho, to West Yellowstone for $2.5 million, as well as an OSL line from Rogerson, Idaho, to Wells, Nevada, at $1.2 million.

By 1930, the Utah Construction Company had established itself as a trusted, competent railroad builder. Its successful legacy of far-flung railroad ventures provided a powerful base for meeting diverse challenges and opportunities in the decades to come. With their company assets totaling nearly $7 million, the Wattis brothers had traveled far from tiny Uintah on the banks of the Weber River. A larger river, not far away, would inspire the next chapter in Utah's story.

The Hoover Dam became the world's largest arch-gravity concrete dam at 730 feet in height and 1,244 feet in breadth. Six Companies completed the dam a year ahead of schedule.

Chapter 4

The Dam Builders

The Roaring Twenties came to a staggering halt in late October 1929. With unprecedented abruptness, panic seized Wall Street as more than twelve million shares of common stock passed across the block in a frenzy of selling. Within the week, solid companies by the score had absorbed catastrophic losses in the market, often exceeding two hundred points. A colossal sum of $40 billion in paper wealth disintegrated in the shaking hands of its holders—investors who had believed just weeks before that the inflationary spiral in stock prices would last indefinitely. Aftershocks of the crash struck to the core of American society as millions lost their savings, banks closed, factories locked up, unemployment exploded, mortgages were foreclosed, and tax revenues dwindled. During the next two dismal years, national income decayed to half in the face of five thousand bank closures and 32,000 company failures, all of which compounded the misery of more than twelve million unemployed workers and their families.

In the midst of this alarming period, the Utah Construction Company embarked upon perhaps its greatest adventure, a bold attempt to transform the Southwest. In partnership with other firms, Utah prepared to bid on a massive concrete dam across the Colorado River at the Arizona-Nevada border. When completed, the dam would create a reservoir 120 miles long, containing five thousand gallons of water for every person on earth. The 700-foot-tall structure would supply water to a quarter million acres of arid land and vast quantities of electrical power to western cities and farms. Planning for the project began in September 1930 under the name Hoover Dam, but as the Depression deepened and the incumbent president failed to achieve reelection in 1932, it became Boulder Dam, then by joint resolution of Congress in 1947 became Hoover Dam again.

While the gigantic Hoover project certainly represented a huge step for Utah, the company was hardly a newcomer to dam building. In addition to filling relatively minor contracts on irrigation projects, Utah had erected several substantial dams by the time bidding for Hoover took place. In the aftermath of the great San Francisco earthquake in 1906, city engineers began plotting a dam for power and water on the Tuolumne River. Utah subsequently teamed with Transbay Construction Company to build the O'Shaughnessy Dam (usually called Hetch Hetchy, after the reservoir behind it), a 675,000-cubic-yard structure with a price tag of $6.1 million. A gravity dam 430 feet high with a crest length of almost one thousand feet, it holds back more than 360,000 acre-feet of water and delivers an installed power capacity of 67,500 kilowatts. The company's first major dam project turned into one of its longest jobs ever, with preliminary work in 1914 and its dedication not until 1938. Another Hetch Hetchy footnote relates to the ongoing discomfort over the dam among Bay Area environmentalists, although Utah was never more than peripherally involved in the controversy.

Work on another major dam near Mackay, Idaho, began in 1917 after a turbulent history dating back to 1906. At that time, the Big Lost River Land and Irrigation Company organized in response to the Carey Act of 1894, which provided federal irrigable land if a state would develop it with private capital. The irrigation company planned a dam to water some 100,000 acres in Butte County. Land advertised for 50 cents an acre and water rights for $25 and $35 an acre in Powell Tract—30,000 acres named for their proximity to the Powell Station of the Oregon Short Line Railroad, also a Utah Construction job.

When Big Lost River could not raise the necessary funds, its Chicago-based bonding company, Trowbridge & Nivers, took over and contracted with Corey Brothers Construction Company on May 28, 1909. Corey had never built a dam before, but apparently its ability to grade road bed for the Canadian and Western Pacific Railroads qualified it to construct a dirt-filled dam. When water behind the dam began to rise, rumors circulated that the dam was faulty, naturally alarming the residents of Mackay, four miles downstream. In addition, hundreds of farmers below the dam who depended on the flow of Big Lost River waters were outraged when the stream dwindled to a trickle. These concerns brought the Big Lost River Water Users Protective Association to life in April 1910 at the same time a court case evolved over the title and value of the land covered by the reservoir.

The water users group managed to have engineering firms from New York and San Francisco evaluate the dam's structural integrity, but their reports differed widely. Then another committee of engineers submitted a report in September 1910, documenting serious defects in the dam, most notable that it rested on gravel rather than bedrock, causing leaks in the downstream toe or base. These findings sent the region into near panic. Now nearly everyone was upset, including the promoters who had sold $1.4 million in bonds to investors, the sixty upstream families who had filed on three thousand acres and now wondered when they would receive water, and the stockholders, to say nothing of those downstream. All these considerations forced the Idaho State Land Board to halt construction on the Mackay Dam in May 1911. Soon afterward, an adjacent, much smaller Darlington Dam diverted upstream waters to irrigate 45,000 acres—a dissatisfying contrast to the unfinished Mackay Dam.

When construction ceased, Corey Brothers filed a $500,000 lien against the Lost River Land and Water Company. In the spring of 1914, when the company went into court-mandated receivership, these liens totaled $700,000. At the court sale, Corey Brothers (represented by the Utah National Bank of Ogden) gave the high bid of $35,000 for Lost River's assets. In February 1915, Utah Construction interceded for the Coreys when W. H. Wattis proposed to complete the project, given certain stipulations: Utah Construction would provide two acre-feet at $40 per acre, to be paid over a fifteen-year period at 6 percent interest on the unpaid balance. The Idaho State Land Board rejected Utah's offer, saying there would not be that much water in the river. Eventually, the federal General Land Office insisted upon completion, or the land would return to the public domain. In November 1916, Utah Construction posted a completion bond for a new dam and finished it on time in May 1918.

Unfortunately, 1918 brought record lows in available water, and so, in the spring of 1919, Utah Construction petitioned the United States District Court to confirm the company's rights to claim title to and store water from the Big Lost River and its tributaries. When it became evident the court would rule for Utah Construction, the upstream water users formed the Big Lost River Irrigation District and, on July 9, 1920, also petitioned the court. On March 15, 1923, the federal court awarded 566 water rights to the irrigation district, granted Utah the absolute right to store water, and named a commissioner to distribute the water. The drought lasted through most of the 1920s, forcing many farmers to sell their land and many others to lose their patience. As a result, the Mackay Dam Club formed in the winter of 1928–29 to bring those people together socially and to discuss remedies. Sobered by legal expenses, the club turned to political action. Soon the Big Lost River Irrigation District and the club united as the Big Lost River Reclamation Association to seek solutions through fact finding and rational discourse.

The irrigation district and the reclamation association joined with state reclamation interests and agencies in convening a panel of experts in the spring of 1931. The experts' report proposed a water-users' organization to purchase Utah Construction's holdings, the dam, diversion dam, reservoir, canals, storage rights, and so on. Utah agreed to sell for $2.5 million, granting options to purchase to the irrigation district. Lacking funds, the irrigation district applied to the federal government, which viewed the petition favorably. At last, it appeared that the whole mess might be headed for a happy resolution. In the spring of 1933, however, word spread that the Big Lost River's volume would drop 50 percent during the forthcoming summer and fall irrigation period, barely sufficient for upstream users and insufficient for downstream users. Late on the afternoon of June 21, around thirty unidentified men went to the dam, overpowered the watchman, cut the telephone lines, and then blasted out the dam's tower gates with dynamite. In a few seconds, 14,000 acre-feet of water—half the reservoir's contents—burst like Niagara down the river's course. Simultaneously, another group damaged three of the four gates controlling the water leading from the Darlington Dam to the canals upstream.

An article in the *Arco Advertiser,* on June 23, 1933, stressed the seriousness of this vigilante action, investigated by several law enforcement agencies. When the reservoir finished draining, Utah Construction repaired the dam, and two years later, the federal Reconstruction Finance Corporation allowed the Big Lost River Irrigation District to bond itself in order to pay Utah $258,000 for the repairs. On January 25, 1936, the district court declared the irrigation district the legal owner of the Mackay and Darlington water systems and rights. The company finally walked away from the Mackay fiasco, having learned the hard way many important lessons in the dam-building business.

The smaller Guernsey Dam played an even more significant role in Utah's story. Built for the Bureau of Reclamation as a power, irrigation-storage, and diversion unit, and finished in 1927 on the North Platte River in eastern Wyoming, the $1.5 million Guernsey paid dividends well beyond its profit value. It marked the first of many joint-ventures between Utah Construction and the Morrison Knudsen Company of Boise, Idaho (M-K). Also, this project represented the last on which Utah employed steam power for heavy construction. Following Guernsey, the firm modernized with diesel-powered, internal-combustion equipment. Perhaps most importantly, the new dam-building techniques Utah Construction tried at Guernsey highlighted the company's innovative capabilities. Dam construction commonly required diverting the river so that crews could excavate a dry work area down to solid rock. With diversion impractical for the North Platte, Utah used an underwater bucket on a drag-line cable way to dig the river bottom to a depth of thirty feet. Railway cars on a trestle then dumped rock (combined with finer stone and sand) from the tunnel and spillway onto two parallel ridges that formed the upstream and downstream faces of the dam. In the pool between, a hydraulic monitor on

H. W. (Harry) Morrison, co-founder of the Morrison Knudsen Company, teamed with Utah Construction on many projects.

pontoons sluiced the finer materials from coarse rock and formed the impervious core of the dam.

Another project, a mile high in the Idaho Rockies, tamed the wild Deadwood River, which the Bureau of Reclamation's Boise Project managers marked for an irrigation dam and power facility some sixty miles northeast of Boise. With the nearest railhead at Cascade, also more than sixty miles away, the dam site could be reached only by traveling over mountainous terrain where snow banks remained as long as six months of the year. In 1929, for instance, workers barely finished foundation stripping before winter drove them out; so the following spring, Utah and Morrison Knudsen decided to get an early start by hauling a concrete mixing plant and two-inch cable ways to a close-in location. Even by using the first bulldozers, diesel trucks, and gasoline-powered shovels, crews could not beat the onset of winter, and the last group of men

Felix Kahn, co-founder of MacDonald & Kahn, became treasurer of Six Companies and oversaw much of the work on the dam.

had to hike to Cascade when the only tractor broke down. Deadwood, a gravity-arch concrete structure 165 feet high and eleven hundred feet long, finally reached completion in 1931 at a cost of just under $5 million.

During this period of growing occupation with dam building, Utah developed a healthy capacity for multiple and diverse activities on a major scale. For example, it moved cautiously into highway construction. Between its first road contract in 1914 and the end of 1931, the company had built roads mostly in California and the Intermountain West amounting to contracts in excess of $1.5 million. Of course, Utah's mother industry of railroad building continued well into the 1930s. Hank Lawler, for example, upon his hasty return from Mexico, had ramrodded the $5 million Keddie-Bieber Cutoff in California for Western Pacific, completing the job in 1931. Utah had also begun work on the Dotsero Cutoff in

Colorado for the Denver and Salt Lake Railroad, a $1.75 million project. Significantly, both of these jobs developed as joint ventures with the Bechtel Company. Other minor railroad jobs, many of them related to dam building, continued as well, but with decreasing frequency.

In the midst of all this dawning growth in the Utah Construction Company, two of its principal founders had arrived at the dusk of their lives. E. O. Wattis had struggled with health problems incident to aging for some time, but W. H. Wattis, who had been generally vigorous, spent part of 1931 in a hospital battling cancer. They had presided over one of the most meteoric yet hard-won successes in the history of American business. While transforming themselves from farm boys to captains of industry, they had carved for themselves and their associates an empire of respect and wealth. By their time in life, most men had hung up their sickles to rust, but the Wattises, true to their rural origins, always looked ahead to one more harvest.

As the Wattis brothers and their colleagues crisscrossed the West with railroads during the first three decades of the twentieth century, men and nature were scripting a drama on the Colorado River that would cast the Utah Construction Company in a leading role. For millennia, the mighty stream drained a vast portion of the Rocky Mountains into the Pacific by way of the Gulf of California. Eroding a river basin one thousand miles long, the drainage encompassed one-twelfth of the land area of the continental United States. With awesome power, the Colorado's silt-laden waters frustrated early attempts at control, devastating the Southwest with floods. Late in the nineteenth century, the Colorado River Irrigation Company tried to channel its torrents into a canal for use in southern California. Within a decade, the river had demolished the canal and created the Salton Sea, requiring $8 million to shut off the flow and return the river to its normal course.

Following that disaster, President Theodore Roosevelt urged Congress to authorize a study of the Colorado and the building of a federally funded waterway. The signing of the Colorado River Compact on November 24, 1922, brought to a meeting representatives of Arizona, California, Colorado, Nevada, New Mexico, Utah, and Wyoming to divide equitably the river's flow, benefitting each state's agricultural development. As a by-product, the compact would minimize future controversies over water allocation and flood damage. Seven years later, when Arizona refused to agree to the Colorado River Compact, President Calvin Coolidge signed the Swing-Johnson Act, inaugurating a study that quickly recommended building a massive dam for flood control, power generation, and water storage.

The Bureau of Reclamation chose Black Canyon, on the Arizona-Nevada border some thirty miles from Las Vegas, as the site for the new dam, because it was located near irrigable lands and would provide a firm bedrock foundation. At that point, the Colorado had cut a sheer gorge eight hundred feet deep and one thousand feet across through desert country that baked in 100-plus degrees much of the year. When the bureau advertised for bids in December 1930, few doubted that the job would be incredibly difficult. After all, said skeptical observers, this would be the eighth wonder of the world. It might not be done at all, at least not with a profit.

As soon as the Wattises and their long-time friend and vice president Andrew H. Christensen heard about the proposed high dam on the Colorado, they followed every development with interest. W. H. seemed to believe that Utah and Morrison Knudsen could build Boulder Dam just as they had constructed the Guernsey and Deadwood Dams. "This is just a dam," he told *Time* magazine in an interview published on March 23, 1931. "It's no different than any other dam.... There's just more of it, that's all." But M-K's chief ramrod, a battle-hardened Bureau of Reclamation veteran named Frank T. Crowe, looked at preliminary specifications and concluded the dam could cost as much as $50 million—a sum far too large for the two companies to finance together. Harry Morrison agreed with Crowe and apparently tried to convince E. O. to invite in additional partners. W. H. remained skeptical. "If we can't do the job alone," he swore, "to hell with it." He believed that Utah could raise the necessary capital by drawing on a resource peripheral to its construction enterprise—the company's large ranching operation.

In 1913, David Eccles had purchased property located in the northeast corner of Nevada from Jasper Harrell, successor to the

Sparks Harrell Company. Covering some hundred square miles, the ranch raised more than 100,000 head of cattle. In purchasing the land, Eccles incorporated Vineyard Land and Cattle Company, with himself as chief shareholder; the Utah Construction board essentially comprised the other shareholders. Vineyard continued to acquire land in Nevada and Idaho, and while the ranching operation made little money, it provided a form of financial diversification that could provide ready cash.

W. H. was not the only Utah Construction leader to favor selling land to finance the Hoover project. At that point, however, Marriner S. Eccles (a son of David Eccles and now a forty-year-old financier) urged Utah executives, by letter and in a personal visit, to find additional partners. After further assurances from E. O. Wattis, Harry Morrison, and Hank Lawler that the scheme felt good to them, W. H. relented. "All right, boys," he agreed, "Utah will go in."

Tentatively, Morrison had begun lining up other partners. He figured the combine would need $5 million, of which Utah would

Normal Gallison, Henry J. Lawler, Brig Young, Charles Shea, E. O. Wattis, Elwood Mead, Frank Crowe, R. F. Walters, and W. A. Bechtel line up at the Hoover site. Young, Mead, and Walters represented the Bureau of Reclamation, Crowe was project superintendent, and the others were officials of Six Companies.

put up one million and Morrison Knudsen another half, leaving $3.5 million to raise. He soon found another million: half each from the J. F. Shea Company of Los Angeles and the Pacific Bridge Company, two highly respected West Coast operators with a working alliance. Morrison called MacDonald & Kahn, a San Francisco company that had previously subcontracted for Utah, and found it was already considering bidding on at least part of the Colorado River project. Partner Felix Kahn quickly agreed to put up a million, which, he chuckled, "made me one of the family right away."

Not surprisingly, other large contracting firms were debating partnerships to bid on the dam. Among them were Henry Kaiser and W. A. Bechtel, close associates and powerfully connected contractors in California. After convincing Bechtel to come in, Kaiser invited in Warren Brothers of Cambridge, Massachusetts. Kaiser hoped to round out his group with other East Coast contractors in time to get bonded and make a winning bid early in 1931. But upon his return to California from finishing a $20 million highway project in Cuba, Kaiser learned of Morrison's activities. Recognizing the expanding power of the Wattis-Morrison group, Kaiser approached Morrison about a possible alliance. W. H. Wattis then parleyed with Bechtel and apparently liked what he heard. As a consequence, the Kaiser-Bechtel-Warren union threw in the remaining $1.5 million, and Six Companies, Inc. became a reality.

Three major tasks loomed before the new collaborators—organization, preparing a workable bid, and bonding. With remarkably little disagreement, they cleared the first hurdle in February 1931 when Six Companies incorporated under the relatively easy laws of Delaware with six officers: President W. H. Wattis, First Vice President W. A. Bechtel, Second Vice President E. O. Wattis, Secretary Charles A. Shea, Treasurer Felix Kahn, and Assistant Secretary-Treasurer K. K. Bechtel. With the exception of Bechtel, these officers were also named directors. Stephen D. Bechtel, Henry J. Kaiser, Alan MacDonald, and Philip Hart (representing Pacific Bridge) rounded out the board.

Amicably, the principals agreed to establish the following holdings: Utah, 20 percent; Kaiser-Bechtel-Warren, 30 percent; M-

K, 10 percent; Shea, 10 percent; Pacific Bridge, 10 percent; and MacDonald & Kahn, 20 percent. M-K later distributed 4 percent of its share to two individuals: Graeme MacDonald, the brother of Alan MacDonald of MacDonald & Kahn, and Sydney Ehrman, a San Francisco attorney.

The new conglomerate comprised more than five thousand employees, a permanent staff of officers, and 156 engineers with a combined technical experience that covered much of western America. The group entrusted the task of assembling a winning bid to Utah Construction's chief engineer John Q. Barlow, a gruff railroader who never used a calculator, figuring everything longhand. Each company took responsibility for bidding a portion of the job and feeding the figures to Barlow. If Barlow's compilations differed from the figures received, his experience prevailed. The bid took form in the late months of 1930, with Crowe and an engineer from MacDonald & Kahn hammering out independent estimates for confirmation. Meeting in February 1931 at the Engineers Club in San Francisco, the partners were both astonished and encouraged to discover that the difference between the high and low cost estimates amounted to only $700,000 ($40 million versus $40.7 million). In the meantime, Crowe and other engineers had constructed a working model of the dam to demonstrate their attention to the engineering details. This model often appeared in W. H. Wattis's hospital room in San Francisco, where he battled cancer even as he participated in important discussions.

The third aspect of the bidding process, providing a performance bond, brought a significant challenge as word filtered west from the eastern financial establishment that the surety companies felt little enthusiasm for the Six Companies plan. They worried that $5 million initial capital might not justify the bonding, thinking as much as $8 million might be necessary. They doubted that this combination of companies would work together well enough to see the project through, and they viewed Utah Construction's ranch holdings with urban disdain. They felt highly skeptical about the Shea operation, which appeared to consist of Charles Shea himself, who ran his company from a hotel room and boasted that he never went near a bank. Finally, they did not like M-K borrowing $100,000 from a brother of Felix Kahn's deceased

S. D. (Steve) Bechtel joined his father, W. A. Bechtel, at the Hoover site, and chaired the transportation committee.

partner and Pacific Bridge's selling 40 percent of its interest to its lawyer to produce its share of the initial capital.

To counter this pessimism and to generate support and confidence, Six Companies dispatched Leland W. Cutler, vice president of Fidelity and Deposit Company and president of the San Francisco Chamber of Commerce, to the east coast to visit with the chief officers of two dozen major surety firms. To assist him, Cutler enlisted Edwin C. Porter of the United States Fidelity and Guaranty Company, and A. C. Posey of the Hartford Accident and Indemnity Company. Also, Cutler carried with him Utah's certified check for $1 million—its full share. After innumerable meetings, twenty two bonding companies agreed to provide bonds for the entire $5 million. The Fidelity and Deposit Company of Maryland assumed $2 million, while Hartford Accident and Indemnity Company, National Surety Company, and United States Fidelity and Guaranty

Company acted as co-suretors. The final underwriting set a record for a construction bond issued in the United States.

With the bonding issue settled, the principals had only to decide upon a final bid. To guard against a leak, they agreed to leave this step until the last moment. Consequently, a few days before the deadline for submission, the group met in W. H. Wattis's hospital room and settled upon the figure of $48,890,996, which was $220,000 under the government's estimate, yet still included a profit of 25 percent for Six Companies.

On March 4, 1931, three Hoover Dam bids lay in sealed envelopes on a table in a vacant retail store beneath the Denver office of the Bureau of Reclamation. Only these three bids qualified, though the Bureau had invited more than one hundred firms to bid, chosen from two hundred companies that sent representatives to the initial announcement meeting. The qualifying candidates were Arundel Corporation, Woods Brothers Corporation, and Six Companies. When the envelopes were opened, Six Companies had underbid Arundel by $5 million and Woods by nearly $10 million. Stories circulated after the meeting that Six Companies executives had developed cold feet on the train from San Francisco and chopped $2 million off their bid—making it the most expensive train ride in history. The story was untrue but illustrated the bewilderment surrounding Six Companies' dramatically low bid for the gigantic project.

On March 11, 1931, Secretary of the Interior Ray Lyman Wilbur officially awarded the contract to build Hoover Dam to Six Companies. Two weeks later, seventy-two-year-old W. H. Wattis signed the contract in San Francisco. Confident that his cancer treatments were working, he talked exuberantly about his imminent return to work on the greatest construction project in American history. "Twenty years ago," he said, "it would not have been possible. Modern machinery and modern engineering methods have made it possible." Wattis knew, however, that Six Companies needed to create a lot of possibilities from scratch. The government timetable was short, calling for completion of the four diversion tunnels by October 1, 1933, the cofferdams by May 1, 1934, the high dam for water storage not later than June 15, 1936, and power generation by 1938.

Before actual work could begin, the company refined its organization. Six Companies put together the Boulder City Company, headed by Henry Kaiser, to handle housing, food, commissary, and related activities, and the Hoover Dam Transportation Company, chaired by Steve Bechtel. General Superintendent Frank Crowe served in both subsidiaries, as did Felix Kahn and K. K. Bechtel. The corporation next created a construction committee with Hank Lawler at the helm, assisted by E. O. Wattis, Charles Shea, Harry Morrison, and W. A. Bechtel, Jr., and a purchasing committee consisting of Chairman Steve Bechtel, Les Corey, and Alan MacDonald. A streamlined plan linked the various components together.

This arrangement underwent almost immediate revision. With so many high-powered builders on the Six Companies board, Crowe found himself answering to too many bosses, who often disagreed with one another. Worried that Crowe might quit in frustration, Charlie Shea persuaded his colleagues to stop intervening. Felix Kahn, who had been one of the worst offenders, agreed: "A board of directors can establish policy," he mused, "but it can't build a dam." The board relinquished its privileges in favor of a four-member executive committee to coordinate with Crowe: Shea over field construction; Kahn over money, legal affairs, food, and housing; Steve Bechtel over purchasing, administration, and transportation; and the diplomatic Kaiser as chair. Few conflicts surfaced after that.

As Six Companies awaited its mid-summer start on heavy construction, late spring and early summer of 1931 bustled with preparations. Temporary quarters went up to house the three hundred men who erected camps, removed loose rock from Black Canyon's walls, and prepared areas for heavy equipment. A Stockton, California, builder raced to finish a highway into Boulder City from the dam site even as government contractors laid ten miles of track from the Union Pacific terminus at Boulder to the canyon rim. Late in June, electrical power coursed over a 240-mile transmission line from San Bernardino. Meanwhile, Six Companies crews built a $600,000 tram to connect the canyon to the Boulder City–Las Vegas railroad line. This double-track construction line, much of it through tunnels, ran along the canyon wall at the 720-

foot level of the cofferdams (temporary dams to de-water the work site) and linked the entire operation. Utah Construction also built an aggregate producing and batch plant to supply 4.5 million cubic yards of concrete and grout, locating it upstream eight miles beside sand, gravel, and cobble deposits.

In the meantime, government contractors erected Boulder City, which the Department of the Interior quickly promoted as a model city and "moral Utopia," with boarding, medical, recreation, and shopping facilities for a population of five thousand. In addition, Six Companies spent approximately $250 per worker to buffer the harsh climate, seven-day workweek, and the danger inherent in many jobs. Six Companies contracted with Anderson Brothers Supply Company to fill the cafeteria and soda fountain with a variety of fresh and canned foods, drawing upon a dairy farm Anderson established eighty miles from Boulder City. A dining room, barbershop, reading room, and billiards room rounded out the accommodations, which, along with a private room, cost each worker $1.50 per day. By late summer, more than three thousand workers transformed the dam site into a disturbed anthill, moving the earth and changing forever the face of the Southwest.

At about that same time, death brought another milestone to Utah Construction's history. William Henry Wattis, who had led the bidding effort from his hospital room, never returned to work as he had planned, but succumbed to cancer on September 13, 1931. At a board meeting September 21, his brother and partner for half a century suggested that Marriner S. Eccles be elected company president. The financier agreed, on the condition that E. O. become board chairman, despite his advanced years and problematic health. Lester S. Corey became vice president and general manager, and the indomitable Hank Lawler took W. H.'s seat on the board.

In Black Canyon, the work continued on an impressive scale that W. H. surely would have relished. Excavation work required the removal of six million cubic yards of earth and rock, including more than 1.5 million for diversion tunnels. To channel water into the tunnels and to keep the dam site dry, two cofferdams, each bigger than most conventional dams in the United States, required 1.236 million cubic yards of earth and rock fill. When the concrete dam was built, the lower cofferdam was then removed. The double-curvature gravity dam itself gobbled up 3.4 million cubic yards of concrete, with another 900,000 yards going into the U-shaped powerhouse, the four intake towers, and the plugs for the tunnels. In an ingenious innovation, engineers devised two-inch icing tubes to lace through the curing concrete. Without them, it might have taken up to a century for the concrete to set completely. The pouring alone took nearly two years. Almost 100,000 tons of steel

In the initial stages of building the Hoover Dam, drilling jumbos and crews excavated tunnels to divert the Colorado River from its bed.

also went into the project. As W. H. Wattis predicted from the beginning, the toughest jobs turned out to be the foundation and tunnel work. Workers drilled and pressure-grouted foundations and abutments at five-foot intervals up to 150 feet deep. After this, the dam construction itself began. Crews poured the "mud" in columns or sections and set them with a water-gas tar mixture between expansion joints.

Frank Crowe, the project's colorful superintendent, explained the precise ordering of tasks. "We had five thousand men jammed in a four-thousand-foot [wide] canyon. The problem, which was a problem of materials flow, was to set up the right sequence of jobs so they wouldn't kill each other off."

The Hoover's tunnel system alone stands as an engineering and construction feat. Four diversion tunnels, fifty feet in diameter, punch through a total of nearly three miles of rock. When the dam reached completion, the two upper tunnels were plugged at the intake ends, then linked to the spillways on either side of the dam so they could continue to carry excess water out of the reservoir. Two thirty-foot penstock tunnels, 230 feet long, and two shorter penstocks connected to the four intake towers to deliver hydropower to turn Pelton wheels that drive the dynamos. To control water flow at the four canyon outlets of these penstocks, Crowe and his men installed eight great needle valves on each unit, each valve six feet long.

When complete, the dam stood 730 feet above bedrock and stretched 1,244 feet across the crest. At its base, it was 660 feet thick, tapering to forty-five feet at the top. When Lake Mead filled behind the dam, the lake extended 115 miles upstream and contained 30.5 million acre-feet of water, with a further flood capacity of 9.5 million acre-feet. The dam's power plant capacity of 1.835 million horsepower could generate enough electric current (1.350 million kva [1 kva = 1,000 volts]) to qualify it as the largest concentration of power-generating units in the world.

Historians still debate the number of men who lost their lives building Hoover Dam, a number certainly in the scores. The food concession, for example, lost six men to heat exhaustion in its kitchens. Falling rock in Black Canyon killed two men only days after the project began. Searing heat in the canyon and often precarious heights took an additional toll in human life and injury. Despite such casualties amid rugged and hazardous conditions, the government continually complimented Six Companies on its tireless safety efforts. In a way of thinking, another casualty related to the project came on February 2, 1934, when Edmund Orson Wattis died suddenly in Ogden of a heart attack. Also passing during the Hoover Dam project were Andrew H. Christensen (1932), a close friend and confidant of the Wattis brothers almost from Utah's beginnings, and crusty Henry J. Lawler, who died in 1935. The Hoover Dam became their legacy of ingenuity and determination.

On September 30, 1935, President Franklin D. Roosevelt dedicated the massive dam in cadences reminiscent "of Deuteronomy and the triumphant prescription for the Promised Land," as television commentator Alistair Cooke later put it. Under tough Frank Crowe, the combine cut two years from the government's timetable. The Department of Interior accepted the structure as complete on March 1, 1936, three days short of five years from the opening of bids.

When the hot dust of Black Canyon settled, Six Companies' profit after taxes came to $10.4 million. That outcome was not accidental. In preparing its original bid, Six Companies had cut everything to the bone except anticipated excavation costs, which it inflated. As E. O.'s grandson Edmund Wattis Littlefield explained:

> What Six Companies did was to "unbalance the bid," which means that it had a higher markup on some of the work items and a lower markup on others in contrast to spreading the estimated profit evenly throughout the work items. Unbalanced bids are not uncommon and were used here in order to gain the profits in the early part of the job to alleviate the need for additional capital which would have strained the resources of all the partners.

This strategy paid substantial dividends, inasmuch as the tunnel excavation was finished early in 1932, capturing perhaps as much as $6 million in profits the first year and returning the total invested capital plus net earnings of $1 million. Also, Crowe's expertise

On September 30, 1935, President Franklin D. Roosevelt dedicated the Boulder Dam. The Hoover name (recalling FDR's predecessor) was later restored by Congress.

allowed the workmen to complete virtually every portion of the job well ahead of schedule as he made every nickel count. Six Companies rewarded Crowe by adding to his $18,000 annual salary a bonus of 2.5 percent of the gross profit, amounting to something more than $300,000. In a comment that summarized the enlightened management of Six Companies and its remarkable achievement, the lanky Crowe said, "When you work for that crowd, your work is appreciated."

Chapter 5

A Changing Company in a Changing World

Even as the huge dynamos of Hoover Dam began to whir in the late 1930s, changes of massive proportions were sweeping the nation and the rest of industrialized world. The Great Depression, in spite of the New Deal's stop-gap remedies, affected virtually every family in the United States. A new president took office in 1933 determined to use federal power to alleviate the suffering of millions of Americans. Franklin D. Roosevelt hoped that a huge expansion of the national government and massive spending programs would restore confidence in the democratic-capitalist system. To do this, his men had to devise countless new ways for the government to spend money on public projects, which would have the concomitant effect of bettering people's lives.

In the midst of all this historic drama, swift change also visited the Utah Construction Company, bereft of all of its founders. Some familiar surnames remained at the top of the company roster as a second generation of corporate leadership guided the enterprise into the rapidly evolving environment of the 1930–40s. For decades, W. H. Wattis, E. O. Wattis, Andrew H. Christensen, and Henry J. Lawler "really ran the company," according to E. O.'s grandson, Edmund Wattis Littlefield. "They were the 'know-how' management." By 1935, all were gone, "and they really had not provided for any management succession." Two of W. H.'s daughters, Estella Hope Wattis Bowman and Mary Jane Wattis Brown, nevertheless told Marriner S. Eccles that it was their "father's wish that, if anything happened to him, Marriner become head of the company."

The board's subsequent selection of Eccles as company president was astute in any case. Self-assured, thoughtful, broad-gauged in his thinking, and intellectually challenging of his associates, Eccles was such a formidable financier that the government named the Federal Reserve Building in Washington, D.C., after him in 1982 to honor his long tenure as chairman of the "Fed." Born in Logan, Utah, on September 9, 1890, Marriner was the eldest son of Ellen Stoddard Eccles and industrial magnate David Eccles, one of Utah Construction's founders. Marriner was twenty-two when his father died suddenly, leaving behind diverse and extensive holdings in banking, lumber, railroads, sugar, food processing, and livestock, in addition to the Eccles interest in Utah Construction. Stepping forward to manage those assets, Marriner soon controlled a large portion of his father's enterprises.

Financier Marriner S. Eccles (left) was appointed by President Franklin D. Roosevelt to lead the Federal Reserve System. Simultaneously, Eccles served as Utah Construction's president.

With his brother George S. Eccles, and the Browning family of Ogden, he formed the Eccles-Browning Affiliated Banks in 1924, forerunner of the First Security Corporation, perhaps the first multibank holding company in American history. Before age forty, Eccles had become one of the nation's shrewdest and most successful banking entrepreneurs. His ingenious efforts saved not only First Security but also the Deseret National Bank of Salt Lake City from disaster with the onset of the Great Depression. Eccles came to believe in the necessity of national compensatory monetary and fiscal policy to prevent the complete collapse of the American banking system. Consequently, he helped draft the Emergency Banking Act of 1933 that created the Federal Deposit Insurance Corporation (FDIC). In doing so, Eccles caught the attention of President Roosevelt, who in 1934 appointed him to the board of governors of the Federal Reserve System. Two years later, Eccles became chairman in time to be instrumental in countering the effects of the recession of 1937–38. The Utahn headed the board until 1948 and remained as a governor until 1951.

Although as president of the Utah Construction Company he had no direct managerial responsibility, Eccles kept a close eye on the firm, regarding it as one of his father's most important investments. In addition to his duties in Washington during the 1930s, Eccles oversaw the Amalgamated Sugar Company, First Security Bank, and the Eccles Investment Company. To run Utah Construction, Wattis cousin and veteran company executive Lester Corey assumed the role of general manager, "whose duties," read the corporate by-laws, "shall be to look after and superintend all operations of the company." Eccles attended most Utah board meetings and rose in September 1940 to chairman of the board when Corey became both president and general manager.

With Corey in charge and despite the ongoing Depression, Utah's activities escalated after the completion of Hoover Dam as dam building continued to dominate its work during a decade of big dams, not only for Utah and its partners but for the United States as well. Promising electrical power, renewed agricultural bounties, jobs, and insurance for the success of an industrial democracy, the giant dams captured the imagination of President Roosevelt and Depression-weary Americans. "After Boulder," observed historian

Alistair Cooke, "Roosevelt was consumed with a passion for more dams.... The dam may be taken as a symbol of Roosevelt's New Deal, a majestic exemplar of the doctrine that ... more electricity, more power, was to be the guarantee of what Roosevelt called 'the more abundant life.'" With the dam complete on the Colorado River, America's attention focused on its other Pacific-bound river, the Columbia.

Learning that the Bonneville—the first big dam across the Columbia—would be built forty miles east of Portland, Henry Kaiser immediately contacted his associates in Six Companies about a new joint venture. Utah and four other companies joined to form the Columbia Construction Company. As with the Hoover, the group faced problems in financing the project. Bonding companies feared that the size of the Bonneville job precluded individual companies from bidding on other projects without permission from each member of the bonding syndicate. Once the articles of incorporation were amended to allow each firm to negotiate its own bonding arrangements, the United States Treasury Department approved the bonds and Columbia Construction prepared a successful bid of approximately $17 million.

Actually constructing the Bonneville Dam to government specifications also posed a major problem. The United States Army Corps of Engineers dictated that the project provide a constant flow for downstream navigation and power generation, regardless of seasonal shifts in water level. To accomplish this, the Army located the dam at a point where the river divided. Most water flowed through the north channel, so Columbia Construction built a slab-and-buttress dam there, 197 feet high and 1,450 long. The dam diverted the water into the south channel, where a powerhouse and power plant controlled the distribution of federally-generated electricity. When completed in 1940, Bonneville included eighteen spillways for water-level adjustment. Another challenge lay in preparing the foundation for a dam on a river measuring sixty feet deep with velocities up to twelve cubic feet per second. To de-water the site, the company constructed cofferdams and wooden cribs to receive tons of river silt from barge-mounted clamshells. As pumps dried the beds, earth-moving equipment extracted more than six million cubic yards of dirt and boulders down to bedrock.

The Bonneville Dam was only the first effort on the Columbia. A second, even larger, job began upstream in 1938, some ninety miles west of Spokane. Kaiser again sponsored a joint venture known as Consolidated Builders to erect the mammoth Grand Coulee Dam at an approximate cost of $65 million. The group included Utah (with an 8 percent interest), Morrison Knudsen Company (M-K), Shea, MacDonald & Kahn, Pacific Bridge, and General Construction Company, as well as another association of contractors that had already accomplished the foundation work at the dam site. Among the technical challenges was freezing an entire hillside to prevent slides by pumping refrigerant through buried pipes.

Perhaps the greatest challenge came with the massive volume of the dam itself. Consolidated devised an enormous concreting process that placed more than ten million cubic yards of concrete—three times more aggregate than had ever gone into a single structure in all of history. For two years, a couple of 270-ton, double-cantilever cranes moved along a trestle two hundred feet high and thirty-six hundred feet long, with 356-foot booms from which poured almost four hundred cubic yards of concrete every hour, day and night. During one twenty-four-hour period, 20,697 yards of concrete sloshed into the forms, an all-time record. As the dam rose from the river bed, workers latticed the concrete with 2,200 miles of steel pipe to carry cold water through the "mud," speeding the curing which, unaided, may have taken up to 150 years. Finished in 1941, Grand Coulee stands as tall as the Washington Monument—550 feet above the river bottom—with spillways twice as high as Niagara Falls. With the capacity to irrigate more than one million acres, the dam also powered eighteen generators that could produce in excess of 1.9 million kilowatts of electricity.

While "big dams"on the Colorado and Columbia captured the American imagination, Utah and its associates also built many smaller dams during this period, including the Cooney Dam on Montana's Red Lodge Creek. A half-million-dollar operation completed in 1936, Cooney required an earth fill less than one hundred feet high but almost half a mile long. Working in partnership with M-K a year later, Utah crews finished work on another earth-filled dam, a three-year project just seven miles up the Ogden River from corporate headquarters. Under the auspices of the Bureau of Reclamation, Pineview Dam was erected in a $1.5 million joint venture to provide irrigation water and power for Ogden City. Another significant water project was the Imperial Dam in California. Prior to its construction, California water companies spent up to $1 million a year to remove tons of silt from the water emerging through the All American Canal. Located over terrain difficult to de-water, Imperial demanded as many as twenty-eight hundred well-points connecting sixty pumps to blot seepage. To cope with the silt, the combine installed fifty-five control gates on the dam canals to operate four settling basins where seventy-two scrapers moved 70,000 tons of mud per day into underground galleries; from there, it flowed back into the river bed below the dam. After the dam's completion in 1938, the Imperial Valley received clear water from a chocolate-brown river.

Throughout the Depression, New Deal spending spawned a whole string of such dam-building adventures for earthmoving companies like Utah. As Cooke intimated, FDR seemed intent on taming every wild river in the country. Two additional examples of federal projects were Taylor Park Dam near Gunnison, Colorado, and Seminoe Dam on the North Platte in Wyoming, not far from Rawlins. The 200-foot Taylor Park reached completion in 1937 at a cost of about $1.2 million. Three of Utah's Six Companies partners, M-K, Bechtel, and Kaiser, also participated in the project. As the Gunnison job ended, Utah was almost two years into the Seminoe dam, another joint venture, this time with M-K and Winston Brothers Company. Winston had provided the sponsoring impetus on Seminoe but enjoyed the other two companies' proven expertise in concrete dams. A 300-by-530-foot arch structure, it required an installed powerhouse—a kind of miniature Hoover. When finished in 1939, Seminoe cost almost $4.5 million.

Roosevelt's water reclamation agenda also included dams to restore and electrify flood-damaged regions outside the West, particularly in the impoverished Tennessee Valley, a region almost as large as the United Kingdom. To aid him in this aim, Congress established the Tennessee Valley Authority (TVA) in 1933. This brought Utah Construction eastward to participate in a number of

The Pineview Dam, completed by Utah and Morrison Knudsen in June 1937, caught waters from several forks of the Ogden River.

projects, the largest being a scheme to erect a dam, power plant, and tunnels on North Carolina's Nantahala River, primarily for power production. Nantahala initially appeared to be a routine earth-filled operation, yet by the time Utah completed this project, the firm had wrestled with a series of problems and delays that threatened an over-budget financial disaster. Satisfied with Utah's efforts, the TVA and the Nantahala Power and Light Company agreed to a settlement that produced a reasonable profit for the company.

Next in the water-project category, Utah and M-K undertook the Norfolk Dam, a flood-control structure across the destructive Northfork River in Arkansas. A torrential rainstorm, hurling a thirty-four-foot wall of water through the construction site, and a second flood a few months later, amply demonstrated the need for the dam. While the cofferdams prevented a great deal of damage to downstream farms and homes, the contractors lost valuable work time. A wartime decision to add power-producing capabilities to Norfolk for strategic metal processing meant the dam builders must accelerate the concrete pouring by 60 percent. To counter the high heat generated by the concrete mix, pumps forced near-freezing water from a refrigeration plant through a web of steel pipes and sent crushed ice, replacing carefully calculated proportions of water, directly into the concrete. The Norfolk Dam was dedicated in 1945, creating a forty-mile-long lake and generating more than 35,000 kilowatts of electricity.

Smaller TVA projects also contributed to Utah's overall dam-building program with its associates. In 1942 Utah and M-K jointly contracted to construct the Watauga and South Holsten diversion spillway tunnels near Knoxville, Tennessee. The following year, Utah relocated the Southern Railway line between Bryson City and Wesser, North Carolina, before Fontana Dam, a major part of the TVA system, inundated the site.

The company's dam-building enterprise continued well past the Depression and war years in such places as Angostura, South Dakota (completed in 1947), Sonora, Mexico (1947), Davis, Arizona (1951), and Grace, Idaho (1959). Dam work also brought Utah Construction to its home state to build the $2.6 million Gateway Tunnel near Ogden. Completed in 1954, work consisted of driving, lining, and constructing portal structures for the tunnel, which measured more than three miles in length with an approximate diameter of ten feet. Then, in 1957, the company also built the $3 million Wanship Dam, east of Salt Lake City and part of the Weber Basin complex. This earth-filled structure rose 156 feet and stretched two thousand feet at the crest. Behind it, Rockport Reservoir filled for use in irrigation and recreation. That same year, Utah raised the height of Ogden's Pineview Dam, which it had built during the 1930s, to make it a key element in the Weber Basin system.

Table 2
Dam Projects Completed 1936–59

Dam	Location	Completion	Contract Amount
Cooney	Montana	1936	$478,000
Hoover	Nevada	1936	$48.9 million
Pineview	Utah	1937	$1.5 million
Taylor Park	Colorado	1937	$1.2 million
Imperial	Arizona	1938	$6.3 million
Parker	Arizona	1939	$8.8 million

Seminoe	Wyoming	1939	$4.5 million
Bonneville	Oregon	1940	$17 million
Missouri-Broadwater	Montana	1940	$692,000
Grand Coulee	Washington	1941	$65 million
Nantahala	North Carolina	1942	$6.1 million
Ross (expansion)	Washington	1943	$7.1 million
Norfolk	Arkansas	1945	$10 million
Angostura	South Dakota	1947	$5.4 million
Hermosilla	Sonora, Mex.	1947	$3.8 million
Davis	Arizona	1951	$31.3 million
Wanship	Utah	1957	$3 million
Grace	Idaho	1959	$275,000

As dam building followed in consequence of railroad construction, so did road building. After a tentative move into highway construction before Hoover Dam, Utah undertook twenty-four highway projects while working at Black Canyon. Although corporate management did not emphasize this endeavor, road projects enhanced Utah's public recognition. They also solidified the company's reputation among government officials in the western states and prepared Utah for larger projects to come. In addition, much of its highway-related work went forth as part of joint ventures. For example, Six Companies of California organized in 1934 (with the same partners in building the Hoover) and bid successfully on a $3.7 million contract with the State of California to construct a highway and tunnel. Simultaneously, Utah joined with two of its Hoover partners, Kaiser and Bechtel, to form Bridge Builders, Inc., in order to acquire a $5.5 million contract to construct a portion of the San Francisco-Oakland Bay Bridge. The group's responsibilities in the massive $77 million project included building the piers and abutments for the east span of the bridge and painting the superstructure. This project demonstrated Utah's capabilities as a regional general contracting firm of considerable stature.

As further proof of its diversification and managerial expertise, the company continued its traditional railroad contracting by submitting the winning bid for the Dotsero Cutoff in Colorado and the Niles-San Jose branch in California. For the Utah Copper Company's Bingham and Garfield Railroad, Utah Construction extended mining dump lines and tunnels and built bridges, tunnels, piers, and railroad lines. Another mining client, the Union Pacific Coal Company, hired Utah to finish air shafts and entrance slopes in Wyoming. Other projects included building a jetty off the coast of Washington State, erecting three bridges in California, and digging eight water-project canals and tunnels in Utah, Wyoming, California, and Colorado, as well as the Moffat Project for the Denver Municipal Water Works, the West Iron Mountain Water Tunnel, and the Los Angeles Aqueduct for the Metropolitan Water District of Southern California.

An important step outside the region came in 1938, when Utah formed a joint-venture partnership with three other firms to construct an $11 million, seven-mile portion of the Delaware Aqueduct, an eighty-five-mile pressure tunnel to augment New York City's water supply. The partners installed access shafts and appurtenant fixtures on the tunnel as it ran between three to fifteen hundred feet under the surface, often below sea level. Measuring twenty feet at its outside diameter and fifteen feet at the interior, the tunnel required a two-and-one-half-foot reinforced concrete lining to deliver water from the upper tributaries of the Delaware River. At least the men and women selling apples and pencils on the poverty-ridden streets of New York would not go thirsty.

After nearly a decade of such public works projects, Utah Construction and most of the country were still struggling to find their way in the new world the Depression had created. Elsewhere, worldwide economic chaos had unleashed a whirlwind of revolutions. In Europe, Adolf Hitler and his National Socialists charted aggression and ethnic cleansing as ways to regain the eminence Germany had lost in the Great War, while Benito Mussolini promised the Italians new glory and security in the fascist deification of brute force. Half a world away, militarists in Japan adopted imperialism as the means to make the sun rise for their nation. By the end of the 1930s, World War II had engulfed much of the planet. In response, President Franklin D. Roosevelt called on America to become "the arsenal of democracy" against totalitarianism.

Then, on December 7, 1941, Japanese bombers swooped over Pearl Harbor, and the United States found itself fighting a two-front war. Already, Utah Construction was in the thick of things, with the War Department as a major client. Safe inside volcanic cliffs, Utah personnel worked without interruption for eleven months during the crisis as they labored on top-secret fuel depositories known as the Red Hills Storage Vaults on Oahu, Hawaii. Construction began in January 1941 on four underground fuel tanks, 250 feet deep (about the height of a twenty-story building) and one hundred feet in diameter, with fifty-foot radius domes at top and bottom. Additional contracts with the Navy Bureau of Yards and Docks for sixteen more vaults made Red Hills one of Utah's largest—as well as the most unusual—defense contracts of the war.

Confronting challenges outside Utah's previous experience, company engineers and site superintendents developed ingenious construction methods at Red Hills. For instance, the project required excavating more than 1.7 million cubic yards of red volcanic rock. Utah saved time and effort by placing the blasting charges so that the discharged rock fell directly onto a conveyor belt, which moved it to a crusher in an adjacent tunnel. Also, Red Hills required 10,000 tons of reinforcing, structural, and tunnel steel plus enough quarter-inch steel plate to cover forty-five acres. It took 413,000 yards of concrete and nearly eighteen million sacks of cement for grout and gunite lining. The facility, completed in October 1943, stored up to six million barrels of diesel fuel for vessels of the Pacific Fleet.

To defeat the Axis, the Allies would need all the fuel and all the ships that industry could supply. Even before Congress declared war, Utah began building ships. In 1939, as Hitler's war raged in Europe, the firm joined in forming the Seattle-Tacoma Shipbuilding Company, the first of many such joint ventures during the war years, often with Utah's dam-building partners. As with most early war contracts, Seattle-Tacoma's initial business came from the British government. As the American role increased, so did the contracts the government offered, leading to the eventual creation of nine other shipbuilding firms, most located on the Pacific Coast and involving Utah with an interest between 3 and 10 percent. The names of these companies became legendary as the United States

Henry Kaiser, a major force when Six Companies built the Hoover Dam, teamed again with Utah Construction to build ships during World War II.

launched hundreds of new ships to aid in the war effort: Joshua Hendy Iron Works, Permanente Steamship, and Todd-Bath Iron Shipbuilding, as well as the California, Houston, Oregon, Richmond, South Portland, and Todd-California shipbuilding companies.

By November 1941, these nine companies, along with Seattle-Tacoma, had undertaken defense contracts worth more than $750 million. By war's end, companies in which Utah participated had completed work on contracts worth billions of dollars, many of them for Liberty ships that set sail from the Richmond yard in California at the remarkable rate of one every four days. "There was no miracle formula available to the shipbuilders," observed the British-American writer Alistair Cooke. "The government kept insisting upon a miracle, however, and got it in the shape of a lumbering, undramatic tub called a 'Liberty ship.' In its final form it was a brainchild of Henry Kaiser, a bald bullfrog of a construction man who liked nothing better than the word of an expert that something couldn't be done."

The secret to success lay in the adaptability of the assembly line, long the butt of European jokes. "The Americans cannot build airplanes," Air Marshal Hermann Goering had assured Hitler, "They are very good at refrigerators and razor blades." Both Nazis would live to regret that judgment. Years later, Cooke recalled his own visit to the Richmond shipyard:

> The place was laid out like a gigantic chessboard, with cranes hovering overhead depositing parts, engines, and booms in alphabetically marked and numbered squares. Thirty thousand components came in this way, and it was like something out of Disney: trolleys whizzing, and hooters honking and buzzing, a whole deckhouse moving to the ways upside down. It would then be upended while the welders descended upon it like an army of woodpeckers. You'd have a stem and a keel and then part of plate A-1 would be welded to A-2, and S-13 to S-14, and so on. The workers knew even less about shipbuilding than Kaiser. Only one in two hundred had ever been in a shipyard. Kaiser himself talked about the "front" and "back" end of a ship. Roosevelt said, "I don't care what he calls them, provided he delivers." And he did.

Within a few months after America's entry into the war, the joint venturers in these nine companies realized that, for the sake of efficiency, the East and West Coast operations should function separately. As a result, Utah and the other western companies agreed to a plan whereby the Todd Shipyards Corporation (a major eastern member of the consortium) would purchase the stock of the shipbuilding companies located in the East and sell its interest in those located in the West. In this manner, "Atlantic" and "Pacific" groups evolved, coordinating yet operating independently.

In addition to helping to provide the Allies with "instant" ships, Utah won many other joint-venture defense contracts. The most profitable lay within the Pacific war zone, where Utah and its associates rebuilt, fortified, and equipped bases that American forces needed for the ongoing assault against the Japanese. All told, Utah joined in building more than $550 million worth of naval air bases on Pacific islands, from Hawaii and Midway to Guam and Samoa, erecting hospitals, barracks, supply depots, airfields, and many other facilities.

Military construction also proceeded at a feverish pace on the mainland and outside the Pacific war zone. Perhaps Utah's most visible of many home-front jobs came in 1942, when the Public Roads Administration selected Utah as one of several contractors to build a military highway from Dawson Creek, Alberta, to Fairbanks, Alaska—a major portion of what became the Alaskan-Canadian (Alcan) Highway. Utah set about building a rugged 150-mile portion of the highway just east of the Alaskan-Canadian border. Though sparsely inhabited, that stretch included beautiful lakes and marshes, swift rivers, areas of dense virgin timber, and a challenging climate—scorching midsummer days and dark, bitter cold during the long winters. The $8.4 million project was completed ahead of schedule in 1943, earning Utah Construction a certificate of merit from the Public Roads Administration.

Many other stateside military projects came to Utah and its associates, including the construction of dry docks on Mare Island, California, and a naval air station at Corpus Christi, Texas. The Texas project required a diverse range of activities, including the erection of buildings, hangars, ramps, and other accessories, in addition to runways and training fields. In California, Utah Construction built dry docks in San Diego and Alameda, a shipyard at Alameda, and a temporary staging area at Pittsburg.

The influx of military personnel immediately strained military housing facilities, and so construction companies began framing hundreds of temporary buildings, most at California's Fort Ord and Camp Roberts, and Washington's Fort Lewis and McCord Field. Long supply lines into the Pacific also demanded increasing storage and shipping capacities in military depots. Utah participated in several depot projects, including the Oakland Supply Depot, Navy buildings and warehouses at Clearfield, Utah, and the Deseret Chemical Warfare Supply Depot at St. John, Utah, south of Tooele, which also involved building a half-million-dollar railroad.

Ironically, Utah's largest military contract came after the war ended. Early in 1945, American forces under the command of General Douglas MacArthur drove the Japanese from the Philippines. The urgent need for the United States to reestablish and bolster its military presence there necessitated an enormous rebuilding program. Transforming Clark Field into a modern air force base became an essential priority of reconstruction. Located near Manila Bay, the badly damaged base was strategically crucial to the future of American interests in Southeast Asia and the South Pacific. During 1945–46, Utah participated in joint ventures that performed $136 million worth of work in the Philippines, primarily at Clark Field.

Also during the war years, although only indirectly related to the war effort, Utah began to involve itself in domestic mining. During the 1930s, it had undertaken railroad construction for mining outfits, particularly in connection with the Utah Copper Company (Kennecott) operation in Salt Lake County. Between the completion of its work on Hoover Dam and the end of the decade,

Utah Construction joined other companies in an all-out effort to build the Alaska Military Highway (later the Alaskan-Canadian Highway) in just over eight months.

Utah had built bridges, tunnels, piers, and railroad lines for the Bingham and Garfield Railroad, which serviced the mining operation, for total contracts in the amount of $1.4 million, and had constructed a highway tunnel for the copper company for another $1.2 million. In 1938, Utah finished air shaft and entrance slopes in Wyoming for the Union Pacific Coal Company on a $311,000 contract.

Its first large mining contract came from the Pittsburgh Coal Company in western Pennsylvania. Opening in 1943, the operation lasted until 1949, as the company made its initial steps into stripping and open-pit coal mining. During those six years, the mine produced more than 3.2 million tons of high-grade coal using a process that required the extraction of nearly thirty million cubic yards of overburden, enough material to bury a square mile under a mound of earth three stories high. The total contract amounted to more than $6.7 million.

In 1945 Utah set up an exploration and development fund to support a search for mining properties; meanwhile the company continued to perform mining operations as outgrowths of its construction activities at mines. In the late 1940s, Utah undertook more than $5.5 million of iron ore mining for the Colorado Fuel and Iron Corporation (CF&I) through both stripping and mining operations at the company's Iron Mountain Mine in southern Utah. This contract led Utah into a coal strip-mining operation near Ozark, Arkansas, in 1948, where Utah crews stripped a layer of very high-grade coking coal from the Ozark-Philpott Coal Mine for shipment west to Colorado Fuel. In Arkansas, crews removed overburden up to fifty feet deep, a significant challenge. As shallow coal reserves became increasingly scarce at Ozark-Philpott, the company ventured into underground mining.

Utah's 1948 explorations also located iron ore deposits near Vancouver, British Columbia. By 1951, Utah created its wholly owned subsidiary Argonaut Company, Ltd., to work extensive magnetite ore deposits. Although Utah operated this mine only until 1957, the experience would lead to greater ventures. Also, near the war's end, Utah began its own iron ore extraction program at Iron Springs, located ten miles west of Cedar City, Utah, to supply the Kaiser Steel Plant at Fontana, California. The first sales to Kaiser averaged 26,000 tons per month, but ore shipments temporarily halted in late 1945 and 1946 due to post-war steel strikes. When shipments resumed in 1947, they increased to about 50,000 tons per month.

Although the company's worksheet remained full, many of the projects Utah undertook during the 1930s and 1940s were small in revenue, raising the company's net worth only slightly—from $6.7 million in 1929 to $7.3 million in 1939. The more lucrative military contracts of the 1940s helped, yet Utah's diversification did not bring a powerful identify nor substantially increase the company's net worth. Indeed, much of its work had been in joint ventures where outfits like Kaiser and M-K cast huge shadows, eclipsing Utah's sense of identity and purpose.

Following the war, Marriner Eccles participated in establishing the World Bank and the International Monetary Fund, then left the Federal Reserve Board in 1951. Widely recognized as the most talented and energetic business and financial analyst in America, he then turned his full attention toward his family's business interests, high among them the Utah Construction Company. Eccles was convinced that, if Utah was to succeed in the postwar world, the company must find stronger management and set a clear direction. In terms of shareholder votes, he needed support from at least one of the Wattis families and all the other shareholders. One thing was certain—the Utah Construction Company, now a half-century old, was struggling to find its bearings in a vastly changed modern world.

Section II

Utah Construction & Mining

Utah Construction acquired its first mine in 1944 near Cedar City, Utah. The Iron Springs Mine developed over several decades.

Chapter 6

Reinvigorating Management

By the midpoint of the twentieth century, the world had arrived at a critical juncture. Advancements in science and technology made it possible for humanity to alter nature to such an extent that many observers worried that developments such as the atomic bomb symbolized only a bleak future for a planet gone mad. Others believed that humans would instead use their newfound knowledge and skills to make life immeasurably better. Among the latter were the leaders of the Utah Construction Company, now at a crucial crossroads in its own history. Despite a lengthy list of achievements in railroad and dam building in the 1930–40s, annual company profits never exceeded those in 1919, when black ink totaled $1.6 million. In fact, Utah's books showed a net loss in 1945. From building the Hoover Dam on through the war, events swept Utah along, as they did many firms. Some, like Bechtel and Morrison Knudsen (M-K), adjusted their strategies and took advantage of the rapidly growing economy, but Utah—which had provided major leadership in the Six Companies—did not advance. Understandably disappointed in such a performance, Marriner Eccles began talking of selling the company as early as 1943.

Perceptibly, the slide began with the changing of the guard in 1931. The new management came essentially from the ranks of the founding families. While no one questioned the competence and dedication of any of these men, and in particular general manager Lester S. Corey, their relationships with major shareholding groups, often with diametrically opposing views, sometimes paralyzed decision making and kept Utah from moving aggressively to stay in the game with such competitors as Bechtel and M-K. Although Eccles had played a visible role in the management of the company as president, his personality, talents, ambition, and accomplishments kept him so busy before he retired from the Federal Reserve Board in 1951 that he limited his direct function as a real guide of Utah's destiny. In addition, until 1971 corporate bylaws gave to the general manager "duties ... to look after and superintend all operations of the company." The office of president existed primarily to satisfy corporate regulations within the state of incorporation and held no managerial implications beyond that of advising.

When Corey became president as well as general manager in 1940, Eccles assumed the chairmanship of the board. This and other appointments served to emphasize the continuing importance of family members at the top of the company, with the natural idea that one of them would become heir-apparent. For example, W. H. Wattis's son-in-law George P. Bowman became a member of the board in 1931 and in 1936 received a charge from his colleagues "to advise, confer with and assist the General Manager in any manner possible in the management of the corporation's real estate and livestock holdings." This gave Bowman, then in his forties, considerable authority and stemmed from his position as manager of Utah's huge Vineyard ranch, headquartered at Montello, Nevada, where, according to Thomas D. Dee's son Lawrence (Larry), he enjoyed playing the role of the rough, tough cowboy.

Another example of this second-generation effect was E. O. Wattis's son Paul, who came to the board at the age of thirty-two in 1931. Like Bowman, he had considerable experience working for the company, continued to perform actively through the 1930s, and became a vice president in the 1940 shuffle at the top. A year later, increasingly frustrated and disappointed with Utah's decline from dominance, Wattis resigned from the board and the vice presidency to become more involved in his insurance business in San Francisco. As a matter of ethics, he frankly admitted to the board that he was no longer giving Utah top priority. E. G. Bennett, representing the board, suggested that he retain his directorship and continue as a vice president in name only but with continuing salary for another year. Wattis agreed, and, with repeated invitations, kept the vice president's title until 1945 and his directorship until 1971.

With Corey aging and showing little innovation, the limited scope of Bowman's involvement and the departure of Wattis from active management raised a big question of successorship. Into the midst of this uncertainty came other vexing crosscurrents. The E. O. family suffered from a nagging bewilderment over why E. O. had not received the presidency upon the death of W. H., while the W. H. group wanted Bowman to become general manager. Eccles, on the other hand, hoped to preserve the financial strength of Utah with a competent general manager, who—in his mind—was not Bowman. All of this had kept Corey in charge while the company invariably drifted.

To break this impasse, the W. H. family moved to create an alliance between the two Wattis families against Eccles. During the Christmas season of 1943, Stella and George Bowman contacted Ezekiel (Zeke) Dumke (E. O.'s daughter Edna's husband) and Paul Wattis to arrange a meeting of the two groups in Ogden. Wattis and Shephard (Shep) Mitchell (husband of E. O.'s daughter Veda Ruth) invited Edmund Wattis Littlefield, son of Edmund A. and Marguerite Wattis Littlefield (E. O.'s daughter). The younger Littlefield was then busy in Washington working for the Petroleum Administration for War, but he agreed to attend as a representative of the E. O. family. At the meeting from the W. H. side were the Bowmans, their son Donald Wattis Bowman, and Martin McNamara, representing his mother-in-law, Mary McNamara Brown (W. H.'s granddaughter).

Shortly after the meeting began, the W. H. representatives recommended that the two families unite in replacing Eccles and Corey with their own management group. "With all the confidence of a twenty-nine-year-old," Littlefield later recalled, he listened to the discussion and then said, "I think we ought to talk about getting together, but I want to observe that there is too much nepotism in this company. As a guiding principle, we should find the best qualified person, outside of the company, to run it." By his own assessment, "Everyone agreed to that proposal, but it wasn't thirty days before Jerry Seale (George and Stella Bowman's son-in-law) was to be hired away from Kaiser and to be made assistant to Les Corey. All of a sudden, it was clear that the W. H. family didn't have the same ambitions that we had."

News of Seale's appointment enraged Paul Wattis, who planned to challenge the move at the next board meeting. In an attempt to calm the waters, Ed Littlefield (E. O.'s grandson) wrote to Wattis from Washington, D.C., on February 18, 1944:

> You have indicated that with or without the support of the other family [W. H.] you plan to battle on March 7th. What is your strategy? What can you possibly achieve by fighting alone? I see no earthly reason in this case to fight unless you can win. If, without hope of success, you further antagonize Eccles and the existing management, the result is merely to expend your ammunition, alienate possible allies, lose your position, and impair your ability to strike effectively at some future strategic moment. You may lose everything and you can gain nothing.
>
> Let's make haste slowly. Let's not commit the blunder of leading the attack. Either the Eccles group or the W. H. interests or ourselves must find an ally in the other two to assume control. At the moment the two of them are split asunder, and I suspect that sooner or later one or the other will seek our support. You have diligently tried to get the two families together, but the W. H. family will not move to a joint attack on the comprehensive problem [of which person manages the company]. Certainly the past experience points to the fact that they are difficult to work with.
>
> Why don't we just sit tight for once? As long as the Eccles interests are at odds with the W. H. interests, we are in a beautiful position for neither one dares to antagonize us too far. I am quite sure that we would find MSE [Eccles] quite receptive to our suggestions, and we might well accomplish much of our program on a friendly basis. Certainly this is a wiser course than fighting without chance of victory.

While he thus worked to keep the lid on tempers, Littlefield suggested to Dumke and Wattis that he visit with Eccles in

Washington to pledge the support of the E. O. family for a reorganization that would be in the best interests of the stockholders, that did not seek offices for family members, and that would reduce or eliminate the internal friction. Mitchell persuaded Wattis and Dumke of the wisdom of this approach, and Littlefield was off to broach the idea to Eccles, who later met with Wattis and Mitchell in Ogden to ratify the concept.

In the meantime, the Bowmans continued to hold to the old pattern of family succession and hoped to secure for the W. H. side a major management position in the company, perhaps for their son Donald, who had become a director in 1938 at age twenty-seven. Then, to signal his new alliance with the E. O. group, Eccles informed George Bowman on May 15, 1944, that the board, with the exception of the W. H. representatives, was dissatisfied with his management of the ranch and livestock division. Twenty-four hours later, Donald Bowman resigned his vice presidency and directorship in a letter to the board, saying he did not care to work with the present management. The committee accepted the resignation and nominated Seale (husband of Donald's sister) for a board membership. This clever and conciliatory gesture was approved on September 28, 1944, although Seale remained with Kaiser in California.

In a rancorous and intemperate reaction, with unfortunate financial costs to them and their descendants, George and Stella Bowman sold their stock "in a cold fury." The Bowmans asked William H. (Billy) Harris, a Utah vice president and secretary/treasurer (married to E. O.'s daughter Mattie Cassidy Wattis), to help them dispose of their shares. Harris told Marriner Eccles, who passed the word on to Eccles S. Browning, who then purchased the 2,594 shares. Saying later he was not sure they had readily available money, Harris did not inform the larger E. O. Wattis family nor the Dee family. Browning kept 2,357 shares, and distributed 237 shares to his own family, to the W. H. family, and a few to one of his secretaries. With the former block of W. H.-based shares now fragmented, the gap between the two Wattis families widened.

In the aftermath of all this, and in reaction to Donald Bowman's outspoken criticisms of management and other members of the board, a shareholders' meeting convened on October 13, 1944, to review his status as a director. Eccles read a prepared statement describing the board's dissatisfaction with the existing arrangement, after which the shareholders ratified Bowman's resignation from his directorship. In the board meeting that followed, George S. Eccles replaced Bowman, Marriner Adams Browning (son of Marriner Sandifer Browning) took Seale's chair, and R. B. Ford (a son-in-law of Thomas D. Dee) assumed another directorship. With that, the dust began to settle, but the rift between the families had widened. The W. H. group resented its loss of office, while the E. O. group felt confused at holding the largest block of stock yet still looking in from the outside. So, despite their differences, both families seemed to have lost their place in the sun.

In spite of this new clarity as to who controlled the board, company management remained fairly static into the postwar years. Corey remained at the helm as president and general

In 1951, engineer Allen D. Christensen (center) became general manager and executive vice president. He is flanked here by Marriner S. Eccles and Edmund W. Littlefield.

manager, and the company's fortunes continued to sag. In the midst of this dim situation, however, appeared a promising yet familiar name. Allen D. Christensen had followed his father, pioneer engineer and company leader Andrew H. Christensen, into the engineering profession and into the ranks of Utah's management. Something of a visionary, the younger Christensen possessed a creative imagination and an ability to conceptualize. Convinced that Utah's future lay in mining, where its enormous earthmoving experience could pay healthy dividends, he persuaded the board to undertake mining at Iron Springs near Cedar City, Utah, in 1944; at the Ozark-Philpott Mine in Arkansas, in 1946; and at the Argonaut Mine in British Columbia, in 1951. Wisely, he organized these moves in ways that did not threaten Utah's client companies already in the mining business.

Promoted to general manager and executive vice president in 1951, Christensen's confidence clashed with his sometimes shy and reticent demeanor. Ed Littlefield saw this characteristic as a "cultivated mystique ... at times impenetrable." This personality trait frequently caused board members, although they had no reason to mistrust him, to believe that he "was either withholding information or did not have it at his fingertips." As a result, according to Littlefield, they felt that they were being asked to make project decisions without adequate information. By design or personality, it was certainly Christensen's personal style to keep his information close, doling out only what was necessary.

Christensen's assistant treasurer, H. N. (Bert) Stronck, followed his boss's lead by preparing financial statements that were "not illuminating," as Littlefield put it. Although the board generally approved of Christensen's leadership, it felt a growing need for more information to offset any concern that the general manager either was not forthcoming or not in possession of the facts. This situation became acute as board members spent long hours at quarterly meetings debating moot points on potential projects that never materialized.

Marriner Eccles watched all of this with growing discomfort. While he liked Christensen's aims and vision, Eccles sought long-term stability and strength in the company's management. As he thought about solutions, his mind repeatedly came back to the bright career successes of thirty-six-year-old Ed Littlefield. Eventually, Eccles determined to draw him into the family business.

Littlefield had graduated from Stanford University with distinction in 1936, beginning as an English major and ending up in economics. Awarded a master's degree in business administration from the Stanford Business School in March 1938, he became the first in his class to find a job when Standard Oil of California hired him at $150 a month. Littlefield was soon working for W. E. Bates, an assistant to vice president Ralph K. Davies, both of whom worked for Henry T. Judd, the corporate treasurer. The new executive's job involved "sales investments," exclusive sales contracts with undercapitalized companies (early clients were Yellow Cab and Pacific Greyhound), which drew financial support from Standard. Both Bates and the treasurer cleared the investments through Davies before they went to the board for final approval. In one illuminating incident early in Littlefield's career, Judd did not believe the inexperienced man could handle a certain complex negotiation. Judd later apologized: "Mr. Littlefield, I want you to know I protested your being sent on this assignment.... I also want to say to you now [that] no one could have done better work than you did." The young executive consequently became an assistant both to Judd and to his boss Victor Palmer. Littlefield always believed that his relationship with Palmer prepared him for working with Allen Christensen: "The two managers had an extraordinary genius, were extremely creative, yet they could not manage well what they created."

Littlefield's next career stage seemed even more promising. When the president of Standard of California died, the two heirs-apparent launched a bitter fight for the office. In the wake of the realignment of power, Littlefield had the opportunity to become assistant treasurer of the company. His two immediate superiors recommended the advancement, although he was only twenty-seven. As Littlefield himself ruefully recalled, "The eighteenth floor of the Standard Oil building was not quite ready for a twenty-seven-year-old assistant treasurer. The matter had not been approved, but it was being debated." The question suddenly became moot. Littlefield was Henry Judd's house guest on the fateful Pearl Harbor weekend of December 7, 1941. Before that memorable Sunday morning, their conversation had revolved around Judd's confidence "that I would ultimately be acceptable by the board of Standard as assistant treasurer." When the announcement came on the radio that Pearl Harbor had been bombed, Littlefield immediately went on active duty as a Naval Reserve officer, and Standard's plans for him went on hold.

After some eighteen months of working for Naval Intelligence in San Francisco, Littlefield received a letter from Ralph Davies, now deputy petroleum administrator in the War Department, asking if he would accept a transfer to Washington. Davies had struck a deal with the Secretary of the Navy to attract qualified people in the armed forces to the petroleum side of the war effort. Littlefield jumped at the chance and left for the nation's capital, where he learned invaluable management lessons under Davies's farsighted, painstaking tutelage."It's not what you do now," Davies told him. "You think of the years in the future—ponder what you're getting into." Davies also taught him by example many valuable skills and leadership principles. For instance, his mentor would "rewrite a one-paragraph letter several times, changing words, just to get them right. In a sense I learned a kind of perfectionist technique from him."

In spite of his admiration for Davies, who later became chairman of the board at Stanford, Littlefield was ready to move out of his orbit at war's end, so he accepted in August 1945 a managerial position with Golden State, a processor and distributor of dairy products. As he thought back on his time with Davies, he realized that remaining with him had held great opportunities. "He taught me a great deal," Littlefield acknowledged. "He taught me a lot about thinking, of thinking for myself, but ... he was a tough taskmaster [and] I decided I didn't want to work for such a demanding boss. Life was too short."

As a division manager at Golden State, Littlefield acquired operating experience in contrast to his previous background as a staff officer. From this perspective, he discovered he had a talent for solving problems that he tested in six different jobs in five years at Golden State, including director of marketing, although he confessed that he "had no taste for managing salespeople all of my life." He later said, "I got a lot of experience painted on me pretty fast." He also credited his work at Golden State with creating his expertise at putting the right people in the right places. While Littlefield enhanced these abilities, Marriner Eccles watched from afar with another plan for his future, but the Wattis grandson was not looking for a new opportunity, particularly in the family business, "because I was succeeding in my own right with the Golden State dairy company and knew something of Utah's slowdown during the late 1940s."

In 1951, thirty-seven-year-old Ed Littlefield was living in Los Angeles with his wife, Jeannik Mequet Littlefield, and their two children. One day, Marriner Eccles called and arranged a round of golf at the Los Angeles Country Club for Littlefield, himself, George Eccles, and Arthur Stoddard, president of Union Pacific Railroad.

> I have been told that Shephard Mitchell suggested to Marriner that the company "needed someone like Ed Littlefield but you probably can't get him." Marriner remembered me from our two or three meetings in Washington and, without saying anything to the Wattis family members of the board, set about to see if he could persuade me to come in. He had cleared the idea with the directors who represented the other families, but only checked with the Wattis family directors after we had come to an agreement.

After the game, Littlefield joined the Eccles brothers for cocktails. Littlefield recalled that Marriner "didn't beat around the bush" but bluntly asked him if he had any inclination to work for Utah. Littlefield remembered being both surprised and flattered, but said, "No." Paul Wattis had offered him a job with the family-owned corporation prior to his graduation from business school, but he had refused it, wanting to see if he could make it in the business world on his own steam. Besides, his uncle's invitation was hardly an offer on a silver platter—"$100 a month, when and if they had some work to do."

Eccles persisted, and, as the conversation continued, Littlefield became increasingly intrigued. Disclosing the concerns of the board about the quality and quantity of information they were getting from management, Eccles said it was looking for someone with the right qualifications who "had a stake in the company." Littlefield considered the problems built into such a job and countered with two conditions: "I have to know precisely what my job is. I have to know to whom I report, and I have to know precisely and particularly who reports to me. I'm not going into a fuzzy situation and find myself in the middle of some backbiting thing. It's got to be straight out front." He then looked Eccles squarely in the eye and said, "The second thing is that I have to be under no pressure to hire anybody's relatives, yours or mine."

Eccles grinned and said, "Fine." (Only later would Littlefield find he was the only person at Utah with such a clear job description and reporting line.) Satisfied enough, Littlefield accepted Eccles's invitation, although he believed that he had little hope of becoming general manager, inasmuch as Christensen was only seven years older. He sensed that Eccles had confidence in him as a leader, but "he never promised the presidency to me."

The necessary clearance process for hiring Littlefield began, but Eccles seemed to know in advance that the other family shareholders, Les Corey, and Allen Christensen would all concur. Eccles then had Littlefield interview with both Corey and Christensen about the board's offer to install him as a financial vice president. Corey had known his young relative personally for a long time and welcomed the prospect of his joining the firm. Christensen, however, was concerned about Littlefield's conditions. He tried hard to convince Littlefield to come in with an undefined role and report strictly to him, not to the board. Littlefield adamantly refused to dicker. "Allen, I'm not going to come in on that basis," he said. "I didn't seek this job and don't really care much whether I come or not. I've been asked by the board to come in as financial vice president—which requires a definite description of my job and authority." Finally, at 2:30 in the morning, Christensen "realized that on those points I could be as stubborn as he was and so he yielded."

Littlefield was formally elected financial vice president and treasurer at the next board meeting, held in Ogden on March 22, 1951, with a salary of $18,000. In comparison, Corey and Christensen received $25,000 each, Stronck, $16,000, and Harris,

$10,000. The company also paid incentive bonuses annually to top management. The board meeting became an ordeal Littlefield would never forget. It took a full, laborious day for the board to extract the necessary information from senior management about the projects at hand. Littlefield later remembered that "finally, the second day, they ... approved the various actions." He also observed that Christensen, in seeking board approval for the Argonaut iron ore mine project, for instance, made a completely verbal presentation; none of the board members "saw a thing" on paper. Littlefield needed no clearer demonstration of why the board was dissatisfied with senior management's communication.

Littlefield spent the next week mapping his strategy before formally reporting for duty on April 1. Before the next quarterly board meeting convened in June, he put into the hands of each board member a comprehensive, relevant summation of the state of the company titled *COMMENT and OUTLOOK,* which he hoped would lead to more prudent decision making. Detailed, factual, and timely, the report impressed everyone. As one family member said, Littlefield "provided more information than has been or perhaps will be given to any board in the United States." Believing that such written communication between management and the board would ease strained relationships and clarify decision-making, Littlefield went on to overhaul the entire reporting system, requesting that any important action be reported in writing.

In keeping with this philosophy, Littlefield also insisted that scrupulous records be kept on every project. For example, just after his arrival in April 1951, management faced increased costs on two projects—a dam on the Lower Bear River southeast of Sacramento for Pacific Gas and Electric, and the Argonaut mine in British Columbia. Christensen brushed off these concerns, saying these projects had just begun, and higher costs were to be expected. In contrast, Littlefield encouraged Christensen to "look into the numbers," to study thoroughly the information available on revenues, historical costs, amounts invested, and the projected costs. He particularly urged a review in the context of the larger and more detailed financial picture that was causing the cost overruns. Not only did he introduce many fresh and original ideas, but he implemented what he considered to be conventional business practices learned during previous experiences, such as a funds flow analysis.

As it turned out, however, reporting directly to the board as financial vice president and treasurer placed Littlefield in an awkward position.

> It was understood that I reported directly to the board of directors and not to Allen Christensen who was executive vice president and general manager. This was not an arrangement that could have pleased Allen Christensen, but the board had given him no choice. I was the one who recognized that this had to be an unsatisfactory situation in the long term, and that I should make every effort to convince Allen that I could and would work with him as if I were responsible to him. Naturally, he was suspicious in the beginning; but before too long, he realized that I could be useful to him in helping him become more effective in obtaining the backing of the board for what he was trying to do. I was careful to go through him and not to go around him—and it paid dividends.
>
> The person that was in fact demoted when I came on the scene was H. N. (Bert) Stronck, who had functioned as the financial vice president and treasurer. He was advised that he had to report to me as did the chief purchasing agent, the director of personnel, and the company's chief legal counsel, at least on the organization chart. John M. (Johnny) Horrigan was controller and technically reported to Stronck. My uncle William H. Harris had the title of secretary; but Stronck, as assistant secretary, did the work. Stronck was told that, at the end of 1951, Billy Harris would resign as secretary and Stronck would take his position. This was not a happy solution for him, and that was understandably the cause of his dissatisfaction over staying with the company.

The sixty-year-old Stronck, despite the appearance of a promotion, was actually losing his powerful financial function to the newcomer, Littlefield. Consequently, when Stronck received a

Utah Vice President Weston Bourret developed and oversaw mining explorations and projects.

job offer from J. H. Pomeroy, another construction company, he announced to Christensen that he would leave Utah Construction and go to Pomeroy unless he got "more running room." Rather than quickly capitulating to the ultimatum, "Allen asked me [Littlefield] if I felt I was ready to operate the administrative responsibilities of the company without Bert Stronck on hand. I said that I wanted to talk to Johnny Horrigan before I replied. When I asked Johnny for his opinion, he said, 'Let's go!'" Christensen told Stronck he was free to accept Pomeroy's offer, and Stronck left in June 1951.

This incident highlighted Christensen's style of pitting corporate executives against each other to create internal rivalry, saying, "You can ... let them run a race and maybe they'd both run faster if they thought they were running against each other." In another case, when Littlefield came aboard, Frank Keller was competing against Charles S. (Chuck) Davis, another vice president. Their personalities differed considerably, Davis being "a heavy construction guy ... gregarious, personable, a strong personality," Littlefield related, while Keller, was "a soft-spoken fellow, a bit of a loner, the opposite of a hard-drinking construction guy." The fierce rivalry for projects and profit margins led Keller to find a specialized niche in commercial construction—stores, garages, office buildings, and housing. Then he proposed treating construction fees as equity and subsequently selling that equity at a capital gains rate of 25 percent. The federal Wherry Act passed Congress, accommodating Keller's tax strategy. Under the Wherry Act, Utah constructed buildings during the Korean War for the United States government—mostly what was termed "critical housing" around airbases. Once the war was over, Utah acquired titles to the homes, rented them, and finally sold them at a profit. Eventually, Utah constructed parking garages and even hotels under government auspices on the same tax basis, a profitable venture at the time.

As the September 1951 board meeting approached, Marriner Eccles proposed forming an executive committee to facilitate decision making at the board level. (Eccles had assured Littlefield a place on this committee during their job negotiations.) The board agreed to a committee that was to meet monthly comprised of Eccles, Corey, Christensen, and Littlefield. According to Littlefield, this group

> had all the powers of the board and could act in the board's stead if it chose to do so. It did take many actions particularly in the approval of bids for construction jobs, etc., when construction was the company's principal business. Later on, when mining became so important, the executive committee had much more lead time before a final commitment was necessary, and it then served the very useful

> function of being the organization that screened and evaluated the important decisions to be made and made its recommendations to the board of the action that should be taken.

Nearly two years later, in January 1953, Littlefield, who was already financial vice president, treasurer, and secretary, and a member of the executive committee, also became a member of the board of directors. He put the appointment in perspective:

> Not being a director really had no practical effect one way or the other on my ability to perform, since I attended all of the executive committee meetings and board meetings and usually had a key role in preparing and presenting the material to both bodies. The urgency to elect me to the board came about because of some banking regulations concerning conflicts of interest that prohibited a bank from making loans to a company if a majority of that firm's directors were also directors of the bank. I was needed on Utah's board since the majority of its members were also directors of First Security Corporation [in Salt Lake City].

With these modifications, Utah's top management by 1953 consisted of Littlefield, Corey, Christensen, and vice presidents A. H. Ayers (also chief engineer), Charles S. Davis, and George R. Putnam, who headed construction divisions. Littlefield saw his role as guiding strategy formulation, along with his day-by-day management responsibilities. While there is no doubt that his vision led to much of the firm's success in the fifties and sixties through "establishing corporate objectives ... and having a detailed master plan," he modestly stated that Utah merely responded in many cases to "fortuitous circumstances which came along."

As that master plan developed, sharp divisions persisted among company leaders over pursuing construction versus mining projects. The anti-mining group had some ammunition. In 1951, the Argonaut mine in British Columbia recorded a backlog of two million tons of magnetite iron ore, yet saw no profit from the output, which went to Japan. Other Utah mines, however, showed increasing profitability. Consequently, a small geology section organized in 1952, gradually expanding under the leadership of Vice President Weston Bourret. Its primary mission was to search for, acquire, and develop mineral deposits that would create new wealth and establish profitable long-term mining operations—largely producing iron ore and coking coal for the steel industry and steam coal for electric power generation.

Giving truth to the old saying that old habits die hard, Corey determined to keep the company in heavy construction, regardless of continuing losses. He remained convinced that "this field should not be deserted, that we should still keep in touch with it, and hope the present low bidding cycle will pass over before long, and then we can obtain some worthwhile business of this class." To cut operating expenses, improve efficiency, and realign its organization, Utah's management discontinued the operations of the West Coast District headquarters, merged its bidding and accounting functions with the San Francisco office, and placed them under the control of Vice President Davis. Additional organizational changes brought Guy Sperry, previously manager of the West Coast District, into headquarters as chief engineer. A. H. Ayers, who had served as vice president and chief engineer, continued to work for the company as a consultant on special engineering problems. During the fourth quarter of 1952, the financial condition of the company improved rapidly. Its net worth and working capital climbed to all-time highs of more than $16 million and nearly $7 million, while the long-term debt was reduced to just below $4 million.

Despite this news, company officials did not foresee a respectable net income in 1953 and feared that Utah would merely endure in a world of increased competition. Littlefield broached the subject bluntly in the 1952 *Annual Report,* over the signatures of Marriner Eccles and Les Corey: "Unless we are unusually successful in our effort to obtain new work, we cannot sustain the rate of construction activity and the earnings experienced during the last two years." Additionally, a pending steel strike could sharply cut demand for the output of the Ozark-Philpott, Iron Mountain, and Iron Springs mines. Littlefield commented on the value of Iron Springs:

> The principal customer of the Iron Springs Mine was the U.S. Steel plant at Orem, Utah; but the Japanese were desperately in need of importing iron ore, and Allen found out through Ted Takahashi [a sales agent] that our surplus production of ore from Cedar City could be shipped to the Japanese at a price profitable to Utah. This was also the intended market for the ore from Argonaut. Originally, Utah passed title to the ore at Long Beach, but Allen learned that there was a profit to be made in ocean shipping since the Japanese were really only interested in the delivered cost at final destinations. Consequently, Utah considered chartering its own fleet of ships to give us some flexibility over where the overall profit in the transaction was reflected. For instance, part of the profit could be allocated to a Panamanian company where it would not be taxed until it was ultimately repatriated to the United States.

Although the Utah Construction Company enjoyed limited prosperity in the first few years of the 1950s, senior management realized that the company persistently lost money on various construction projects, even though it was making enough profit on its mining ventures that income was breaking records. Still, the board, except for members of the executive committee, remained unconvinced that mining should become the company's principal business and grew disenchanted with management, even skeptical of its ability to identify and manage mines properly. Despite the success of the Cedar City mine, Littlefield recalled, the board emphasized that "the record of the company at the Ozark-Philpott mine ... was one of vastly over-running the investment originally contemplated and under-earning the profits promised. But, worse, Argonaut in British Columbia had really been a disaster."

Littlefield's assessment of Argonaut was that "we relied almost exclusively on construction personnel to handle the mining venture" when specialists in mining management were really what the job demanded. He admits that "it took longer than perhaps it should have to recognize the need for company mining people." Littlefield often said in speeches, "Little mines are more trouble to run than big ones. The last thing you want in a mine is used equipment selected for construction jobs. We soon learned there were damned few construction fellows who can be successful miners." Construction men "were great if someone told them what earth to move, but they couldn't do the mine planning and ore treatment."

In spite of all the difficulties in mining, Littlefield looked at the company from a wide perspective and concluded "that this mining business was the way to go because the construction business wasn't." It was clear, however, that the problems at Argonaut had to be solved before he could propose any other mining venture to the board. Christensen had sent J. A. (Tony) Mecia, a Stanford engineering graduate in his early thirties, to British Columbia to assess Argonaut. Littlefield read his analysis and reported:

> There was no way we could operate the mine profitably during the winter months. It was Tony who found out that the mill through which the ore was processed was improperly designed for the kind of ore it was treating [a matter of wet versus dry processes]. Additionally, the mine operated used trucks which were totally inadequate for haulage requirements. As a result of his findings and the steps taken to correct them, Argonaut became profitable and finally even broke even as a project before the ore was exhausted, but the board still had a very sour taste in its mouth.

Nevertheless, Littlefield always promised the relevant facts for the board, the shareholders, and the financial community—and he delivered them in Utah's annual reports, its in-company publications, board minutes, and senior management commentaries. Those relevant facts portrayed not only a company remaking its management, but now a company turning steadily from construction to mining.

During the six years the company operated the Argonaut mine on Vancouver Island, it shipped nearly two million tons of beneficiated iron ore to the Japanese steel industry.

Chapter 7

A Change of Course

Into the 1950s, as the world recovered from the ravages of World War II and adjusted to the realities of the Cold War, the industrial economies of the so-called "Free World" craved ever-increasing quantities of minerals and fossil fuels. In addition to the insatiable needs of the arms race, the domestic demand for durable goods such as automobiles and televisions, and energy to power them, pushed a burgeoning industrial machine to new heights. In the United States, for example, the gross national product nearly doubled between 1950–60 to one-half trillion dollars. Americans enjoyed economic growth during the 1950s that averaged more than 4 percent annually, as real wages rose during the decade by 30 percent. Other industrial nations were experiencing similar good times. As a result, companies in a position to enter into the mineral and energy extraction business had a very good chance of making a lot of money.

Fully comprehending this opportunity, leaders of the Utah Construction Company determined early in the decade to focus increasingly on mining. Significant changes in management combined with this new resolution to galvanize the company's strength and sense of purpose. Extensive new operations brought forth copper, coal, uranium, and oil, as well as iron ore, until, in 1959, the company changed its name to Utah Construction & Mining. As profits from domestic and foreign mining ventures rolled in, leadership began to catch a glimpse of the company's destiny. Given their view from the valley floor of modest profits, however, Utah executives could not know that, by the decade's end, earnings would begin a climb, eventually leading to the summit of a financial Everest.

Although prior to 1951 the company had dabbled in mineral extraction, often in conjunction with other firms, the 1950s would see a dramatic expansion in both the variety and number of Utah's mining enterprises. Its move into copper, for example, exemplified the enthusiasm management held for this new emphasis. In the beginning, its copper mining work followed the traditional pattern of joint ventures and contract stripping. Such efforts led the firm into Arizona in the mid-1950s, where it joined Stearns Rogers Manufacturing Company in a joint venture. The San Manuel Copper Corporation awarded a $60 million contract, to design, engineer, and construct mine surface structures, including mills and a smelter. The project included erecting head frames and hoisting

In 1965, the company acquired a 25 percent interest in the Pima Mining Company near Tucson, Arizona. Here, Edmund W. Littlefield and other company officials tour the site.

machinery; maintenance shops; a change house; a compression house; and a seven-mile, standard-gauge, ore-hauling railroad. Utah used subcontractors for certain specialty work, such as electrical installations and painting. The contract also included constructing thirty miles of railroad to transport product and supplies, two major bridges, several smaller wooden trestles, and many concrete and corrugated steel culverts.

In 1957, Utah completed the initial stages of stripping for another Arizona copper mine, the Pima Mining Company near Tucson. Between 1955–57, $5.5 million in work put the open-pit mine into production. Discovered in 1950, Pima was one of the first large-base metal deposits in the western United States located through geophysical methodology, a highly technical process of measuring the physical properties of the earth's crust. At the outset, geologists estimated that Pima had colossal reserves of some 220 million tons, extracted early on at thirty-eight hundred tons per day. Utah's geologists and geophysicists also used advanced technology to find subterranean minerals without indications of their presence on the surface. The scientists measured one or more physical properties, such as variations in gravitational force, electrical and magnetic properties, velocity of seismic waves resulting from test shots, and radioactivity. Steady plant expansions (at a cost of $50 million by 1970) increased the mill's total capacity to sixty-three hundred tons daily. In little more than a decade, Pima became one of the major copper producers in Arizona.

In 1965, Utah acquired a quarter share of Pima, which became the Cyprus Pima Mining Company, with Cyprus holding a 50 percent interest and the Union Oil Company of California owning a quarter share. Cyprus Pima's mining properties consisted of thirty-four patented, royalty-free mining claims on federal lands and seven mining leases from the state of Arizona, due to expire in 1990-91. The leased areas contained approximately 29 percent of the estimated reserve and required a 5 percent royalty payment to Arizona on the net value of produced minerals. During ensuing years, the Cyprus Pima Mine would remove as much as twenty million tons of ore per year. Concentrates, processed in Arizona smelters, contained 176 million pounds of copper, 900,000 ounces of silver, and 1.8 million pounds of molybdenum. Between 1964–

74, the amount of copper sold increased by 400 percent and the earnings from the mine increased by 700 percent.

Such extensive involvement in the copper business put Utah on the list of America's major nonferrous metal production firms. In addition, the company's domestic copper activities had an impressive counterpart north of the border in Canada. By the mid-1970s, Utah Mines, Ltd., a wholly owned subsidiary, would complete its development of the Island Copper Mine. This mine, the second-largest copper mine in Canada, had a production capacity of 230,000 tons per year of copper concentrates and eighteen hundred tons per year of molybdenum concentrates.

Utah Construction's history of mining in western Canada stretched back to 1949 when the company acquired the Argonaut iron mine on Vancouver Island, near the Campbell River. Almost two million tons of beneficiated iron ore from this mine went to the Japanese steel industry during the six years (1951–57) the company operated the mine. About the same time that the Argonaut Mine shut down because its iron ore reserves were spent, an exploration office opened in Vancouver with the objective of finding and developing iron properties near tidewater to serve growing Japanese markets. During the late 1950s, the major efforts of the exploration group aimed at developing iron deposits in southeastern Alaska. In the early 1960s, however, exploratory efforts began to concentrate on western Canada and increasingly turned to the search for copper, molybdenum, and other important nonferrous and precious metals. The bonanza came with the discovery and subsequent development of the Island Copper Mine, located at the northern end of Vancouver Island and accessible by both land and sea. Companion mill facilities rose on Rupert Inlet, about ten miles south of Port Hardy, British Columbia.

Utah Construction became interested in the Island Copper deposit in 1965, when a local prospector, Gordon Milbourne, made a classic discovery of mineralization in the tangled roots of two overturned trees. Digging by hand in the depression under the trees, he exposed a small system of narrow pyrite and chalcopyrite veins. Milbourne submitted his claims on the area to the company. After concluding an agreement with Milbourne, Utah began an extensive field examination, which included a systematic program of geologic mapping, geochemical and geophysical surveys, and diamond-bit drilling. Exploratory drilling led to a small ore body of one million tons at slightly more than 1 percent copper ore; but while Utah's exploration team was drilling in this first area, it located several target areas through geochemical sampling. In early 1967 the first diamond drill hole penetrated what eventually became the main Island Copper ore body, more than a mile to the southeast of the initial discovery.

By late 1967 Utah had confirmed the presence of this potentially large, low-grade copper deposit. The company greatly accelerated diamond drilling while simultaneously developing plans for a feasibility study and development program. In the summer of 1968, drilling crews sank a 225-foot exploratory shaft and crosscut the

By late 1967 Utah Construction & Mining had confirmed the presence of a potentially large, low-grade copper deposit, and began developing the Island Copper Mine.

upper portion of the ore body with several tunnels (drifts). The material from this work was shipped to a Utah pilot plant at Cedar City, with selected samples going to equipment manufacturers for grinding and crushing tests. During this same period, the company entered into initial negotiations with Canadian provincial and federal agencies to comply with various mining regulations. By early 1969, studies of marketing, housing, environmental considerations, metallurgy, and plant design considerations were complete. The ore body would contain approximately 280 million tons of ore within the proposed pit limits at 0.522 percent copper and 0.029 percent molybdenum sulfide. Utah's board of directors approved continuing with the project, and work began in June 1969. Eighteen months later, the task reached completion at a cost of nearly $80 million to cover a 33,000-ton-per-day copper and molybdenum concentrator and related mine facilities. Visitors to the site marveled at the six largest autogenous (self-fusing metals) grinding mills ever installed in the mining industry. Also, the dock facility could accommodate 40,000-dead-weight-ton ocean-going vessels, required for transporting the copper concentrates to smelting facilities throughout the world.

Planning the mine's operation presented some imposing problems, although the Island Copper Mine was typical of many large copper deposits. With a stripping ratio of overburden to ore of more than two to one, the open-pit operation called for removing more than 100,000 tons of ore, rock, and overburden each day. After drilling and blasting, the ore itself would be loaded into trucks and hauled about one mile to the mill, where Utah's plans envisioned a unique operation to dispose of the tailings by discharging them into the sea through a submerged outfall. Following public hearings concerned with ecological pollution problems, the company received a permit from the government of British Columbia to carry out its marine tailings disposal system on condition that the company retain an independent team of scientists from the University of British Columbia to evaluate data and guide the company's own on-site environmental group.

Over the next twenty-five years, the pit came to occupy about 490 acres—seventy-five hundred by thirty-five hundred feet wide and eight hundred feet below sea level, a depth roughly equal to the height of the Empire State Building. When mining operations terminated, Utah planned to fill the pit with water, creating a lake. As a guarantee that it would carry out its proposed reclamation plans for the area, the firm posted a $110,000 bond with British Columbia's minister of mines. In the meantime, Island Copper produced enormous quantities of copper and other nonferrous metal ore efficiently and profitably. According to its production plans, the ore moved from the pit to the mill, where crushing and screening isolated a copper-molybdenum concentrate. This concentrate was then separated and stockpiled for shipment. The copper concentrate was stored in a large building with a capacity of 30,000 tons, while molybdenite concentrate was loaded into steel drums for shipment. Island Copper's molybdenum contained a significant quantity of rhenium, a rare metal with unique physical and chemical properties useful in electronic and bimetallic catalytic applications. The concentrate also contained significant amounts of gold and silver. In 1973 alone, Island Copper recovered and shipped approximately 44,000 ounces of gold, enough to offset nearly a fourth of the original cost of the mine and mill facility.

Inasmuch as the Island Copper Mine and Mill were situated on an inlet, vessels of up to 40,000 dead weight tons could load with ease at the wharf, although vessel size ultimately depended upon the width of the narrow channel linking Rupert Inlet with the Pacific Ocean. As for the concentrate's destination, Utah procured two long-term contracts for sale of the copper concentrate. The first was with Mitsubishi Corporation of Japan, which covered fully one-third of the mine's production before the contract expired in 1976. A second contract with Mitsui Mining and Smelting Company, Ltd., of Japan covered the remaining two-thirds until 1981. The contracts linked prices to quotations on the London Metal Exchange and gave Utah the option of offering up to 16 percent of the product to other customers.

The molybdenum output of the Island Copper Mine was sold on short-term contracts. The rhenium content was sold, either to molybdenum buyers or, after separation, to more specialized clients. The Island Copper Mine had considerable impact on the small town of Port Hardy, which had in the past depended on logging and fishing for its income. The town population of eighteen

The development of the Island Copper Mine brought new residents, new jobs, and new housing to Port Hardy in British Columbia.

hundred residents doubled with the mine's development, creating more than four hundred permanent new jobs. As part of the project, Utah added an entirely new housing subdivision to Port Hardy and gave the town a grant that helped cover the cost of new water storage facilities and a modern secondary sewage treatment plant. Also, Utah donated land for a new medical clinic and helped with overall town planning.

To return to the beginnings of all of this success in copper and other minerals, by the mid-1950s it became increasingly clear that the transition into mining was having a salutary effect on earnings. For example, in 1956 Utah set a new profit record—$4.2 million. Changes in top management reflected the clear dawning of this era. Becoming executive vice president, secretary, and treasurer,

Edmund W. Littlefield's titles reflected his increasingly pivotal role in the firm as he solidified corporate objectives and promoted diversification. Marriner S. Eccles and Allen D. Christensen continued their responsibilities as chairman of the board and president/general manager, respectively. Meanwhile, Salt Lake City construction functions merged into San Francisco's and began operating as the Heavy Construction Division, headed by Charles S. Davis. Tony Mecia headed the mining operations at Ozark and Cedar City, while Frank Keller took responsibility for land development.

As Utah's mining ventures multiplied, so did its possibilities. For instance, the acquisition of the Lucky Mc uranium mine in Wyoming and its shareholder base raised a question that company leaders had debated earlier—issuing public stock. Wanting shareholders to have enough of a market if they had to sell, or wanted to sell their interest in Utah Construction, Littlefield and Eccles began grooming the company for increased public attention. They published enhanced annual reports, cultivated investment banks and large stock brokerage firms, and made more detailed presentations on "going public" to the board. They also encouraged appointing more directors from other firms, selected "strictly for their talent and ability to function with the board, and not necessarily [for] having a large amount of shares," as Littlefield put it.

Two impediments stood in their way: the small number of shares outstanding to meet the New York Stock Exchange listing requirements and the cyclical nature of construction's sometimes unpredictable swings in demand. The board solved the first problem by issuing one hundred shares for each share held by both Utah and former Lucky Mc investors. Since there were only about 150 shareholders in 1956, the number of shares issued was not significant. But the construction division was a different problem. As Littlefield said, "It would make some money and then lose some money, make some, lose some ..." The company boasted no exceptional engineering talent, and the competition became increasingly lethal. As Henry Kaiser said of this cut-throat business environment, "Whenever you beat out ten contractors on a job, you got it too cheap." Littlefield realized that "it was nothing for very large jobs to receive ten to fifteen bids." Obviously, it made sense to sell this faltering branch of the business; and the board of directors urged Littlefield to take this course during a number of turbulent meetings.

Littlefield agreed except for timing. He knew that the market simply had no willingness to pay any kind of high price-earnings ratio in the construction business. There had never been a successful publicly-held construction company, although Morrison Knudsen came as close as any. Littlefield consistently tried to convince the directors that the company could not simply sell a business that was not making money. "The only way to get out of the construction business," he argued, "is to put it on a profitable basis and then sell, given the nature of the business we're in."

Littlefield and Eccles knew that very little of the company's stock ever changed hands, although Paul Wattis (E. O.'s son) accumulated some shares during the 1940s because he was the only buyer. He acquired thirty-two hundred shares soon after joining the company and held 16,000 shares by 1954. Most of the shareholders remained relatives or close friends of the founding families, with the E.O. Wattis family as the largest shareholder. Littlefield observed that "no real market existed for these shares although the local newspapers carried bid and ask prices that were usually below the book value of the company. But the fact was that no stock was really being traded." To illustrate, Littlefield had served on a private company board with a broker in Los Angeles. When Littlefield went with Utah, the broker decided to buy shares in the Utah Construction Company. He "ran the price from $65 to $115 ... and he was never able to buy one share," Littlefield explained. "This was alarming because inheritance taxes could be influenced by a published stock quote; but without an assured market, there was no guarantee that the stock could actually be sold in quantity at this price."

Determined to obtain a listing on the New York Stock Exchange, Littlefield began working with brokers and security analysts, having already cultivated the bankers. Palmer Weber, a San Francisco friend of Eccles, also became interested in Utah's significant progress. After a career in government, Weber had gone into the brokerage business looking for special situations to

Edmund W. Littlefield (center) took the company from its status as a construction firm with a lustrous history to becoming the most successful mining firm in the United States. Here, he inspects the Navajo Coal Mine along with Ed Raymond and Sterling Grogan.

promote. During the late 1950s, Littlefield and Weber teamed up on trips to the East to stir up interest among big brokerage firms. Closer to home, a San Francisco broker named Jerry Brush committed to preparing and promoting the company to outside investors. "Jerry believed in the company," Littlefield recalled, and "became a national source of information about Utah and the market." Littlefield knew that the company's future depended on the marketability of its stock throughout the United States. He also knew that many investors who lived in the state of Utah would be attracted to a company with local ties.

During all of these negotiations, Littlefield and Eccles made a tight and effective duo. Eccles remained the dominant force on Utah's board, but as their working relationship matured, Littlefield became the company's driver while Eccles became more contemplative, concentrating on strategic matters, particularly those with economic consequences. Calling Eccles "a very conscientious overseer," Littlefield remembered him as "a completely independent person. He was not swayed by the mob; he did not think like the mob thought; he didn't care what the mob thought. He did his own thinking...." He was also proficient at judging potential projects, the man on the board who had to be convinced of a project's profitability—"the obstacle you had to get by to get something done." Eccles always demanded the answers to tough questions, although intuition remained an important factor. If, when his questions were answered, "something about the deal [still] made him uncomfortable," Littlefield observed, "I would not try to sell him the project, but took it back for further study to see if we could find what might be bothering him. By the time we got it to where Marriner was willing to give his blessing, you had a lot of confidence that the thing had really been thought through by someone who was objective."

Another quality Eccles demonstrated was an ability, once convinced, to fight for a project, even one about which he had been initially doubtful. His value was usually in appraising ideas rather than initiating them. "Marriner was unusually far-sighted in recognizing the general economic atmosphere in which business would be operating nationally or internationally," said Littlefield, "but [he] really was not an initiator or author of the idea that the Utah Construction Company should acquire raw materials or develop land." Rather, "Marriner was the highest hurdle to be leaped in the approval chain. He ultimately believed in the ideas and was effective in promoting them with the board because the directors had so much confidence in his wisdom."

Perhaps the most significant role Eccles played during this crucial transitional period in company history was in his assistance to Littlefield as a financial counselor and "someone to bounce ideas off." Consequently, Littlefield took the company from a construction firm with a lustrous history but a blunted competitive edge, to the most successful mining firm in the United States by the 1970s. Not only did Marriner have the knowledge and abilities to aid the company's success, but he also had extensive contacts with high-level business executives and government leaders across the United States. As Eccles and Littlefield contributed complementary talents and experiences, they developed "a great relationship," as Littlefield termed it. "We didn't always agree on things, but I think that we not only had a great trust and respect for each other, but also a personal affection for each other."

As the 1950s wore on, it became even more clear to this capable team that traditional money-makers were becoming sluggish, with newer ventures paying off spectacularly well. The company was building considerable muscle with successful new operations in dredging, uranium mining, and iron ore mining, yet world markets rode a roller coaster. Competition, plummeting steel prices, and disappointing international sales of iron ore and crude oil transported by Utah's carriers took their toll. In 1958, corporate net income dropped $663,000 to $54.8 million, after a record high of $55.5 million in 1957. The continuing nationwide steel strike rippled through all economic sectors, including offshore installations. As expected, losses from the overall construction division also meant decreased earnings, although domestic construction experienced a banner year, enhancing the profit picture by more than $1 million. All in all, Utah ended the year with its fourth-highest level of net income, largely due to profits in uranium mining.

The situation in the domestic construction arena underscored the growing inclination of top management to retreat from heavy construction into mining. Ironically, given Christensen's leadership in that direction, other aspects of his management style raised concerns especially in Eccles's mind. This all played out after August 12, 1958, when Littlefield was named executive vice president and general manager, the traditional top position. Tony Mecia, Charles W. Robinson, and Albert L. Reeves all became vice presidents, with Orville L. Dykstra as treasurer. Christensen resigned as general manager, but remained president. This was a lame-duck office, however, for Littlefield's promotion resulted, in part, from the board's disapproval of some aspects of Christensen's management. He had been particularly ineffective in dealing with Cyprus Mines.

Littlefield later explained that Eccles, in particular, felt that, "even though Allen had some very good points about him as far as concepts were concerned, he really couldn't run what he could

Senior Vice President and Secretary Albert L. Reeves also directed staff functions.

create, and that he was not the fellow on which to build Utah's future." This appraisal represented a dramatic departure from Eccles's earlier view, expressed at the January 20, 1950, shareholders' meeting, when he described Christensen as having "unusual qualities of foresight, leadership, imagination, and knowledge of construction and mining operations." Although Eccles traveled extensively and spent much of his time in Washington, D.C., he chaired the executive committee and closely oversaw the company. As his confidence in Christensen dipped, his confidence in Littlefield rose. Other board members shared the chairman's views, and starting in late 1956 and building slowly until the summer of 1958, personal animosities between Eccles and Christensen exacerbated their differences.

Hoping to avoid corporate trauma and perhaps disruptive change, Littlefield encouraged Christensen to talk through his differences with Eccles: "Allen, you're getting in terrible trouble, and I think you ought to go in and make your peace with Marriner." From Littlefield's perspective, Christensen made the grave mistake of deciding that he was indispensable. He felt that "he could defy Marriner and the board because Utah couldn't run without him. What he didn't realize, at that point, was that the board had pretty well decided that Utah could run better without him than with him." By the time Littlefield finally persuaded Christensen to meet with Eccles, the chairman had his back up and put him off, saying, "I'll talk to you when I'm ready." Meanwhile, Eccles informed Littlefield in direct terms that he was the best-qualified candidate for the job of general manager. Littlefield later reflected on this open invitation with mixed emotions:

> I really wasn't even sure I wanted the job. At that time, I was confident I would be a very good financial vice president. I wasn't confident that I could be a general manager and chief executive officer. Utah was in turmoil, and I didn't know much about running the construction business or, for that matter, the mining business. I had a serious question in my mind whether the organization would accept me because I had never tested those waters. And secondly, I certainly had a question as to how I would be seen by the industry and the people on the outside. So I resisted and tried to get the two of them together.

Eccles remained insistent. "Just make up your mind," he said. "If you don't take the job, we're going to go outside and hire somebody. I've talked to all the members of the board. They all think you could do it; you're the only director who doesn't think you can."

After careful thought, Littlefield decided to take the job on three conditions. First, the board must unanimously agree to the move and agree that Christensen no longer had their confidence. Second, Christensen must remain as president to provide as much continuity and as little disruption as possible, at least for a time. Third, the board must rewrite the by-laws and transfer all corporation-wide decision making to the general manager. The board readily agreed to these stiff conditions, rewriting the by-laws as requested.

Littlefield now faced the task of threading his way through the sensitive circumstances of Christensen's de facto removal, knowing that many in the organization probably had no idea about the board's intentions. Littlefield genuinely appreciated Christensen's strengths, especially his vision and negotiating prowess that had led the company into new ventures. He also knew how significantly Christensen's father had contributed to Utah Construction. Yet Littlefield also recognized that changes in competitive conditions often demanded new management. Christensen's unwillingness to communicate with, confide in, or really inform the board of directors had brought Littlefield into the company. That flaw now loomed as the chief reason Christensen could no longer lead. "[Allen] had everybody reporting to him," said Littlefield. "He wanted to keep it all like spokes in a wheel. However, despite his faults as a manager, he was a tireless worker, with creative ideas, a man of action, a man of decision.... He cultivated a mystique of being a loner, yet Allen has a place in Utah's history."

When Littlefield's promotion was made public, Vice President Wes Bourret remembered Eccles calling a meeting of all department heads at Number One Montgomery Street in San Francisco. "The meeting lasted thirty-five or forty minutes, and it was a genuine bombshell," Bourret recalled. All of the longtime employees but one immediately jumped on the Littlefield bandwagon. Those who had worked for a shorter time, reminded Littlefield that Christensen had hired them and that he was still their friend regardless of who managed the company. More than they could ever know, Littlefield respected those who spoke truth about their feelings, regardless of what might seem politically expedient.

While he expected the financial group to approve his promotion, Littlefield was startled and pleased when the mining leaders stepped forward to embrace him. Utah's clients also easily accepted Littlefield as general manager, and many associates in joint ventures now expressed interest in establishing new partnerships. "All of a sudden, I am accepted by the Kaiser group ... by Bechtel ... and among all of Utah's potential joint venture

Alexander M. (Bud) Wilson served as senior vice president and mining division manager.

partners. They just accepted it as a fact of life that I'm the person that makes the decisions." Although Littlefield braced himself for a tough transition, it simply did not happen. Indeed, by the end of 1958 it was all over.

A corporate vice president said, "Littlefield is a brilliant man who operates in keeping with his fifteen-year track record of careful analysis, who maintains statements of capital costs, market studies, and sales of products. In short, he wants all bases covered." The board had similar confidence. "Ed Littlefield," commented Lawrence Dee, longtime board member, "was the driving force behind the success of the company since the early fifties." He characterized Littlefield as "a smart man who knows his way around."

Ernest C. Arbuckle, former dean of the Stanford Business School, chairman of Wells Fargo Bank, and a member of other large company boards, such as Safeway, was repeatedly impressed with Littlefield's "great analytical capabilities. He doesn't waste his time on insignificant data. He knows how to interpret the information." Arbuckle also noted Littlefield's "extreme powers of concentration." Perhaps the key to understanding Littlefield's extremely positive effect on the fortunes of the company was his unique blend of competitiveness and competition. "He took up bird hunting and resumed golf late in life," mused Arbuckle, "and he hates to get beaten." Unlike many competitive men, however, he had a remarkable ability to work with the people around him.

"He creates an environment in which they can feel secure and be responsive," remarked Arjay Miller, another longtime board member. "I think the whole Utah organization is different from most, due to the characteristics he has built into it." Miller particularly noted a familial warmth Littlefield brought into his speeches and other management activities. "That is an important characteristic that not all CEOs have." Miller was also greatly impressed with the way Littlefield related to the board. Recalling his own background with six other large company boards, including Ford Motor Company, where he was vice chairman, Miller lamented the tendency of some companies to rubber stamp various projects without thoughtful and prudent discussion.

Among all of Littlefield's companions at Utah, none could see more clearly his effects on the company than Marriner Eccles. The board chairman never made any secret of the fact that he considered persuading Ed Littlefield to come into the company "the most fortunate thing which could have happened to Utah.... He should be given the credit for its fabulous growth and success. He has proven to be an outstanding executive, a great administrator, with excellent judgment and great foresight." For his part, Littlefield always credited company successes to team work, saying, "everybody worked hard, including me, but all of them were pretty damn good." He discouraged clutter from "a lot of committees and procedures, and I think I had the capacity and the willingness—the guts, if you will—to make decisions. We kept the communications channel very clear, very clean."

On the eve of 1959, upper-level management cautiously predicted that "1959 profits may well be the highest in the company's history." The Lucky Mc uranium mine's first full year of successful operation, plus satisfying results from mines at Ozark and Pima, led to this exuberant projection. On the other side of the ledger, however, a decline in international iron ore purchases, meaning that their Peru operation faced serious problems in disposing of its product, cast a long shadow. On top of that, Peruvian politics seemed threatening. Also, land development profits had slumped due to a reduction in land sales.

Management decided to adjust its land development operation and make other changes. On March 13, 1959, the board approved moving the corporate offices scattered across the Bay Area to 550 California Street in San Francisco, a 29,000-square-foot facility on one-and-one-half floors. These new offices would facilitate communications, reduce office space, and modernize the technology linking all the offices. Second, on July 29, 1959, the board authorized the name change to Utah Construction & Mining, as management increased the number of common shares from two to ten million to facilitate the expanded operations. Additionally, Littlefield announced the creation of three separate operating divisions, "designed to keep pace with Utah's expanding operations and the demands posed by a continuing pattern of growth." Littlefield had sensed the need for three divisions immediately after he became general manager, but hired McKinsey and Company, international management consultants, to analyze the company and recommend a course of action. He nevertheless drew his own organizational plan and put it underneath the blotter on his desk. "And after the plan was received from McKinsey, it was damn near the same as the one I had produced." With the subsequent reorganization of the staff, it was the first time the company was organized in recognizable and reasonably well-defined divisions.

In the wake of the reorganization, Littlefield described the changes as part of a strategy for preserving the company founders' "priceless legacy, a reputation for technical competence and integrity." In the March issue of the company newsletter, *Utah Report,* he laid out the corporate challenge in plain and stirring language: "Nothing but our own limitations can stop us from making a record in construction, in mining, in land development, in fields yet un-ventured that will bring to all those who contribute ... a genuine sense of satisfaction for a job well done."

Before the new organization was a year old, vice president Tony Mecia and Homer Mann, manager of mining services, were killed in January 1960 when their company plane, en route to Cedar City, crashed near Minersville. Keith Wallace, also on board, survived and would become very important to Utah's success in mining. With Mecia's and Mann's deaths, Littlefield lost two longtime and respected colleagues, and the loss temporarily crippled the mining division. Mecia's passing struck Littlefield particularly hard. He remembered that, soon after his appointment as general manager, Tony had asked approval for undertaking a technical mining project. Surprised that Mecia, with his expertise, would even ask, Littlefield answered, "You know more about mining than I do. Why do you seek my approval?" Mecia quickly replied, "I've never had the authority to proceed without the specific approval of the general manager." Littlefield responded: "You do now!" Littlefield recounted this story to illustrate Mecia's insight, but it also revealed Littlefield's operating style. He appraised his team's expertise and then felt perfectly confident delegating decisions and authority. "It is critically important to be aware of the knowledge and skills of others," he said. "You can't keep a highly competent individual around as a vassal, because he won't stay."

Realizing how difficult it would be to replace the men, Littlefield even looked outside the company for individuals equal in competence and experience. In the meantime, Vice President Alexander M. (Bud) Wilson, moved forward with stepped-up "technical capabilities and the drive to make decisions." The more Littlefield searched for replacements, the better the insiders looked. Seven months later, on August 1, 1960, Wilson was named general vice president in charge of the Mining Division, with exploration activities under the supervision of Wes Bourret, also a general vice president. Littlefield later called these promotions an illustration of men being thrust into the front lines of the company at a very young age. "A man of thirty-two years of age would have the responsibilities that a man of forty-five would have at other firms."

It might have been a gamble for Utah and Littlefield, but it paid off handsomely. Wilson later became company president and Bourret director of long-range planning and development.

The picture of mingled sunshine and shadow resolved itself in a bright final image in the 1959 annual report. The company posted net income figures exceeding the previous year's record by $3.6 million, the largest annual earnings figure to date. These achievements made it possible to reduce bank loans by $8.8 million to $3.5 million. At the end of August, the company had a bank credit line of $9.5 million. Utah's financial managers summarized the firm's financial status with an optimism that shines through the sober institutional prose: "Our debt is now easily manageable and our problem has become one of finding attractive opportunities for investment of funds in order to perpetuate our earning power and to replace those assets which are presently being consumed."

In other words, the effect of the executive team's competency shone in some remarkable figures: profits, for the previous ten years exceeded the total earnings of the previous fifty years by 175 percent; assets more than quadrupled the total earnings of the first five decades; shareholders' equity rose from $12 million to more than $51.4 million; and the number of shareholders increased from 150 to 2,550, primarily due to the merger with the Lucky Mc Uranium Corporation, made final on February 1, 1960. The whole world seem to lie at the feet of a company reborn and striding confidently into a new decade and a new future.

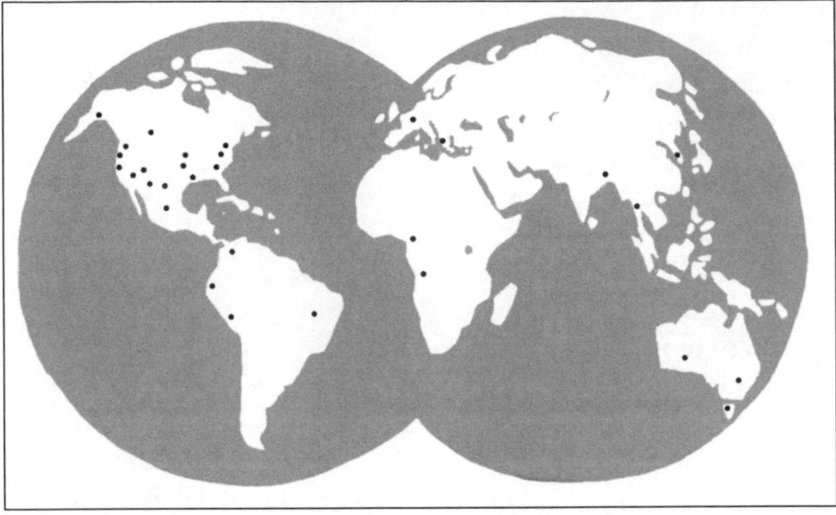

Utah's *1959 Annual Report* used this map to show construction, mining, exploration, and land development activities in sixteen countries on six continents.

Chapter 8

Land Development

Long before the Wattis brothers left their Uintah home to learn the rudiments of earth-moving from railroad builders, the Dutch devised a silt-clearing process for their canals. Using a bag held open by a metal ring attached to the end of a pole, the Dutch would *dregghe* the canal bottom from a stationary barge, which then delivered the silt to a disposal area. Dredging technology expanded greatly by the twentieth century (witness the massive dipper dredges that helped cut the Panama Canal), but land-fill applications did not become popular until after World War II when urban population growth led to demands for desirable waterfronts. On the eve of major diversification, Utah's move into dredging was logical, given its excavating background, but the company's post-war entry into the land development business in the San Francisco Bay Area provided the catalyst for this remarkable new endeavor.

The story began on November 15, 1950, when Utah purchased for $300,000 from Stanley Hiller and J. J. Coney 872 acres on the northwestern tip of the tidelands near Bay Farm Island, not far from the present-day Oakland Airport. Utah planned to extend the shoreline for commercial purposes, inasmuch as developable land in the area was extremely scarce. The eventuality of a third bay bridge, Southern Crossing, with Bay Farm Island as the eastern terminus made the investment seem foolproof. The company thus reentered the land-holding business for the first time since it sold its Nevada ranch properties in 1945.

Utah Construction's plans for Bay Farm Island, however, encountered a series of obstacles—intense public resistance, Oakland's intended condemnation of the land for its airport extension, the delay of the Southern Crossing bridge, a lack of return on Utah's previous investment in the project, and the return of high interest rates in the mid-1960s. Out of patience, Utah diverted its attention to other nearby development opportunities.

In December 1954, Utah acquired 150 acres of South Shore property not far from its Bay Farm holdings. Shortly afterwards, company executives and the board determined to take the lead in dredging for land development in the Bay Area. On tap was a bold proposal to fill the tideland around and along the shoreline near Alameda, a densely populated community of 70,000. Eventually, Utah's giant machines would deposit on a new coastline some thirty-six million cubic yards of material from the bottom of the bay—enough sand to fill a cylindrical hole one thousand feet across and one thousand feet deep. That would not happen, however, until after local opposition to the project threatened to scuttle it before it could get underway.

A few old-time residents of Alameda who were markedly unhappy with the prospects of radical change in the topography organized a campaign to stop the undertaking. Ironically, their slogan—"Alameda is old, Alameda is tired, Alameda is ugly, but I love Alameda just as it is"—helped convince a majority of the residents to favor the development. As the referendum approached in late spring, the *Alameda Times Star* editorialized on May 20, 1955:

> Young people—our sons and daughters reaching maturity and getting married—are leaving the city to establish their homes in new modern districts. Why? Because a self-appointed few refuse to accept what comes—and fight change. They want the city just as it is, old, tired, and decaying, a community in which 61 percent of the homes were built before World War I, or worse still, 83 percent before 1929. These and other percentages spell obsolescence, and youth wants no part of it.

Happily for Utah, pro-development forces waged an intense

political campaign, pulling mobile billboards about the city. During the heat of the debate, the *East Bay Labor Journal* featured the facsimile of a check made out to "East Bay Labor" for $23 million and signed "South Shore Bay Farm Island Project." The text read: "This means jobs for labor—this plan means prosperity." On May 25, 1955, the vote for development carried 7,002 to 5,385, with local labor organizations supplying crucial support.

Because the California dredging industry lacked the capacity to perform the work within feasible cost limits, the way opened for the creation of the Utah Dredging Company, a wholly owned

In the 1950s, Utah Construction undertook dredging and land development projects. Over the next two decades, land development became a major form of diversification.

subsidiary of the Utah Construction Company. Unwilling to use antiquated local dredges, the firm decided to build its own modern machine. Of custom design and with a price tag of $2.7 million, the *Franciscan* sported state-of-the-art technology, including a discharge line that pumped longer distances at greater capacities than any existing dredge in the area. Completed in November 1955, it moved into the bay as the largest hydraulic dredge on the West Coast, equal to any other in the United States.

The massive machine took less than a year to dredge the bay floor fifty feet below the surface and transfer the fill onto the reclamation area. In some months, the dredge placed more than a million cubic yards of fill. When the project's first phase ended, the *Franciscan* had converted an expanse of wetlands into sixty-eight choice acres of commercially zoned property and 308 acres of highly desirable residential land. Nevertheless, work on the Bay Farm Island project slowed due to political resistance, primarily from environmentalists and Alameda landowners unhappy about losing the shoreline in front of their properties. This, plus a lagging real estate market, prompted the company to find other jobs for the *Franciscan*.

Utah executives readily defended the Alameda project as benefitting local communities. Charles T. Travers, Utah's manager of commercial land development and vice president of South Shore Center, saw the Alameda enterprise as wholly successful. In a 1964 *Utah Report,* Travers wrote that the South Shore area now contained nearly one thousand homes and twenty-two hundred apartment units in developments that often featured swimming pools and recreation areas. He argued that a shopping center built on the reclaimed land allowed nearby residents to park and shop with ease. He persuasively described the former tidelands at low tide as nothing more than "ugly mudflats" with "a very unpleasant odor," while the company had constructed a public beach.

"Where no one could have used the mudflats before," he wrote, "now literally thousands of people from Alameda and from other parts of the bay area come ... to enjoy it throughout the summer and it provides healthful and relaxing weekend recreation for a great many citizens." The company created nearly half of the accessible public beaches in the Bay Area, he claimed, plus a large lagoon,

Vice President Charles T. Travers oversaw commercial land development.

three and one-half miles of "sparkling waterfront property," wide streets, and a modern street-lighting system. "We literally gave this community 28 acres of land for schools and parks," Travers wrote. "That land is today worth over $2,000,000; and in return for that, we received only the right to dredge useless sand from the bottom of the San Francisco Bay to fill the property."

Despite Travers's glowing defense of the company's South Shore project, "Alameda became an albatross around our necks," Littlefield later observed. Political power in the city shifted with the resignation of the mayor, he explained, "two or three incumbents were defeated, and soon we were in a battle for our lives." Utah wanted the land re-zoned from single family to multifamily housing, but the voters said no. Despite this stalemate, by the late 1960s, Utah would sell most of the land at a profit, including its original and still largely undeveloped Bay Farm Island parcel, which it sold to Shoreline Properties, Inc., in 1965 for $6 million.

While all of this land development energy in the Bay Area added to Utah's bottom line, the heavy investment in the *Franciscan* also served to draw Utah into the contract dredging business. When political opposition and other difficulties stalled work at Alameda and Bay Farm Island, Utah Dredging looked for commercial contracts that would keep the massive machine busy. The first major contract came in 1956 when the company landed a $4.5 million job to prepare land for the Metropolitan Oakland International Airport. The *Franciscan* began dredging in June 1956 and completed the job two years later, after Utah Dredging placed nearly fourteen million cubic yards of fill to create enough land for a terminal and an 8,600-foot runway.

The Oakland project's success inspired company executives to have a second dredge built, similar to the *Franciscan* but with its own self-contained power plant. Ordered in 1956, the *Alameda* began operating in late 1958. By then the company also had acquired a clamshell dredge called the *Californian,* as well as barges, tugs, and floating cranes. The *Alameda* immediately went to work on a second stage of the Oakland Airport. In 1958 the new portion—including the runway, the taxiways, and the building areas—resembled a series of sand spits linked by mud or water at high tide. Complicating the Oakland project was the need to deposit the sand and mud in sections, leaving space for a proposed bridge between Oakland and San Francisco. Also, tractors occasionally sank when they hit a pocket of soft mud, and the dredged sand was so abrasive that the pump shell, liner, and runner had to be replaced as often as twice a week. These sinkings happened often enough that Utah mechanics installed Cummins 270 HP diesel engines in the tractors and sealed them to minimize damage when submerged. This process resulted in "down time" about one day in seven. Despite such challenges, the powerful *Franciscan* came through magnificently as it pumped sand and fill 26,600 feet without the aid of a booster, including a stretch across two miles of tidal flats over a crib line on timber piles.

In August 1959, Utah Dredging moved the *Alameda* to the East Coast principally to dredge a federally sponsored ship channel on

By 1963, the company's land development on the Alameda South Shore boasted a shopping center and land for single and multiple housing projects.

the Delaware River near Glenside, Pennsylvania. A host of complications arose, and the undertaking brought a net loss, later alleviated by a substantial government claim award. Not only was it costly to tow the *Alameda* east, but large areas of boulders and ledges marked the site, requiring blasting before the dredge could go to work on the Army Corps of Engineers project. Once the Delaware contract ended, the *Alameda* sat idle due to keen competition, both foreign and domestic. The manufacturer had designed the *Alameda* and its ancillary plant for large contracts, and the company failed to bid successfully on jobs big enough to accommodate the vessel.

While the *Alameda* idled temporarily on the other side of the continent, its counterpart, the *Franciscan,* moved down the California coast to participate in the Long Beach Port Authority's program to build large new pier areas. The cost of the project was $2.7 million, but the rock removal contractor could not stay ahead of the dredge, idling the project and dragging down the profit. From there, the *Franciscan* went to Redwood City for similar harbor work. Again, bay mud flats at the project called for innovation. This time, the company turned for the first time to an answer that would eventually become common in such operations—using helicopters to haul and position pipes. The bulk of the work also required the company to rent a smaller dredge to accompany the *Franciscan.* Utah later bought this craft and changed its name from the *Palmer* to the *San Mateo*. Inasmuch as the *Franciscan* (unlike the *Alameda*) required utility power from shore, Pacific Gas and Electric Company built a 12,000-kva substation to supply the huge implement with its required power, enough electricity to light a community of 26,000 people. Even with these added expenses, the Redwood City project finished in the black. Shortly thereafter, Utah entered into a joint venture with Olympian Dredging Company to construct retaining levees, rip-rap, and rock dikes at the San Leandro small-craft harbor. Work on the half-million-dollar contract wrapped up in 1962, also in the black.

Utah Dredging next found itself occupied on the Sacramento River. Although it did not dredge deeply, it sucked up enough material to cover a residential street to a depth of six feet for a distance of 160 miles. That silt included large amounts of peat moss permeated with gas, created by the decomposition of the organic material in the peat. Occasionally a chunk of the muck would tumble through the pipes, where it would break up and release the gas, which produced a terrific banging and rattling as it bubbled its way out of the system.

In the meantime, the *Franciscan* was kept busy on jobs that earned a $370,000 net profit in the Los Angeles West Basin. After working through a backlog in Southern California that included projects worth an additional $5.8 million, the *Franciscan* returned late in 1966 to the Bay Area. Over the next two years, its cutter scooped up about twenty-two million cubic yards of dredged fill, but when the work finished, no one seemed to know whether the enterprise had produced a profit. Constantly plagued with political controversy, Bay Farm Island dredging never managed to escape the same objections that critics had raised ten years before. Quick wits at company headquarters across the bay often exchanged quips about the "troubled waters" off the South Shore. A small note, for example, appearing on one of the final Bay Farm Island reports asked in jest whether it was even possible to tell if the project had reached completion. Someone else then penned under it, "Ask Joe!" a reference to beleaguered Vice President Joseph Allen. Actually, the company had reclaimed nearly nine hundred acres of land under a contract amounting to $2.9 million, although it seemed a new problem emerged every day.

While the *Franciscan*'s continuing productivity secured its reputation as the premier dredge on the West Coast, the smaller *San Mateo* also had little trouble earning its way. During 1964, it completed contracts grossing $480,000—the channel to the Stardust Marina in Isleton, California; Moss Landing Harbor in Monterey County; and the Suisin Point Channel in Martinez, California. During the next year the dredge did three jobs, one at Stockton for the Army Corps of Engineers; another at Santa Cruz Harbor, opening up the entrance; and still another at Redwood City, plowing out a barge channel and dock area for Ideal Cement Company. These three contracts totaled $136,000. Although the company used *San Mateo* on fairly small jobs, it was a workhorse—the busiest in the triumvirate of Utah dredges. In 1966–67 it cut a trench for the Bay Area Rapid Transit (BART) tube across the San Francisco Bay, then went to work for the Port of Oakland, labored next on the Sherman Island Levee and at Stockton, and finally began dredging at the Oakland Middle Harbor.

Across the Pacific, meanwhile, the *Alameda* had left its bitter East Coast experience behind after the long trip to Japan, with which Utah Dredging's parent company was building a lucrative business relationship. Following company philosophy about

Vice President Joseph K. Allen was responsible for industrial land development activities.

matching markets with minerals, ships carrying large quantities of iron and coal from Utah mines on the Pacific Rim arrived with increasing frequency in Japanese harbors. Given the extent of Japan's coastline and limited usable land, Utah's involvement with the island nation naturally led to the possibility of cooperative dredging efforts. Late in 1961, the company negotiated a technical-assistance agreement with Japanese interests and made a 5 percent equity investment in the formation of George Ishiyama's Japan Industrial Land Development, Ltd. (JILD), which leased the *Alameda* to the venture's promoters, then sold plans for the vessel to the consortium so that it could build its own dredge, the *Kokuei Maru,* in the Mitsubishi shipyards. At the launching of the *Alameda*'s Japanese counterpart, Marriner Eccles's daughter, Sallie Eccles Glassie, represented the American company her father and grandfather had served so devotedly.

The Japanese planned an extremely ambitious reclamation project in which a total of thirty-one dredges—fully half of the country's active total—would take part. Due to its advanced design, the *Alameda* served as the flagship of this mud-mucking fleet so effectively that, prior to the launching of the *Kokuei Maru,* it accounted for 15 percent of the monthly yardage all by itself. The fleet dredged for more than a year through high seas and strong winds to create almost eight square miles of new land off the shores of Sakai near Osaka. On this property, homes for nearly two million people eventually rose. A bridge across the lower end of Tokyo Bay, longer than the San Francisco-Oakland Bay Bridge, capped the project and became another symbol of Japan's urban rebirth and postwar modernization.

In July 1965, the *Alameda* left Japan temporarily to dredge new berthing areas at Port Hedland in Western Australia and to deepen the harbor there. Dredging bids coming into the Mount Goldsworthy consortium were so high as to jeopardize the project, so Utah retrieved the dredge from JILD and moved it "down under." Because Utah's Mount Goldsworthy mining project mushroomed in scope, the dredge remained in Australia much longer than expected, scooping ten million cubic yards of material from the bay in order to create a five-mile entrance into the harbor, as well as a turning and mooring basin for ships of at least 100,000 dead weight tons.

While in Australia, the *Alameda* narrowly escaped serious damage when a cyclone hit Port Hedland on March 31, 1966, a few days after Littlefield, now company president, had visited the site. The storm came up with short notice early in the morning. The main concern was for the *Alameda*'s safety; but moving the pipelines that would carry the mud from the bay to the land occupied most of the day, with two-inch tow ropes breaking more than a dozen times as tugs fought against high waves and strong currents. The next day passed without incident as the dredge rode out the swells from the security of two storm anchors. On April 2, the swing wires securing the *Alameda* to the anchor began to break under the strain, forcing crews to spend a rough afternoon weighing anchors and towing the vessel into the harbor. Fortunately only the ship's tree and considerable lengths of swing, quarter, and stern wires suffered heavy damage. A suspected hole in the hull could not be found when the *Alameda* was pumped out, and it returned to work.

On completion of the Mount Goldsworthy project, Utah Dredging, now with JILD as its partner, successfully negotiated a second phase dredging at Port Hedland for the Mount Newman Mining Company. The scope and completion time for this job required that the *Kokuei Maru* come from Tokyo to assist the *Alameda*. This project became one of the most profitable major undertakings of the construction division ($16.4 million profit on $42.5 million revenue), but it ironically led to a bit of a problem. Inasmuch as negotiations for the sale of Utah's construction division to the Fluor Corporation began during its course, the projected profitability of the Mount Newman Project became an issue in the discussions to the degree that the dredging division did not become a part of the ultimate sale. In any case, following completion at Port Hedland, the *Alameda* and the *Kokuei* returned to the reclamation projects in Japan.

In 1971 JILD purchased all of Utah's dredging plants and equipment. The company thus discontinued all dredging activities and sold its operation at a gain of $1.4 million. Although the dredging adventure had been brief by company standards, its wide scope enabled it to contribute many colorful anecdotes to company lore as the three vessels traveled the world creating new shore lands and assisting in the company's internationalization.

*

While interesting and profitable in its own right, the dredging adventure developed as an outgrowth of Utah's expanding commitment to real estate and land development, a determination that rose first out of postwar construction activities around the growing complex of military bases. Housing projects at Sandia and Kirtland Heights in New Mexico, Daly and Lewis Acres in Illinois, and North and South Mathes Heights in California went up to accommodate relatively low-income families. Financed with Federal Housing Authority mortgage money, the homes passed through a rental phase, after which the military purchased them at a handsome profit. Between 1950–54, agencies such as the Atomic Energy Commission contracted with Utah for housing units in Wichita, Topeka, and Salina, Kansas; Joliet, Illinois; San Diego,

California; Allendale, Colorado; Bisbee, Arizona; Davenport, Iowa; and Ely and Ruth, Nevada.

Utah's largest land acquisition during the early 1950s was the Moraga Ranch adjacent to the growing Bay Area urban complex. The spread's title had changed hands only twice between the time the King of Spain gave it as a land grant to the Moraga brothers and Utah Construction's 1953 purchase. In classic Old West fashion, the first transfer came about in a poker game when the winner sold the property to a group that became the Moraga Company. Income from cattle and agriculture covered acquisition and maintenance until residential development began, which is when Utah entered the picture. Owning ranch land, of course, was nothing new to the firm, although few Utah watchers realized that the giant corporation actually had several cattle brands of long-standing reputation—notably the "Winecup" and the "Shoesole"—left over from the sprawling Vineyard ranch in Nevada, where Utah had owned and managed ranch properties almost the size of Connecticut.

While raising cattle might seem an illogical endeavor for a multinational construction and mining company, tending orchards appears even stranger. Nevertheless, at Moraga the company engaged for a time in a profitable pear-raising business that owed much of its success to an effective system of spraying against all types of pests. For a time, the biggest problem the growers encountered were tourists and other passers-by who helped themselves to the crop without paying. This scarcely dented the profitable operation, for the 1965 pear crop brought $135 per ton. On top of this business, English walnut orchards proved second only to cattle as a revenue-producing commodity. Instead of conventional picking processes, tractor belts shook ripe walnuts from the trees. Pickers then gathered them from the ground, after which the dried and sorted nuts sold in the shell for about 29 cents per pound.

Despite these pastoral interim activities, Utah acquired the Moraga property for development purposes inasmuch as the burgeoning population of the Oakland/San Francisco area sought outlying home sites convenient to the cities. Later, the BART system would locate its Orinda Station only half a mile from the Moraga property, giving commuters access to downtown San Francisco in twenty-five minutes. Almost twenty-eight hundred acres of the ranch transformed into residential development by 1970, when Utah sold its remaining property to another developer. In the end, the Moraga venture proved one of Utah's most profitable land investments, producing a gross profit in excess of $12 million in little more than a decade.

In 1959, Utah purchased 1,450 acres in Pauma Valley near the foot of Mount Palomar, home of what was then America's largest telescope. Located in the heartland of California's citrus and avocado industries, Pauma Valley already had a well-known golf course that featured "challenge" matches among such respected golfers as Arnold Palmer, Gary Player, and Jack Nicklaus. Palmer had listed the course as among the top five in the world. When completed, the development also featured an equestrian complex—appropriate inasmuch as John Wayne had once owned a ranch house on the property. Year-round perfect weather combined to round out what was perhaps Utah Construction's most beautiful land development. The company's board of directors enjoyed Pauma Valley enormously, so they consistently scheduled board meetings there and also celebrated Marriner Eccles's seventy-eighth birthday there. When the developers of the golf course pushed to open it to the public, Utah purchased it to maintain it as a private course for the original home buyers. The company also constructed a 2,700-foot private airstrip that further emphasized the community's exclusivity. For all its attractiveness, however, Pauma was not a financial success.

While the company's land development interests were still expanding in the early 1960s, Utah began the construction and development of high-rise apartments for the elderly, providing food, shelter, recreation, and medical services under one roof. Church-sponsored, nonprofit corporations usually became subsequent owners and operators. Canterbury Woods in Pacific Grove, California, was the first such project, built on land bequeathed to the Episcopal Church. Its then distinctive design combined the privacy of separate cottages and apartments with the convenience of central dining facilities. "It is the kindliest human environment I have ever experienced," said one resident. Utah's next retirement center, St. Paul's Towers, opened in Oakland, again with the sponsorship of the Episcopal Church. It contained 286 units, a forty-five-bed infirmary under the direction of the Samuel Merrit Hospital, a solarium and open deck, and a large lounge with a fireplace. The company took much-deserved pride in these efforts. No longer need the elderly be "put out to pasture," said the *Utah Report*. "The new concept is to provide facilities in or close to urban

St. Paul's Towers, a twenty-four-story senior citizen apartment complex, was built at the edge of Lake Merritt in Oakland, California.

areas where the participants may continue their social and civic activities."

Utah also became heavily involved in the development of industrial parks. Its first project went up on land owned by the South San Francisco Land Development Company, which once held title to most of the real estate comprising South San Francisco, where only 350 acres remained undeveloped. Utah saw a chance to use its earth-moving capabilities to increase the land's value, so it bought the company, dissolved it, and then moved more than three million cubic yards of material to fill a marsh. Land values almost instantly appreciated from $4,000 per acre to $37,500 per acre. Notable companies locating their warehouses and other facilities on this development, with aggregate floor space amounting to approximately 1.5 million square feet worth $18 million, included Zellerbach Paper, Armour and Company, Folger Coffee Company, Rome Cable Division of Alcoa, and the Chicago Pneumatic Tool Company. As time passed, tenants included Xerox Corporation and the Pacific Plastics Company. Situated near the Southern Pacific Railroad line, the Bay Shore Freeway, and the San Francisco International Airport, the South San Francisco Industrial Park became one of Utah's most successful ventures, despite intense competition from nearby industrial parks.

The company developed its second industrial park in El Segundo, California. Like the San Francisco property, it lay near an international airport. A clientele focused on the electronics and aerospace industries leased these facilities and employed more than 10,000 people. Built in half the time required at South San Francisco, the park gained recognition for its distinctive and beautiful buildings, some of which featured palm trees along their roofs. The Scientific Data Systems Building won the Governor's First Annual Design Award "for outstanding contributions to environmental design," and two national architectural magazines featured the building. The Aerospace Corporation Building also received plaudits for its beauty and was recognized by the Los Angeles Chamber of Commerce. When the company sold all of its El Segundo properties, gross revenues totaled $18 million.

Profits in industrial land development came also from projects in Martinez and Torrance, California. At these sites, however, Utah did not develop the properties but sold them to other developers. The Torrance property sold at an unusually high price for undeveloped property—$36,000 an acre. Utah's last major industrial land development came about, strangely enough, because of the walnut groves on Moraga Ranch. When Utah learned that the Walnut Growers' Association intended to build a walnut-processing plant, the company located an ideal site in Stockton and built a $5.7 million plant.

Commercial development comprised the final category in Utah's real estate adventure. Its larger projects in this sphere of activity included two multistory office complexes in Phoenix, Arizona, and in Albuquerque, New Mexico, built for Mountain States Telephone and Telegraph Company. Utah held the building in Phoenix as an investment until 1973, then sold it for a profit of more than $1 million. During Utah's ownership period, the building generated more than $1.4 million in rental income. In addition, the company constructed the First Security Bank Building in Salt Lake City, one of the first structures in the intermountain region to feature large glass walls and prefabricated metal materials. Utah also built the Burrard Building in downtown Vancouver, British Columbia, one of its first significant office building contracts outside the United States.

Despite these successes, Utah's land development prospects suffered from the ongoing ordeal at Alameda, where the effort repeatedly bogged down due to continuously vexing difficulties. Also, marginal projects such as Eden Rock Gardens in Tucson, Arizona, prompted executive reassessment. Brigham Young University owned the twenty-acre parcel, on which it had built fifty condominium units in a design unsuited to the desert climate. Utah Construction built twenty-four additional units, then sold its interest.

Gradually, Utah drew away from real estate as a major diversification option. Although its projects were numerous, geographically far-reaching, and profitable, the company increasingly considered mining the path to a more rewarding future.

The *S. S. Allen D. Christensen* was one of several custom-designed company ships transporting ore from the Marcona Mining Company in Peru.

CHAPTER 9

The Peruvian Odyssey

IN THE YEARS following World War II, American businesses and entrepreneurs moved aggressively to establish or to expand international operations. The postwar global economy appeared particularly attractive to American investors for a number of reasons. First, international competition had shrunk to near insignificance as great prewar rivals for the world's markets and raw materials lay financially prostrate, including Germany, Japan, France, Italy, and Great Britain, unable even to maintain their internal economies without American aid. Second, as European empires crumbled, vast markets for exports from the United States and cheap sources of raw materials opened wide. Finally, Rooseveltian economic diplomacy, codified at the Bretton Woods Conference in July 1944, constructed a postwar international financial system capable of funding reconstruction programs and financing a monetary infrastructure in less-developed countries.

The United States alone, among the world's great capitalist powers, had the immediate capacity to undertake global economic expansion. A unique time in international economic history had arrived, promising healthy rewards for businesses with talent, resources, and determination. By the early 1950s, the Utah Construction Company was developing an abundance of all three. It was inevitable, given its new strategic emphasis on mining ventures, that the firm would be among the leaders in the multinationalization of mineral extraction. This process began in earnest in late 1951 when Allen D. Christensen learned from Ted Takahashi and his partner George S. Ishiyama of an undeveloped reserve of iron ore in Marcona, Peru, just inland and 225 miles south of Lima. Utah had been seeking a strategic source of iron ore to satisfy a growing Japanese market, so Christensen dispatched Edgar White from San Francisco to Peru to learn more about the reserve and about La Corporación Peruana del Santa (Santa), which the Peruvian government had chartered in 1943 to manage its raw materials. Edmund W. Littlefield described White "as having a great deal of patience—a must in international negotiations. He could sit in a hotel room for six months, if necessary, without blowing his mind." White did not have to use that ability in Peru. Santa was simultaneously dealing with Bethlehem Steel, but Bethlehem's management had canceled its plans to survey the site at the last minute, even after the Peruvian government had chartered a plane for the occasion. As a result, the government rolled out the red carpet for the Utah Construction official.

White learned that the Peruvian government had declared the Marcona Plateau a national reserve in 1923 after geologists discovered its rich iron ore deposits. Hoping to use the range to develop its internal economy, the regime in Lima had formed Santa two decades later. Ambitious plans called for Marcona ore to be processed in a steel mill at Chimbote in northern Peru. Unfortunately, insufficient local assets and a lack of expertise forced Santa to consider exporting the ore through a concessionaire. With that information in hand, Christensen took the idea to understandably cautious Utah directors. The mine, more than five thousand miles away with no immediate markets, would require a considerable investment to develop. Littlefield explained that the company's earlier experience with the problematic Argonaut mine "was the obstacle that we had to hurdle to get approval for Marcona." Confident of the feasibility of the Marcona proposal, the executive committee (Marriner S. Eccles, Christensen, and Littlefield) estimated an investment of $6–7 million and urged the board to approve. Impressed with what it heard, the board empowered Christensen to negotiate a contract with Santa "for exploration, exploitation, prospecting, and development of the Marcona iron-ore deposits."

In early 1952, Christensen found Peruvian officials willing to consider a Utah proposal if it promised sufficient revenue for the state and ensured that Peru retained (in a reserve agreement or set-aside clause) some of the raw ore for domestic use. Not wishing to rush into an agreement until testing could evaluate the volume and grade of the Marcona ore, the company determined to ascertain precisely the feasibility of a large-scale operation in Peru. After much caution on both sides, representatives of the company and the government reached a tentative accord in February 1952. The preliminary agreement authorized Utah to dispatch engineers and geologists to the region to undertake drilling and survey tests to determine the potential of the range and to assess the potential of nearby San Juan Bay as a shipping site. If the company's findings came up favorable, Lima promised it the right to exercise a concession option to undertake operations for a period of twenty-one years. When, and if, Utah exercised its option, the company would pay Lima a 7 percent royalty on exported ore. Also, it would be obliged to deliver, at 25 percent of market value, a specified annual tonnage of ore to the Chimbote steel works and to leave a stipulated quantity of ore in the ground for future extraction.

The company had only until December 1952 to complete its surveys and exercise the concession option. Accordingly, that spring Utah wasted no time dispatching a team of experts to the region. Early testing determined the commercial quality of the ore and that San Juan Bay could indeed serve as a good port facility. Once engineers assessed the volume of ore to be sufficient, Christensen began to take steps to ensure that adequate capitalization existed and to secure an immediate market for the ore. To enlarge Utah's capital pool he successfully negotiated a $2.5 million Export-Import Bank loan. He then signed an agreement with United States Steel Corporation for the delivery of four million tons of Marcona ore. The latter step amounted to something of a gamble, inasmuch as Utah initially expected to plow large amounts of capital into the Peruvian operation and therefore needed all the short-term revenue it could muster. But the contract with U. S. Steel was good only until that company's own Venezuelan fields came on line in 1953. So Utah had only a matter of months to begin extracting and transporting ore.

The time problem only complicated an already difficult logistical situation. No port or loading facilities existed, no adequate river or road network linked the plateau to the sea, no equipment was in the field, and no cargo vessels were under contract to transport the ore from Peru. In order to realize any profit from the contract with U. S. Steel, Utah Construction would have to arrange for an accelerated placement of substantial quantities of machinery and manpower as well as rapidly building a functional transport and offloading network. Christensen realized that such instant marshaling of necessary manpower and equipment lay well beyond the company's means, so he began floating requests for help in the financial community. Through mutual friend Alfred Thomas at Morgan Guaranty Trust, Christensen came into contact with Harvey Mudd, president of the large and successful Cyprus Mines Corporation of Los Angeles. Like Utah, Cyprus had been searching for promising overseas investment opportunities. Mudd eagerly agreed to discuss the matter with Utah, and negotiations aimed at uniting the resources of the two corporations began immediately.

On October 28, 1952, Utah's board formally approved the investment in Marcona, but only on condition that Utah commit no more than $2 million on top of the original $500,000 already spent for exploration and negotiations. After whirlwind discussions, Christensen and Mudd initialed a partnership agreement and created a joint subsidiary—the Marcona Mining Company. The deal with Cyprus called for each party to invest between $2.5 and $3 million in the project, with each partner receiving 50 percent of the common stock. Cyprus secured the right to 43.75 percent of Marcona's earnings, Utah 41.25 percent. Key officers included Christensen as president, Charles McGraw as vice president and general manager (after the brief tenure of Harlan A. Walker), and Mudd as a director. The new company, headquartered in San Francisco, assumed and exercised the concession option with the Peruvian government in January 1953.

Looking back some years later, Littlefield summarized the year-long drama:

> Christensen and White obtained a concession agreement in February 1952 that had essentially two parts.

First, Utah was to be satisfied as to the nature of the deposit, its size, and how it would be mined. Second, Utah could elect to go forward and assume the obligation for owning, developing, and operating the mine once it was satisfied with the exploration results.... Allen was responsible for betting on "the come" that he could, in effect, bring the deal together in time to meet the obligations under the

Contemporaneous map from company files.

> concession and still satisfy the Utah board. The construction personnel under his instruction would know how to perform the work in Peru, assemble the necessary construction equipment and supplies, charter a ship, load the vessel in the U. S., and unload it quickly when it landed in Peru. It was a courageous decision and one in which I really had no part other than to be advised that it had been done.

Despite Littlefield's modesty, and although Christensen certainly played the lead role, Littlefield's part in the dramatic initiation of the Marcona venture went beyond mere advisement. For example, while Christensen traveled to Pittsburgh to negotiate with U. S. Steel, Littlefield successfully "sold the deal to the Utah board." He retired after a grueling day—an all-day board meeting followed by a black-tie family affair. About 3:30 a.m., Christensen called jubilantly from Pittsburgh. He had lined up U. S. Steel. Littlefield remembered exclaiming, "Wait until I go throw some water on my face!" When he got back to the phone, Christensen said, "You get down to Los Angeles, and I'm going to stay here, and you keep the Cyprus people lined up." Finally, on New Year's Eve, 1952, the parties closed the deal and the Peruvian odyssey got underway.

Now came the heavy lifting. The contract with U. S. Steel specified that Marcona would deliver ore on April 1, 1953, only ninety days away. Utah and Cyprus were starting from scratch, because "we didn't have anything down there," so assembling and shipping equipment took top priority in the next few weeks. In January 1953, the first shipload of heavy equipment arrived at a San Juan port. Road crews began clearing a transit corridor from the port to the mine area some thirteen miles inland. Construction began on offloading dock facilities and a village to house Marcona employees. Simultaneously open pit operations got underway at the mine site as bulldozers scraped surface-zone ore where early cuts indicated that direct shipping grade ore existed in quantity near ground level. This hematite ore required only crushing and sizing modification before delivery. By April, a fleet of cargo trucks began hauling it to the San Juan dock works.

Less than a month later the first of many leased transport ships arrived to receive the inaugural load of ore. To mark the event, Marcona officials arranged a lavish opening ceremony during the first week of May 1953. Even the president of Peru, General Manuel Odria, attended. Everything seemed to be going perfectly. "They cranked up the conveyor belt," Littlefield recalled, "the ore went up the conveyor belt and down the elephant trunk and into the hold of the ship and everybody cheered and then adjourned to the clubhouse ... to celebrate, and the damned thing broke down and we couldn't ship anything for two to three weeks."

Eventually that first ship embarked from San Juan loaded with Peruvian ore bound for the United States. In the short span of five months, Marcona had begun to fulfill successfully its agreement with U. S. Steel. Company leaders realized, however, that although the fulfillment of the contract with U. S. Steel constituted a notable achievement for Marcona, it nevertheless provided only a temporary market for the company's product. The ultimate success of the Peruvian adventure depended upon the company's ability to establish stable, permanent marketing outlets. So they moved swiftly, turning to markets Utah had previously cultivated in Japan, which was rapidly rebuilding its shattered economy and refurbishing its steel industry. In addition to the potentially lucrative Japanese market, other opportunities existed for Marcona in Western Europe, where similar reconstruction efforts were underway. To oversee and maintain the successful penetration of these markets, Marcona officials organized Compania San Juan, S.A. (Inc.), in 1953, with a $250,000 investment. Formed initially to purchase all Marcona ore except that reserved for Peru and to charter ships to deliver ore to customers, a Panama-based corporation with ownership similar to Marcona, Compañía (Cia.) San Juan took title to the ore at the departure port.

The Marcona group, which included Cia. San Juan, earned in excess of $2.5 million during its first fiscal year of operation. During the same period the mining enterprise alone reported earnings of $1,652,178. Beyond that first year the situation only improved. U. S. Steel remained a customer longer than Utah had anticipated, and when that contract expired, Bethlehem Steel agreed to purchase Marcona ore. Littlefield later appraised the entire process, from the delicate negotiations to the rigorous logistical execution, as a "fantastic accomplishment.... The better ore was at the top levels of the ore body, with very little overburden and few impurities. It could be sold as direct shipping ore. But bringing it into production in such a short period of time was a tremendous accomplishment." Moreover it was a key decision in the company's history, because "it was the success of that venture that really changed the board's attitude and the management thrust toward mining activity in general."

Marcona's rich output surprised no one, but the challenges of managing a major project thousands of miles from company headquarters led Littlefield to suggest appointing a liaison over all Marcona matters. Charles W. Robinson, who had been Littlefield's administrative assistant at Golden State, agreed to take the job and immediately went to Panama to learn that country's tax-haven provisions. Given Utah's now extensive multinational interests, the company needed to shield its offshore income from U. S. taxes until

Open pit mining at Marcona became one of Utah Construction & Mining's most successful ventures.

after dividends were repatriated to the San Francisco headquarters. His work became critically important, for every aspect of the Marcona operation passed through his office, and he reported directly to both Christensen and Littlefield. Within a short time, Littlefield related, "Marcona was operated as if it was a branch of Utah," because of Robinson's "very meaningful role in the whole management of Marcona."

With markets for its ore stable and growing, Marcona accelerated production during fiscal year 1954. As a result, the venture's earnings about doubled those of the previous year. To management's satisfaction, the operation on the ground was running smoothly. The dock facilities and road network rounded off nicely, and the employee quarters of San Juan City began to resemble something other than temporary shacks. A crusher at the mine site that had initially caused some problems began to operate more efficiently and increased the quantity of output dramatically. Despite this, a modest downturn occurred in 1955, prompting company officials to evaluate anew the scope of the Marcona gambit. One glaring area of concern was the unstable and volatile nature of shipping costs. Consequently, company officials decided to take a bold step and enter the shipping industry itself. Christensen seemed to anticipate this move from the beginning. After the conclusion of the negotiations in 1952, Littlefield had taken Christensen aside and said, "Allen, we're really in the mining business now"; to which Christensen replied, "Yes, and we also just went into the shipping business."

In June 1955, Utah and Cyprus chartered in Liberia San Juan Carriers, Limited, as a wholly owned subsidiary of Cia. San Juan. The new shipping firm purchased and refitted a small bulk carrier later that year, after which it placed its first orders with Japanese shipyards, in a clever *quid quo pro*, for the immediate construction of large specialized ore carriers. Two sister ships, the *Allen D. Christensen* and the *Harvey S. Mudd* came on line in 1956. Each had a capacity of nearly 32,000 dead weight tons (dwt). Coupled with charter vessels under long-term contract, San Juan Carriers managed to transport Marcona ore during 1956 at a cost below prevailing charter rates. The shipping company earned almost $1.9.million during fiscal year 1956, which combined with

Marcona's earnings of some $3.6 million and Cia. San Juan's $2.4 million to bring the group's total to nearly $9 million.

Buoyed with this success, company officials placed an order for two additional bulk cargo vessels with Japanese shipyards in 1956. Christened in 1958 as the *San Juan Merchant* and the *San Juan Traveler,* these ships (unlike the other three company ships) could handle cargoes of both ore and petroleum, a versatility that represented an increased earning capacity for the Marcona group. Because of the Suez Crisis of 1956, a demand for petroleum tankers to service the Caribbean had arisen. Now company ships could transport ore to overseas markets, back-haul petroleum on the return trip, and earn extra revenue for the Marcona group. By 1960, San Juan Carriers operated five ships with a collective freight capacity of 176,000 dwt; and by 1963, three new 70,000-plus dwt ore-petroleum carriers had joined the San Juan fleet, the capacity of which then swelled to more than 600,000 dwt.

In retrospect, Marcona's intrepid move into the shipping business in 1955 was even pluckier than it seemed, given the dimensions of the ships it ordered. At that time, Littlefield recalled, "the maximum-sized ship used by existing carriers for such purposes ... was 16,000 tons capacity, with most ships being 10,500 tonners." The decision to purchase larger ships was based on economies of scale—larger ships were more cost effective than smaller ships. Littlefield liked to tell of having lunch years later with the chief executive officers of the Dollar Line and General Steamship Lines, who chuckled that Utah's gamble had been a lucky one—for Littlefield did not "know enough to be scared." Even so, San Juan Carriers later acquired 72,000 and 100,000 dwt vessels that dwarfed that first 31,400 tonner.

During these years, markets for Marcona ore expanded to include not only Japan and Europe, but also Mexico and Argentina. Robinson proposed sending the ships with Panamanian registry on from Japan to Sumatra, where they could load crude oil for refining on the West Coast. Next the ships would enter the Panama Canal, where the salt water in the holding tanks would be flushed and replaced with fresh water for use in the port town of San Juan, adjacent to Marcona facilities, thus assuring back-haul profits. Littlefield liked the idea and called Larry Ford, a friend at Standard

Oil of California and a possible customer. After discussing the intense competition Utah would encounter from Greek shipping firms, Ford pledged to do business if Utah would meet worldwide terms and market prices. Hopeful of Standard's crude oil shipment contracts, Robinson encouraged executives at Japanese mills to buy more ore. Utah would then buy more Japanese-made ships, built with the ore they processed into steel.

As this outgrowth industry thrived, Marcona's original mission to mine iron ore in Peru also prospered. Estimates of the ore reserves climbed from some one hundred million tons to 350 million tons by 1962. The company easily obtained export-grade iron ore through open-pit extraction throughout the 1950s, but those surface-zone materials declined rapidly by the decade's end. To continue to meet the quality criteria of the company's customers, Marcona built beneficiation facilities to upgrade the subsurface ores, now the majority of the field. (The beneficiation process results in a more concentrated product that increases the value of lower-grade ores. It generally involves crushing, screening, and grinding the ore, then separating the iron-bearing portion from the rest of the material.)

The necessity for constructing beneficiation facilities in Peru launched Marcona's first major expansion program. After considering the beneficiation question thoroughly, company engineers and executives decided to graft a second branch onto the operation, concluding that beneficiation facilities should go in at San Nicholas Bay, ten miles north of San Juan. The decision to site the plants there instead of at San Juan stemmed from the belief that the Peruvian enterprise would eventually require additional tertiary port and base facilities to augment the beneficiation plants. Centering the new operations at San Nicholas would provide more room for expansion, prevent overlap, avoid strangling off-loading activities at the San Juan dock works, and prove more cost-effective overall. Also this second operations branch and dock works would dramatically increase the volume of ore Marcona could handle and export.

The company successfully negotiated the San Nicholas expansion with the Peruvian government's Santa Corporation, and on February 26, 1960, conferees signed a new contract that extended the company's concession to thirty years. In return, the

Assistant Secretary of State Harry C. McPherson (left) honors Charles W. Robinson, president of the Marcona Mining Company, for developing the private Institute Peruano De Fomento Educativo.

company pledged to invest $22 million in the project, to increase its annual production to a minimum of two million tons (thus increasing Lima's income from the 7 percent royalty agreement of 1953), and to construct a new port facility at San Nicholas. Its designers conceived the San Nicholas facility as a self-contained operation, capable of performing a variety of beneficiation tasks.

A five-stage construction program began July 5, 1960, and by the late summer of 1962 the first three stages reached completion. They included the San Nicholas dock and auxiliary port works, crushing and screening plants, washing and magnetic separation plants, a heavy-media separation plant, product storage facilities, and the world's longest conveyor system. Then workers finished the next two stages—additional crushing facilities, a pelletizing plant, and a steam-generated power plant at San Nicholas. Company officials and Peruvian government representatives, including President Manuel Prado Ugarteche, formally inaugurated the new facility on April 21, 1962. Now serving as president of Marcona operations (having succeeded first McGraw and then Christensen as Peru operations chief executive), Charles W. Robinson delivered the key address, emphasizing the facility's future contributions not only to the company's operations, but also to Peru's current and future economic health.

The new plant added to company revenues immediately. During the twelve-month period ending in October 1963, the Marcona group realized a net after-tax earning of $1 million, a substantial increase over the preceding year, but the new era Robinson promised in his speech—which appeared so conspicuously in the profit statements of 1963—concealed a genuine uncertainty about Marcona's future in Peru. On the surface, relations between the Marcona group and Peruvian government officials seemed solid enough, but they had actually become quite fragile due to dynamic undercurrents sweeping Latin America generally and Peru specifically.

In 1960 Peru represented a classic example of an economy dominated by foreign investors and a domestic oligarchy. American firms were producing and often exporting most of the nation's important commodities—cotton, sugar, silver, copper, petroleum, and iron ore—under an economic policy that encouraged outside investment by offering liberal incentives. In the case of mining operations, provisions for rapid depreciation write-offs and a generous depletion allowance advanced investment considerably. By 1960 total American investment in Peru had reached approximately $600 million, the vast majority of it centered on petroleum and mining. Most Peruvians, however, did not share in the benefits of the program. In fact, the internal distribution of wealth in Peru remained among the least equitable in the world, with 2 percent of the population owning 90 percent of the nation's arable land. The top 1 percent enjoyed 25 percent of the national income while the bottom 20 percent controlled only 2.5 percent. The vast majority of the people lived in dire poverty, and nearly 50 percent could not vote because they did not meet literacy requirements.

In such a setting, a strong reform movement that tilted toward radicalism inevitably evolved. Even officials of the moderate

Democratic party and the reactionary National Union (odrista) party paid lip service to the need for a transformation in Peruvian society, although modern Peruvian reform sentiment clearly stemmed from theories that Victor Raúl Haya de la Torre formulated during the 1920s. Exiled from Peru for anti-government agitation in 1923, he founded a political movement called Alianza Popular Revolucionaria Americana (APRA), which set the Peruvian reform agenda during the 1960–70s. Two of APRA's general principles held direct relevance for Marcona. First, APRA (which became a political party in the 1930s) advocated a policy of "anti-imperialism" in general terms, meaning the retention of Peruvian sovereignty in all spheres. A second principle, deriving from the first, called for a policy of nationalizing all land and industries, including those owned by foreign concerns.

To complicate matters, from the time of Peru's independence in 1825, governments had come and gone at a dizzying rate. During the entire nineteenth century, not one decade passed without a coup d'état. In the twentieth century, military and civilian coups brought different governments to power in 1914, 1918, and 1948, with another governmental change in 1933 due to an assassination, only one of a number against high government officials. This unstable environment led to economic problems that as a matter of course generated labor unrest. The apristas cultivated this troubled ground with promises of national sovereignty over the economy. By the late 1950s, pro-APRA unions had organized one short-lived general strike (1957) and numerous others against individual American firms and subsidiaries.

Although no serious labor problems plagued Marcona, management decided to try to preempt trouble by cultivating good relations with the native work force through a number of initiatives, some of them quite innovative. The company launched educational and job training programs aimed at integrating Peruvians into professional positions inside the company. Marcona also contributed generously to the San Juan school system, to building and staffing a hospital, and to funding and building a Roman Catholic church in San Juan. Robinson and other executives, however, worried most about the expropriation and nationalization of foreign holdings, a pattern occurring with increasing

The company contributed to the San Juan school system and launched educational and job training programs to integrate Peruvians into professional positions inside the company.

regularity all across Latin America. Between 1952 and 1960, Bolivia, Guatemala, Argentina, Brazil, Mexico, and, of course, Cuba expropriated and nationalized American holdings. While this regional tide had not reached Peru, it seemed inevitable.

Storm clouds appeared on the horizon when Peruvian leftists targeted for criticism the International Petroleum Company (IPC), a subsidiary of Standard Oil of New Jersey. By the end of the 1950s, more moderate elements had joined in attacking IPC, which had become a symbolic object of nationalistic wrath. In 1960 the Peruvian armed forces issued a statement condemning the 1922 agreement between the government and IPC, and declared it null and void. Other American companies in Peru watched with increasing concern as the assaults on IPC continued unabated. Despite Marcona's ongoing cordiality with the Peruvian government, the furor over IPC prompted Utah's senior management to issue a warning in the 1960 annual report: "Whether we can ride this storm without being damaged remains to be seen. Obviously, it is a rough sea, but we hope to weather it. Recent developments give some cause for encouragement."

In response to the threat, Marcona officials decided to take active measures to cultivate goodwill among influential Peruvians, and in particular the media. With industry analysts forecasting a dip in the international iron ore market in1963, the company hoped to counter displeasure over any concomitant drop in royalty payments to Lima with a massive propaganda campaign. Enrique R. East,

Marcona's Peruvian manager, proposed to Robinson a campaign orchestrated in the United States to funnel statistics and dire predictions about the international iron ore industry through Utah Construction's press contacts to cushion the shock if the market declined, or if the government called Marcona to account for any other reason. "This would help to avoid any unfriendly campaign against us," East wrote Robinson, "and if such a campaign starts, it would be easier for us to have these people write articles in our defense without having Marcona appear directly."

A veritable whirlwind of nationalistic rhetoric was blowing in the Peruvian congress and press as Marcona completed its $40 million expansion at San Nicholas. Company officials took heart in the cordiality of conservative President Manuel Prado, but in the 1962 election Prado backed the aprista Haya de la Torre, who supported nationalizing all land and industries, including those owned by foreign companies. When none of the major candidates received a majority in the election, the Peruvian congress handed power to an APRA-dominated coalition. Alarmed by Haya de la Torre's ascendancy, the armed forces declared a national emergency and installed a military junta in the presidential palace. The United States immediately condemned the coup, broke diplomatic relations, and canceled $81 million in Alliance for Progress aid, yet Marcona and other multinational companies in Peru felt some relief. At least the coup deflected a growing impulse to "do something" about American-owned firms. Robinson and other executives felt the company's investments were safe as long as the junta held sway, a notion vindicated when wildcat strikes against several American operations—including Marcona for the first time—drew a decisive response from the junta.

The unrest at Marcona began when shovel operators and spotters objected to their transfer to another operations sector, and the managers' unwillingness to discuss the matter led to strikes on both shifts, followed by managers suspending the strikers. When both sides appealed the matter to Lima, the junta backed Marcona, declared the walk-out illegal, and upheld Marcona's refusal to compensate workers for time lost on the job. Beaten, the employees accepted the verdict and returned to work.

Such developments encouraged company officials but did not

completely reassure them. When the junta, for example, issued a decree in February 1963 creating a centralized economic planning agency, Marcona quickly arranged a meeting with its director. East assured the government of the firm's interest in the stable and progressive economic development of the country. The junta leader impressed East by stating his earnest desire for Marcona's cooperation and by promising to involve the company in planning discussions. In a subsequent letter to Robinson, East encouraged close collaboration with such planning agencies. Robinson agreed in his letter of reply but counseled prudence: "There are dangers of misunderstanding, misconception, etc. in dealing with a public body ... [so] this should be approached with extreme caution."

While short-term conditions seemed reasonably secure, Robinson's wariness proved justified when the junta scheduled 1963 elections, partly due to pressure from the Kennedy administration to restore civilian rule. With the election of Fernando Belaunde Terry, the versatile leader of the Acción Popular party, the junta relinquished power peacefully, but the prevailing mood in San Juan and San Nicholas remained one of watchful waiting. Although the new president characterized himself as a moderate, he had obtained crucial leftist support by participating in the campaign to make American firms more responsive to national needs.

These political clouds thus darkened the future of the Marcona group as its first decade in Peru ended. Financially sound and efficiently integrated, Marcona represented perhaps the most valuable component of Utah's growing international empire. In early 1963, company leaders unveiled an ambitious ten-year plan for expanding its Peruvian mining and shipping activities that promised to expand earnings and investment opportunities. The plan called for continued development of the new San Nicholas complex and projected an investment outlay of $80 million between 1963–70. Engineers estimated that this expansion would increase the San Nicholas output from under five million tons to more than twelve million tons per year and raise after-tax profits from roughly $7 million to more than $25 million.

Robinson expressed his confidence in the expansion to Littlefield and Mudd. The mine's reserve capacity was immense, and market forecasts predicted strong demand for Marcona's ore products. In addition to profitability, however, Robinson revealed another motive for implementing the plan. "We must," he said, "carefully consider the advantage of reducing the 'political risk' through [demonstrating a] willingness to continue reinvesting at least a portion of the profits generated in Peru." As early as 1961, Robinson had urged Utah and Cyprus to view Marcona's shipping division as more than a cost-reduction factor. It seemed wise, he explained, to "reduce the risk inherent in an extended operation based almost exclusively on iron ore exports from Peru," a country with a growing consensus for nationalization.

With its problems and prospects clear, Marcona pressed ahead with expansion plans slated for the mid-1960s. Earnings markedly increased as the company brought new facilities into operation at San Nicholas, among them two pellet-making plants, a nonmagnetic (gravity) concentration plant, an extension of the conveyor network from the mine site to San Nicholas harbor (eleven miles total), the installation of flotation circuits to reduce sulphur content in ores, and the general upgrading of several operational units. In addition to reinforcing the dock works at San Nicholas, Marcona dredged to improve the harbor. Work commenced on an auxiliary power plant in 1968, along with a new specialized sulphur flotation unit to meet Japanese air quality standards, further expansion of the San Nicholas docks to accommodate gigantic ore carriers, construction of a bentonite processing plant that created clay from decomposed volcanic ash, and a third thermal power plant. This intense development underscored the firm's intent to center operations at the more accessible site. San Juan continued to be a company town, but processing operations gradually diminished until, by June 1967, it closed shop. Marcona then donated the dock facilities and warehouses to the Peruvian navy as a gesture of goodwill.

Marcona's ten-year plan also included an ambitious scientific research program to develop more cost-effective mining processes. An impressive array of key technical innovations emerged, including the 1963 development of the standardized pelletization process that made handling ore at the blast furnace easier. Perhaps the most significant work emerged with the landmark introduction in 1968 of the company's patented slurry process that simplified handling and transporting iron ore. The process, called "Marconaflo," propelled dry, compacted stationary material through conduits with rotating water jets into pipelines that efficiently delivered the material to waiting ships. By the early 1970s, the application of the Marconaflo process had advanced sufficiently to permit the on- and off-loading of giant vessels a mile or so offshore. This ability enabled the company to purchase three "Vanguard"-class cargo ships of 130,000 dwt each after it sold the aging 32,000-dwt each *Mudd* and *Christensen* in 1968. Shipbuilders constructed these colossal vessels to haul both ore and petroleum, and especially to handle Marcona's pellet and slurry products.

As the physical plant and technical face of the company changed, so did the structure of the business. In November 1965, the Marcona group reorganized into the Marcona Corporation, which consolidated the ownership and management of the Marcona Mining Company; Cia. San Juan; and San Juan Carriers, Ltd., with voting stock distributed fifty-fifty between Utah and Cyprus. At the same time, Utah acquired an additional 3 percent in class B stock, the basis for profit distribution, equalizing its holdings with Cyprus at 46 percent. The Allen D. Christensen interests retained the remaining 8 percent of class B stock. The Marcona Corporation subsequently established two wholly owned marketing subsidiaries, Marcona, Inc., with offices in New York and Tokyo, and Marcona Europe, Ltd., in London. These entities assumed exclusive responsibility for coordinating respective marketing activities in the United States, Japan, and Europe. In 1968, another subsidiary, Marcona Finance, S. A. (Marfin), incorporated in Luxembourg to aid borrowing for expansion programs.

This corporate reshaping improved efficiency by consolidating operations, investing authority in a single board of directors to streamline the decision-making process, and establishing efficient management groups with specialized expertise in administering diversified interests. Marfin, for example, made capital requirements easier to secure and allocate. For another, permanent institutional brokers now handled functions in key countries such as Japan.

Although operations management remained in Peru, the new Marcona Corporation began to operate in Australia, Chile, and New Zealand. It gained the exclusive right in 1966 to transport and market iron ore from the important Mount Goldsworthy concession in western Australia, which by 1970 accounted for approximately 40 percent of the corporation's iron ore sales. In Chile, the company purchased 74 percent (later increased to 76 percent) of Companía Minera Santa Adriana, S. A. (COMISA), a salt-mining operation. In New Zealand, it received the right to begin iron-ore exploration and testing activities on the North Island, backed by Japanese banks. At the same time, it began joint exploratory probes in Alaska, the Bahamas, and in India's Kudremukh Range. All these diversification projects reflected both Marcona's improving capital reserves and its uncertainty about Peruvian politics.

So Marcona's fortunes rose dramatically in the first half of its second decade, as 1963's overall after-tax earnings of around $9 million in 1963 more than doubled to $18.5 million by 1968. (Unusually, Marcona mining in 1968 earned more than San Juan Carriers. In fact, between 1966–70, Marcona mining averaged net profits of $7.4 million annually while San Juan Carriers averaged $12 million, or 60 percent of Marcona's total net income during the period.) "If, in fact, Marcona is [therefore] changing from a mining company with shipping as an ancillary operation," Robinson wondered in a 1970 memorandum, "to a full-fledged shipping company with mining as an ancillary operation, then we must begin exercising our imaginations." He urged careful planning as the company weaned itself from a long dependence on official Peruvian goodwill, but for the moment Marcona's highly vulnerable position forced it to continue to seek positive relations with Peru while simultaneously diversifying its outside earning potential.

While company fortunes had thus prospered, the background noise of radical agitation had risen in a steady crescendo. Since Belaunde's election in 1963, IPC continued to attract much of the flack as Peruvian nationalists repeatedly characterized the Standard Oil (NJ) subsidiary as a villainous foreign leech, sucking the oil of Peru while leaving few benefits behind. While IPC thus diverted attention from other foreign extraction companies, it did not take long before the same critics who were attacking IPC began to ask pointed questions about Marcona. Enrique East moved aggressively and early to parry these thrusts, courting the pleasure of the Belaunde regime and engaging in a largely fruitful public relations campaign to deflect criticisms. Realizing that restraints on Marcona and other foreign companies would certainly harm the economy, both the regime and the opposition gradually backed away from their probes into Marcona's operations, although they unilaterally enacted a tax increase on profits, from 20 to 25 percent. At the same time, to satisfy the radical fringe, they persisted in the highly visibly assault on IPC.

In order to get in front of the problem, company officials inaugurated more frequent discussions with Santa in 1964, hoping these talks would characterize a "good corporation." This meant delivering concessions to the government agency at a steady but slow pace. Marcona guaranteed Santa its commitment to maintain adequate reserves. It also agreed to increase royalty payments from a minimum rate of 75 cents to 92.5 cents per ton and to meet the growing needs of the Chimbote steel mill. The approach seemed to be working when Santa rewarded these concessions with an extension of the concession by an additional decade, to 1982. As part of this extension, Marcona agreed to offer Santa an option to buy 50 percent of the operation in 1982 and to become a full partner. At first glance, such an offer seemed one-sided in favor of the Peruvians, but it also made good sense from the company's perspective. First, the income of the partnership would substitute for royalty payments and would leave Marcona's margin of profit basically unchanged. Second, it would not interfere with overall long-term corporate profit growth projections, which relied increasingly on shipping and non-Peruvian endeavors. Finally, a joint venture with Santa meant government participation, bringing more security for the mining venture.

With relations on a seemingly positive course, East assured Robinson that "we are winning the battle," but events beyond the company's control soon interfered. In late 1966, Peru's economy began to sputter and by spring 1967, Belaunde's government had resorted to massive deficit spending. His opponents noted that this was happening while foreign companies like Marcona posted record profits. In a desperate move, the beleaguered president devalued the nation's currency, a move that backfired badly, prompting the opposition to demand that he raise revenues quickly. So Belaunde stepped up the pressure on IPC, which had decided it was in a fight it could not win. Accordingly it agreed in August 1968 to cede its oilfields to Peru. Unfortunately for Belaunde, this did not satisfy his critics, and the prospects of his re-election dimmed. To avoid an inevitable return to power of Haya de la Torre, the military again intervened, canceled the election, routed Belaunde out of his bed at two a.m, exiled him to Uruguay, and handed power to General Juan Velasco Alvarado. Among the general's first acts was the complete expropriation of all of IPC's Peruvian holdings. He also began to court favor with the Soviet Union and other Eastern Bloc countries, alarming the United States but thrilling Peruvians, now awash in leftist propaganda.

Although these developments blew an ill wind for multinationals in Peru, Marcona officials had enough confidence in their preemptive measures that, in April 1969, Robinson assured worried Cyprus Mines chairman Harvey T. Mudd that no action against Marcona appeared likely, inasmuch as the company had already established a cordial relationship with the Velasco regime. In addition, Velasco was emphasizing that the expropriation of IPC was a unique case and compensatory. "We see no reason to fear the future," wired Robinson, "although there may be actions taken by the government which could adversely affect future profits. We see as an offsetting advantage, a period of increasing stability in which we should be able to proceed with expansion with confidence in the future."

Ironically, Marcona officials worried as much about a U. S. overreaction to events in Peru as they did about the events themselves. As a result, the company lobbied against imposing economic sanctions on Peru with such hawks as Republican Senator George Murphy of California, angry with the regime's harassment of American anchovy seining off Peru's coast. Murphy and others were threatening to invoke the "Hickenlooper Amendment," a rarely used act requiring the U. S. to terminate aid to any country violating the rights of American-controlled property. The danger, of course, was that such moves against Peru would provoke Velasco to retaliate against foreign companies such as Marcona. For that reason, Mudd wrote President Richard M. Nixon in late 1969 to urge restraint: "I believe that American enterprise will be more secure from whatever political hazards there may be if it does *not* seek out the support of the United States Government in the event of a confiscation or the threat of it."

This position developed from Marcona's own healthy relationship with the Velasco regime, from which the operation felt no immediate pressure. So confident were company officials in the future that they pushed forward with general upgrading of ore-processing facilities, completing both a 5,000-kilowatt auxiliary power plant and the third thermal power generator. Things looked so good that planners began to envision for the near future a third pelletizing plant with the capacity of producing an additional three million tons annually.

The Marcona operation helped to fund and build a Roman Catholic church in San Juan.

Although thus fairly secure in its outlook in Peru, Marcona continued to hedge its bets with ongoing diversification. A long-term contract with Midland-Ross, for example, gave Marcona access to Oregon Steel Mills in Portland. Also, after a year's testing proved favorable, the company formally launched its New Zealand mining project in cooperation with a syndicate called the Todd Group, in which Marcona held 75 percent of the equity. Elsewhere, the Alaskan iron ore range at Snettisham revealed a potential reserve of one billion tons, while tests at Kudremukh, India, indicated an even greater reserve. To manage this expanding empire, new corporate components merged in 1969. For the New Zealand project, the company incorporated a subsidiary in Nevada called Marcona Development Inc.–New Zealand. In Liberia, it incorporated three new wholly owned shipping subsidiaries called San Juan Vanguard Corporation, San Juan Venturer Corporation, and San Juan Voyager Corporation.

In the meantime, on-line operations for Marcona approached record levels, as overall revenues of more than $200 million generated net profits of $21 million in 1969, especially impressive in light of Peru's high taxes and royalty rates. Marcona Mining earned more than $8 million from a production high of 9.4 million tons. Shipping accounted for more than half of the company's earnings, with a net of $11.8 million from transporting nine million tons of Peruvian ore and a record four million tons of other contracted products. Significant trends included the fact that one-third of the iron ore Marcona sold came from outside Peru. Also, shipping income, the key source of profits, derived more than 40 percent of its business from hauling non-Peruvian cargoes.

Unfortunately, while all of this positive news came from Marcona's ledgers, and while the company took heart in feeling no pressure from the Velasco regime, it turned out that the reason for the latter centered less around the dictator's positive feelings for Marcona than around his consolidation of power in Lima. Common to most unstable polities across the less-developed world is the willingness of the military to intervene whenever it sees the normal operation of "democracy" failing to promote "progress." By the end of the 1960s, nearly every country in Latin America had succumbed to military juntas at one time or another. Some of those regimes had shown surprising enlightenment and had stepped aside after "restoring order," but the usual course of such revoluciónes was for the colonels, generals, or sometimes sergeants, to translate themselves into "presidents for life," a euphemism for dictator. For multinational companies, dealing with such rulers is tricky business, as Utah soon learned in its dealings with General Velasco.

Through 1969, Velasco and his advisors worked on a major overhaul of bureaucratic structures, attempted to "unify" public opinion by setting state controls over the media, and enacted a number of reforms. Then in 1970, Velasco launched his "third course," a vigorous national reform campaign poised between capitalism and socialism. This aimed to increase greatly government control over much of the economy, and it inevitably increased conflicts with foreign-owned enterprises. As a part of this program, it nationalized International Telephone and Telegraph's 69 percent ownership of Peru's telephone system and ordered all foreign companies to abandon rural landholdings within six months. Generally troubling was the new Industrial Law, categorizing industries as either private, mixed (public and private), state, or private "reformed" (in which workers and management jointly operated the enterprise). The plan clearly aimed at restricting foreign investors by requiring all foreign firms to sell majority control to Peruvian investors over a fifteen-year period, and by requiring the executives of existing investments to file divestment plans. The government also ordered that all foreign currency holdings be declared and converted into sols, even as the state-owned Banco de la Nación bought out Banco Popular, owned by the old Peruvian-based oligarchy, Chase Manhattan's Banco Continental, and the Banco Internacional, which had a minority American participation. (The Velasco régime exhibited a sophisticated approach. For instance, it compensated Chase Manhattan at three times book value, a step that enabled a peaceful withdrawal from Peru and a friendly welcome from Chase's New York headquarters, when and if the military government desired a loan.) These acts brought financing for central economic planning securely under state control.

While these and other measures signaled a clear trend toward a state-owned economy, none menaced Marcona directly until the government abolished Peru's twenty-year-old mining code. The new law significantly expanded government's role in mining and established a state enterprise, Empresa Minera de Peru (Mineroperu), which monopolized foreign mineral trading and metal refining. Marcona executives worried particularly about the probable impact of the mineral marketing provision. After representatives of the Ministry of Energy and Mines clarified this provision and other matters, the company reaffirmed its desire to cooperate with the Velasco régime. In return, the government informed the company that Mineroperu's monopoly in marketing minerals would not immediately interfere with the Marcona-San Juan's profitable marketing and distribution business.

These assurances led Marcona's leaders to conclude they could continue advantageously under the new reforms, yet they sensed that the current changes signaled only the beginning of trouble for foreign firms. As a result, Marcona adopted a repositioning strategy, which included using the media to communicate its position. Inasmuch as the Velasco regime had taken de facto control of the Peruvian media, the company turned to the international press for a forum. In an interview with *Forbes* magazine on March 15, 1970, Robinson hinted that Marcona could and would leave Peru if the revolution's policies became unbearable. "I am really quite discouraged with Peru," he said. "They don't know what they want and may have to go pretty far to learn the economic facts of life." He stressed the firm's new role as a leading international transportation company, saying, "If we had to, we could rapidly deploy our fleet elsewhere in the ore market and not show a substantial drop in revenues." The article then editorialized: "Without Marcona, where would the Peruvians sell the ore and how would they ship it?" Robinson added diplomatically, "It's nice to have a staunch boat, but it's better to have a calm sea."

The Velasco régime responded to Marcona's gentle message with similar restraint. Aware of its dependence on Marcona for its market contracts and especially for its transport fleet, the government assured Marcona that as long as the firm strove to expand production, it had nothing to fear. Consequently on December 28, 1970, Robinson announced that Marcona had reached an agreement with Lima, requiring the company to invest

$25 million for plant expansion and the general upgrading of its mining operation. This would increase Marcona's grinding, magnetic concentrate, and pelletizing capacity, enlarge its storage facilities, and expand its ship-loading ability for both dry and slurry products. "This agreement," Robinson told the press, "reaffirms our confidence in the continuation of a satisfactory working relationship in Peru. Marcona will continue to appraise further opportunities for expansion in the country, based on a continuation of the government's support of private investment." As it had done for some time, however, Marcona continued to bolster its potential earnings outside Peru.

Hoping to stabilize its position by drafting Lima directly into its operation, Marcona sought the first of several preemptive accords in 1971. Drawing on its earlier deal with Santa for the 1982 beginning of a joint Marcona-Peru mining venture, the firm offered Lima an immediate opportunity to purchase 25 percent of the equity. In a letter to the Lehman Brothers investment firm, Albert Reeves, senior vice president of the parent company, now Utah International, Inc., described the proposed partnership as "an intellectual, diplomatic move." Velasco considered but rejected the offer, apparently because of the government's minority standing in the arrangement. Such a decision seemed shortsighted, given that Marcona's consolidated earnings in 1971 exceeded the previous year's $25 million mark by $9 million. Because of labor difficulties and the cancellation of a lucrative Japanese contract (due to stringent anti-pollution laws), earnings from mining operations dropped while other subsidiaries posted higher profits. The overall $34 million resulted largely from the continuing profitability of shipping.

Set upon "diversifying political risk," as the 1971 operations report termed it, Marcona now expanded into additional countries and regions. In Greenland, Marcona signed a fifty-fifty joint mining agreement with the Danish Cryolite Company to exploit the ISUA iron ore deposits at Godthab Fjord. Dramatizing the company's new perspective, "political stability" had played a major role in the decision to proceed. This joint venture, however, never materialized. Using the same criteria, Marcona also undertook a joint venture with S. A. Minerácao de Trinidade (Samitri), a Brazilian ore producer controlled by a Luxembourg steel consortium, to consider a program to transport iron ore 190 miles from the Belo Horizonte mine site in the state of Minas Gerais to an Atlantic port plant for processing and slurry loading. In addition, Marcona's new subsidiary Marconaflo, Inc., began negotiations with Anaconda Copper Corporation and others regarding the use of its patented system. It further submitted European bids for proposed pelletizing plants in Rotterdam, Amsterdam, and Marseilles.

Bold expansion schemes continued throughout 1972–73. For example, the Brazil venture (renamed Samarco) worked to attract Saudi Arabia into a joint enterprise to construct and operate a steel mill. The proposal called for the Saudi state-run Petromin Corporation to own 50 percent of the operation, with the other 50 percent owned by a consortium under Marcona leadership that included long-term Japanese associates such as Nippon Steel. The mill, to be supplied with Samarco ore, was scheduled to open operations in 1976 under the management of Petromar, a joint partnership between the Saudis and a Marcona-Gil consortium called Marsteel (with Marcona holding 40 percent ownership). Although nothing materialized from these negotiations, they clearly demonstrated the propensity of Marcona to develop complicated plans to foster diversification. On the successful side of this effort, Marcona acquired a Bahama-based aragonite (a mineral containing calcium carbonate) submarine mining operation. A newly created subsidiary, Marcona Ocean Industries, Ltd. (MOI), would produce the natural form of calcium carbonate for use in the cement industry as well as for glass manufacturing and acid neutralization.

Meanwhile the Peruvian government launched a new nationalization campaign leading to major expropriation strikes against two American-dominated industries. In May 1973, Lima nationalized fish meal (made from dried and pulverized anchovies) and put all fish-meal companies under a state agency called Pescaperu, thus eliminating the successful operations of twelve American firms, including Heinz and General Mills. For Marcona, the second major expropriation hit much closer to home—the Cerro Corporation, a mining concern with six Andean sites producing lead, zinc, and copper. The country's largest employer with more than 17,000 workers, Cerro's book-value investments of

$250 million ranked highest among foreign firms doing business in Peru. After the laws changed, Cerro executives decided to sell out to Mineroperu and proposed a negotiated nationalization in December 1971. Negotiations quickly broke down, however, when the government offered Cerro no more than $12 million, while the company held out for between $175 and $250 million.

The Cerro stalemate degenerated into an angry war of words in the local and international press, with both parties running self-serving advertisements in the *New York Times* on September 23 and 30, 1973. Frustrated, Cerro withdrew its offer to sell, publicly blaming Velasco's intransigence. Peru responded by charging Cerro with bad-faith bargaining, mistreating its workers, and violating housing laws. This tense atmosphere eased only when James Greene, senior vice president of Manufacturers Hanover Bank, arrived in Lima with orders from President Nixon to review all outstanding expropriation issues between Peru and American businesses. Greene persuaded the parties to arbitrate, with nationalization scheduled for December 31, 1973, so the company could use its losses as a tax write-off. Cerro ultimately received $77.7 million for its holdings.

These developments reinforced Marcona's growing concern for its own future in Peru. Not only had the Velasco regime tackled the largest multinational in the country, but it also unveiled a new plan of socio-economic organization—the so-called "social property" movement, a revised property definition with the potential of radically restructuring society. It envisioned employee-elected general managers and a boards of directors running enterprises, a concept not far from the idea of Marxist collectives. In addition to paying wages, the plan proposed dividing a business's liquid assets equally among the workers at the end of the year. While the new economic structure tolerated private companies, the social property component concerning ownership eventually would prevail.

Marcona leaders viewed the implications as ominous. How could it survive as a capitalist island in a social property state? Also, launching the program seemed expensive, and rumors flew of a pending new tax on export firms such as Marcona. Already Lima struggled with a capital shortage that made Peruvian leaders reckless in dealing with resident multinational firms. For example,

Marcona's huge mine in Peru produced 9.4 million tons of iron products annually. To achieve this production level, the company mined more than 100,000 tons of material each day from four major areas.

when disclosures of Gulf Oil's practice of bribing government officials in other countries hit the news, the Peruvian government used it as justification to expropriate the corporation's local subsidiaries due to "moral offenses."

An additional economic factor further darkened Marcona's outlook. The Yom Kippur War of 1973 and its concomitant Arab oil embargo burdened the Peruvian economy, even as the government sought new and expensive social reforms. The national debt skyrocketed between 1973–75, and consumer prices tripled during those same years, accelerating wage demands and exacerbating labor problems. The incidence of strikes averaged just over three hundred between 1970–72, then jumped to more than seven hundred per annum, idling 29 percent of the work force in 1975 and costing the economy more than twenty million lost worker-hours. So the oil embargo made Peru's financial position decline at the very time it hoped to implement new and expensive social programs.

Due to the sinking economy, the popular Velasco régime began to experience caustic criticism from the now severely restricted press and the old political parties. Finally in 1974, Velasco shut down the nation's private newspapers, a move that provoked open resistance to the régime, including assassination attempts on cabinet officers and bombings of government offices. For the first time, the unity of the armed forces showed signs of cracking as high-ranking naval officers criticized Velasco's handling of the economy. Marcona, virtually the last foreign-owned mining venture left in Peru, consequently came under strong government pressure to increase production so Lima could gain more revenue.

The company wisely responded with caution to the now perilous climate. Again its officers opened talks with the government to consider a joint operation, but their words fell on deaf ears. Still, Marcona continued its Peruvian operations while diversifying in other countries, as Robinson came up with a new tactic. Marcona's strength in Peru depended upon its strategic structure—specialized shipping and market leverage. Hoping to reinforce that structure and thus bolster the firm's security, Robinson proposed building a new facility to produce slurry products requiring the company's own specialized handling. Perhaps more significantly, he proposed that Japanese investors, particularly long-term Marcona customers, become partners in this venture.

This proposal offered Marcona several advantages, for it would reduce the capital outlay for expansion and increase Lima's dependence upon the company's unique skills and fleet. If Lima unilaterally nationalized Marcona's holdings, the Peruvians would face immense problems in selling and transshipping specialized commodities. The proposal also included Japanese customers, who purchased 80 percent of Marcona's iron ore product, and that factor drastically altered the equation, for Japan had very strict laws on purchasing materials from expropriating nations. Early in 1974, Robinson submitted his proposal to the government. When Lima rejected it, he and other executives recognized that Marcona's days in Peru were definitely numbered.

During that year and the next, Marcona offered what it considered generous concessions, but talks eventually collapsed as rumors circulated that Velasco would soon nationalize Marcona's mining venture. The *Peruvian Times*, an English-language newspaper popular with American expatriates in Lima, reported that detailed plans for a Marcona takeover were in a safe at the offices of state-run Mineroperu. Then on July 28, 1974, a government official announced "Plan Inca," which outlined a state policy goal "to place the exploitation, refining and marketing of the great [mineral] deposits in the hands of the state." Reading this message aright, Marcona's senior management tried again in September to negotiate an expropriation agreement, and this time Lima paid attention. Preliminary talks opened on February 28, 1975, with formal meetings scheduled to begin a month later. Marcona officials felt fairly confident, believing they held a firm bargaining position based on the exclusivity and structure of the company's shipping and marketing operations. In early 1975, Robinson sent a realistic summary of the situation to the San Francisco office, saying that Marcona "will be in Peru as long as they believe that they are better off with us than without us.... We are going to work it out, but ... you may get the word any day that we didn't." In case of a non-negotiated Peruvian takeover, the company planned to suspend immediately ore shipments from Peru and not to cooperate with the government until it agreed to adequate compensation.

As the time for the formal talks neared, each party sought to position itself advantageously. In February, Peruvian officials notified Marcona that a government audit revealed the company had underpaid taxes in 1970–73 by some $16.5 million. The national press then accused Marcona of manipulating its shipping records to hide taxable profits. Marcona responded that it had reinvested most of its earnings to develop new technologies that would create a higher demand for Peru's ore. The company presented itself as a benefactor to Peru, one whose discounts to the national steel works had saved the country $10.6 million dollars between 1952–74. This posturing only served to create an adversarial climate before bargaining ever began.

When the talks finally got underway, they became directionless. While company negotiators tried to keep a low profile, members of the Peruvian government's team exhibited a stern, uncompromising demeanor. In response to a query about the lack of movement in the talks, for instance, Minister of Mines Fernandez Maldonaldo indicated no concern, because nationalization amounted only to questions of "how and when," questions Velasco answered on July 25, 1975, with an announcement that the government had decided unilaterally to expropriate Marcona. On Peru's Independence Day three days later, Maldonaldo announced the nationalization of Marcona's mining and processing properties and accused the company of causing "serious damage to our country by actions typical of the immoral conduct that the great multinationals traditionally exercise."

This decree created a new state enterprise, Hierro-Peru, that took over Marcona's operation, froze company bank accounts, and rendered all existing contracts null and void. Perhaps the most serious short-term consequence was the freezing of bank loan guarantees secured by corporate assets, including ships, and the withdrawal of the Samarco line of credit. The bankers asked Utah and Cyprus to guarantee Marcona's debts in exchange for freeing up Marcona's assets. When Cyprus management refused, Marcona declared bankruptcy. Utah then stepped in, bought Marcona out of bankruptcy by repaying its loans, kept Samarco alive, and quietly folded the remains into the parent company.

The official justification for nationalizing Marcona's Peruvian assets was a charge that the company was guilty of "grave non-compliance with its contract obligations." Specifically, the government charged Marcona with failing to maintain adequate iron ore reserves, failing to maintain and replace equipment, failing to pay taxes and royalties, and profiteering on sales and shipping while showing a loss on the mines to dodge Peruvian taxes. It later charged Marcona with manipulating sales commissions, claiming illegal depletion allowance deductions, and engaging in record-keeping irregularities. Utah's executives instantly labeled the charges outright falsehoods and mere pretexts.

Beyond all of the rhetoric, the nationalization of Marcona probably happened for two simple reasons—to gain access to revenue and to rally popular support. Velasco hoped that state operation of Marcona would ease the nation's growing foreign and domestic economic problems and help Peru chart a course of recovery. Ironically, quite the opposite occurred. When Marcona withdrew its ships from service, Peru was unable to replace them, and many of Marcona's Japanese customers refused to sign contracts with Hierro-Peru. Thus, as company officials had predicted, Peru had neither customers for its iron ore nor ships to transport it.

Peru's iron ore exports plummeted from five million tons between January and June of 1975 to a mere 33,000 tons (sold to Romania) between July and December of the same year, at an estimated loss in export earnings of $100 million. In short, Robinson and his colleagues devised a failsafe system that made unilateral nationalization a risky business, something Velasco disregarded. Rather than gaining capital to offset the national financial crisis, the takeover of Marcona intensified his problem.

The seizure also failed to rally political support, for Velasco, who was seriously ill for most of the year, could do little to guide the cohesiveness of national policy-making. This factor combined with tight control over political parties and the press to renew criticism, which then prompted a cruel governmental crackdown on political dissidents. More significant was the growing dissatisfaction among key government officials with Velasco's handling of Peru's economic dislocation. Military unity, the bulwark of the régime, had already begun to crack. The ailing general's bold stroke against the Utah-Cyprus venture postponed his removal, but irritation with his rule continued to mount within official circles.

This lack of direction manifested itself in Peru's post-nationalization dealings with Marcona. No communication with the company, either to settle the matter or to set a date to begin talking, followed the expropriation. In this setting, Velasco's opponents decided to move against him. On August 29, a palace coup removed the president from office and replaced him with his foreign minister, General Francisco Morales Bermudez. Few doubted that the Marcona takeover played a contributory role.

While Morales pledged to continue the revolution, events proved Velasco's ouster to be an important watershed. The reforms initiated after 1968 slowed significantly, and many went into reverse. With this turn to the right under the new régime, talks with Marcona finally began in September 1975, but the two parties held widely divergent valuations of Marcona's assets—the basis for determining compensation. Peru appraised Marcona holdings at a ridiculous $9 million, while Marcona's figure was $167 million. Finally, both sides turned to Washington for mediation. President Gerald R. Ford dispatched officials from both the State and Treasury Departments to steer the parties toward agreement.

Inasmuch as the thorniest problem was establishing the fluctuating value of Marcona's holdings, both parties agreed to defer the issue. The mediators instituted a systematic approach to the negotiations based on the idea that Peru's economic health depended on getting Marcona's vessels back in service. A breakthrough came in December, when conferees signed an agreement calling for the ships to resume transporting ore immediately, in anticipation of an overall agreement within ninety days. The final settlement would include a $1-per-ton shipping charge for materials hauled during the interim.

As the ships weighed anchor, both parties retained independent consultants to assure an objective valuation of Marcona's net assets. Peru employed a French firm, while Marcona executives commissioned the Stanford Research Institute. By March 1976, negotiators reached a consensus. The State Department consequently appointed New York attorney Carlyle Maw to hammer out a compensation package, in consultation with the Peruvian ministry of mines. A three-part settlement soon emerged. Peru signed a $37 million promissory note to be financed by a loan from a group of American banks, a discounted sales contract of $22.4 million with Marcona on 3.7 million tons of Peruvian ore deliverable within four years, and a $2 million payment for the ore transported by the company since December 1975. The total package entitled Marcona to compensation totaling $61.4 million.

The settlement satisfied both sides. Peru would not suffer further on the balance of payments issue, inasmuch as the capital required would not come from the treasury. Peru also received access to the American market and secured transport guarantees from Marcona. In turn, the company retained a guaranteed source of iron ore, with which to fill back orders and provide steady income while Utah restructured and undertook new ventures.

So ended the remarkable quarter-century of Utah in Peru. Through constantly expanding mining, minerals processing, and shipping enterprises, the company and its partner certainly made the most of their intrepid move into multinational business. And while Utah definitely became a mining company during those years, it also held many other irons in the fire.

The company's contract with the Navajo Tribe gave preference to hiring Native Americans. Some one hundred Navajos found jobs during the construction phase, with twice that many jobs planned in mining or power plant operation.

Chapter 10

Black Gold and Yellow Cake

A thousand years ago, the aboriginal inhabitants of what is now northwestern New Mexico burned coal in their kivas, but it was not until after World War II that the presence of vast coal reserves on the isolated Navajo Indian Reservation came to have any meaning for the rest of the world. Early in the 1950s, geologists working for Utah Construction Company became impressed with the feasibility of mining this "black gold" to produce electricity for the growing Southwest. From that beginning, the Navajo Coal Mine became one of the world's largest, as Utah's operation established important firsts and set numerous records in the mining and power industries. A few hundred miles to the north, the company would also enter into another important arena of the postwar energy extraction business when it began to produce "yellow cake" from uranium mines in Wyoming.

When Utah began to investigate the possibilities of entering into a major coal-mining enterprise, the Navajo reservation covered an area equal to Maryland, Massachusetts, and New Jersey combined, yet its population was smaller than that of Berkeley, California. The Navajo Nation constituted the largest Native American population in the United States, with some 90,000 people spread over a vast landscape, largely arid and unspoiled. Concerned about controlling the use of natural resources on their land and deriving maximum benefits from them, the Navajos encouraged the development of industry on the reservation and cooperated closely with Utah from the inception. Their leaders realized that the large mine could dramatically expand employment opportunities on the reservation and improve the local standard of living. Low-cost electricity would become available on many parts of the reservation that would otherwise remain without power.

Although geologists had known of these coal reserves for many years, Utah Construction geologists became the first to map them. Early investigators had a difficult time even finding the area. The first aerial photograph of the region missed it completely. The reserves lay in the mesa country of the mile-high Colorado Plateau, where flat or rolling uplands gave way occasionally to cliffs or badlands. With an annual precipitation of less than eight inches, the entire area under lease supported only three cottonwood trees amid sparse desert vegetation.

Utah's exploration efforts in the San Juan Basin found coal beds dating from the Upper Cretaceous, occurring in the Fruitland area and underlying Menefee formations where the coal was older and consequently of better quality. The deposits, "shaped like two huge lopsided oblong plates, one stacked inside the other," featured seams inter-bedded with sandstone and shale. Comparatively uniform throughout the lease area, the hard and brittle coal ranked as C-grade sub-bituminous, with a bright luster and a heat-content ranging from eight to eleven thousand BTUs per pound. Deposits appeared to vary in thickness from two to twenty feet, with a main seam of thirteen feet. The first usable seam slanted into the earth from beneath a thirty-foot overburden that gradually increased in depth. When actual mining operations began, Utah personnel estimated that the Navajo coalfield held reserves in excess of one-half billion tons.

The saga of the Navajo Mine began in 1953 at Window Rock, Arizona, where Weston Bourret represented Utah in negotiations with tribal leaders for a prospecting permit and option to lease. The following year, the company received permission to explore and drill on 124,000 acres of Navajo land. Because a planned power plant in the vicinity of the mine would be the most practical market for the coal, Utah applied to New Mexico for water rights from the San Juan River. The state subsequently granted Utah 51,600 acre-feet annually of the river's flow.

In the meantime, the firm continued to negotiate a lease. In April 1957 the tribal leadership finally agreed to an acceptable arrangement, but a snag about pipeline rights already granted to an oil company delayed the beginning of the operation. By the end of the summer, a revised lease resolved the problem, and on October 22, 1957, the United States Department of the Interior announced approval of a coal mining and electric power development lease on 24,000 acres of Navajo land. The ten-year lease contained an extension provision for as long as coal production was financially feasible. Allen D. Christensen, representing Utah Construction, and Tribal Chairman Paul Jones signed the compact, which called for payments of 25 cents per acre for the first year, 50 cents per acre for the second and third years, and $1 per acre for each year thereafter.

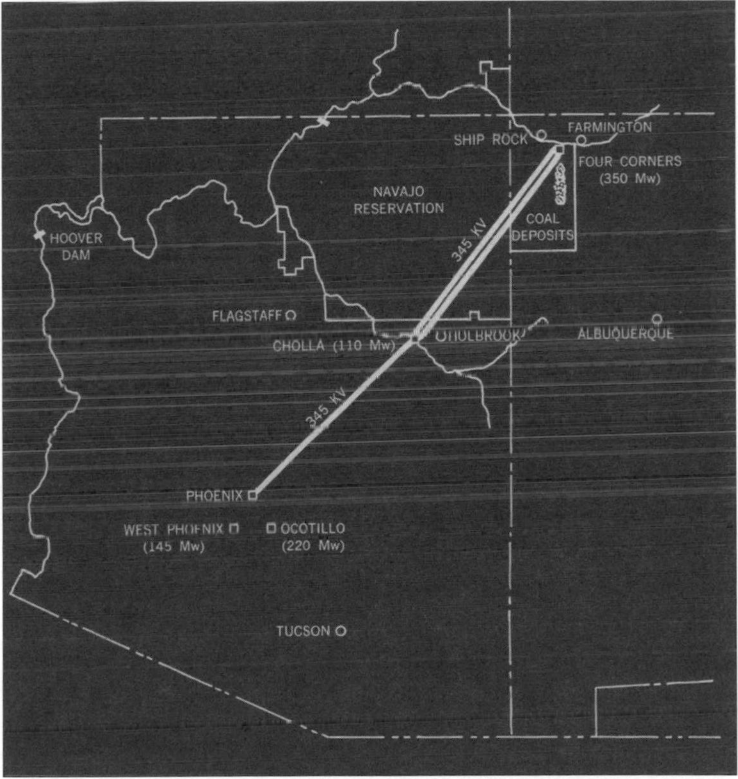

In the 1950s, Utah Construction convinced electrical utilities in the American West to burn coal to produce steam, as was done in the East. Power then flowed three hundred miles to fast-growing Phoenix, Arizona.

In addition, the company agreed to pay royalties on extracted coal at a rate of 15 cents a ton. The tribe retained the rights for leasing oil and gas development, although Utah had to approve drilling and related activities. Utah agreed to hire Navajos to dig irrigation canals and build roads in the area, and also agreed to sell electric power to the tribe. The company also promised to employ local workers when available and qualified, to pay prevailing wages, and to use the services of Native American contractors whenever feasible. In addition, Utah would submit a full plan of development for the area to the Interior Department within five years.

By 1959, crews had drilled holes on one- to two-thousand-foot centers in the northern portion of the lease area. Earthmovers concurrently dug test pits to determine the nature of the overburden and to obtain bulk samples for boiler burning tests. That same year, the Arizona Public Service Company (APS) showed an interest in building a 350-megawatt thermal electric generation station on the Navajo reservation that would burn Utah's coal. Subsequent successful negotiations resulted in an August 1960 contract for the delivery of energy equal to the output of 1.5 million tons of coal annually for thirty-five years, with an option to extend the term for another fifteen years, and to provide additional fuel as generation capacity increased. One month later, the Secretary of the Interior announced approval for the power plant.

To supply water for steam condensation, Utah first excavated a 1,200-acre, 100-feet deep cooling pond for water from the San Juan River. Located about three miles north of the steam plant, Lake Morgan (named in honor of a former tribal chairman) took more than a year to fill as two 15,000-gallon-per-minute, 450-foot head pumps pushed river water up over bluffs thirty stories high and into the basin. Successful plans for the lake included its use and management by the Navajo Nation as a recreational facility for water sports and fishing. Groundbreaking ceremonies for the power plant took place on March 10, 1961, although actual construction began in January. Dignitaries at the ceremony included Christensen, Jones, and Arizona Public Service President Walter T. Lucking.

The Four Corners Power Plant came on line only four months later in July. The futuristic power-generating facility stood on barren plains not far from an earth-filled dam a mile and a half long and 110 feet above ground level. Nearby, 400,000 tons of coal were heaped into a small mountain, awaiting the plant's opening. Huge by industry standards, the facility would generate 350 megawatts by 1963, with an ultimate capacity of 2,085 megawatts. The available water supply set the limit. Designers engineered the plant to produce an enormous 1,270,000 pounds of steam per hour. Most of the energy thus generated would then travel three hundred miles over 345-kilowatt transmission lines to the burgeoning city of Phoenix.

Actual operations at the Navajo Mine got underway on October 5, 1962, when initial box cutting began at the Dodge Pit, named for a Navajo family who had lived in the area. Fittingly, a member of that family, Charley Dodge, was working at the mine on that historic day. That first box cut was about a hundred feet wide and revealed coal depths at from twenty-six to thirty-two feet. The strip-mining operation began with blasting the overburden. To streamline this part of the procedure, the company developed a unique truck designed to measure accurately and mix thoroughly the explosive's ingredients. Workers carefully weighed ammonium nitrate pellets (called prills) and fuel oil while loading the truck, after which two large augers inside the vehicle rotated and mixed the two materials. Two other augers then moved the mixture to and through a discharge pipe which loaded the blasting hole at a rate of one hundred pounds per minute. A typical hole with fifty feet of overburden required seven hundred pounds of the mixture. With varying thicknesses of overburden and differing ground hardness, the charges ranged from 250 to 2,000 pounds per hole, but this ingenious new truck cut a two-day blasting job to half a day, using the same number of men on the crew.

After controlled blasting fractured the overburden, a walking dragline removed the broken earth. Utah began work with a Marion 5323 power shovel from the worked-out Ozark-Philpott Mine in Arkansas while waiting for delivery of the next generation of machine, the Marion 7900 dragline, built especially for the Navajo Mine project. Powerful, flexible, and economical, the 7900 went into operation in double shifts on April 12, 1963. Boasting a 40-cubic-yard dragline with a 250-foot boom and able to dig about

2,400 cubic yards per hour, this machine could remove 16,000 cubic yards of waste each working shift. Every year this dragline moved twice the material Six Companies put into Hoover Dam—or enough to bury a football field under one mile and a half of rock. A second dragline, one-fifth again larger than the 7900, went into operation five years later, and still others followed as the nation's largest coal mine grew.

After the dragline uncovered the coal, ten-yard shovels went into action, loading the fuel into bottom-dump haulage units, each capable of carrying 120 tons. Handling facilities included a 350-ton hopper with a primary single-roll crusher that reduced the mine coal to chunks no larger than eight inches thick. The coal then rumbled along a five-foot-wide conveyor belt to a secondary ring hammer mill that crushed it to less than three-quarters of an inch, then dumped it into one of six 35,000-ton blending piles to ensure a uniform grade of coal for delivery. Utah developed this system for storing and blending mine output prior to delivery—a first in the coal-mining industry. With such efficiency, by 1963 the company was producing seven thousand tons of coal daily at Navajo, with crews stripping during fifteen shifts per week while loading and hauling on five shifts per week.

Finally, on a balmy June 21, 1963, more than five hundred guests assembled at the Four Corners Power Plant for formal dedication ceremonies, which included a tour of the mine and generating facility. Frank L. Snell, APS executive committee chairman, served as master of ceremonies. Although the Tribal Chairman Raymond Nakai was called to Washington, his representative, Carl Todacheene, keynoted the event. His theme was "God made us neighbors; let us be good neighbors," a sentiment that summed up the cordial relationship that had developed between the tribe and the combined industries of the mine and power plant. Then Littlefield summarized some of the many hurdles the project had surmounted due to "the foresight and practical imagination of our engineers and geologists [who] convinced us that advancing technology would provide solutions to most or all of these difficult problems." Littlefield's comments highlighted the broader meaning of the entire Navajo Mine project, pointing to technologies and innovations in the strip-mining industry, which the project enjoyed. Additionally, he emphasized the original goals of the operation—providing low-cost energy and raising the standard of living on the reservation.

The high tone at the dedication proceedings carried the affair, after which Nakai returned from Washington to accompany Littlefield and Snell on tours of the mine and power plant. Utah Construction received many letters praising its role on the

Utah Construction's Navajo Coal Mine fed directly into the Four Corners Power Plant, which was dedicated on June 21, 1963.

reservation and its participation in the continuing success of free enterprise. The laudatory comments were not just talk. A number of significant economic benefits were coming to the Navajo people. Lease payments for the plant site amounted to $116,238 per year, while coal royalties eventually added another $1,235,000 annually. Additionally the three-year mine and plant construction project created jobs for about one hundred Navajos, with permanent jobs for twice that many at the mine and another two dozen at the power plant.

To maintain the positive public-relations momentum that the dedication generated, the Navajo Mine staff put together an impressive exhibit for the 1964 Navajo Nation Fair, including a slide presentation and demonstrations, telling about mine operations and the relationship between the mine and the Navajo community. Stressing the company's concern for environmental quality, the exhibit displayed plans for reseeding and reclaiming the project area. Employees also demonstrated safety equipment and procedures. For the main attraction, a working model of a stripping dragline (similar to the Marion 7900) imitated removing overburden even as a scale model of the power plant, prepared by Arizona Public Service, hissed steam nearby.

In the months following, the project continued to prosper. Although Utah was not directly involved in the process, the power plant became the first to employ computers to determine the best tower sites and designs for transmission lines, an innovation that saved APS almost $1 million. At a cost of more than $43 million, its line to Phoenix became the longest at such voltage in the country and the only line of that voltage carrying steam-generated energy.

As Utah Construction's operation at Navajo continued to grow, so did the generating capacity of the Four Corners plant. In 1965 the mining lease expanded to include an additional 150 million tons of coal under 6,547 new acres, bringing the total leasehold to an area equivalent in size to that of Bryce Canyon National Park. Because some of this new territory contained rich archaeological sites, the expansion agreement included provisions for archaeologists to investigate newly opened sites before mining disturbed them. An extensive archaeological survey resulted in a number of significant discoveries, including one at Cross Canyon, where scientists excavated eight of sixteen pueblos, salvaging more than forty rooms, three pit houses, eight kivas, and two great kivas. This pueblo group offered archaeologists a rare opportunity to study three villages built at the same location, one on top of the other.

To link the strip-mining operation to the power-generating plant as conveniently as possible, Utah's management reached into the company's past and constructed a nine-mile railroad to haul coal. Three 2,500-horsepower diesel electric locomotives powered the trains. Another required change came with the expanding capacity of the power plant. Meanwhile, innovative cooperation developed among six utility companies (Southern California Edison, the Salt River Project, Arizona Public Service, Tucson Gas and Electric, El Paso Electric, and Public Service Company of New Mexico) to increase the generating abilities of the Four Corners facility. In June 1966 these members of the Western Energy Supply and Transmission Associates (WEST) spent $150 million to expand the plant. Four months later, Littlefield signed a coal sales agreement with WEST, quadrupling the tonnage of coal produced at the Navajo Mine.

Another dragline, this one larger than the Marion 7900 by ten cubic yards, went into operation, while the WEST companies set up two new 755-megawatt generators as they planned for the power needs of a nine-state region. Such dramatic project growth brought new benefits to the Navajo Nation by increasing royalties and providing an additional 19,156 kilowatts from each of the two new generators at the low rates established in the basic agreement of 1960. The increased energy amounted to seven times the anticipated needs of the tribe at that time, thus providing the Navajo Tribal Utility Authority with additional power to sell and to continue rural electrification on the reservation.

Coal attracted new attention in the United States in the late 1960s as oil and natural gas reserves dwindled to produce a growing reliance on imported crude oil. It eventually became apparent that Navajo coal could play a strategic role in producing low-cost energy beyond electric power generation. In his June 4, 1971, message to Congress, President Nixon called for "an expanded program to convert coal into clean gaseous fuel" to respond to the national energy shortage. Utah originated a coal

Navajo Tribal Chairman Raymond Nakai (third from left) joined Utah Construction & Mining President Edmund W. Littlefield (center) and other officials for dedication tours of the Four Corners Power Plant.

gasification project, predicting that its uncommitted coal reserves were sufficient to sustain the production of one billion cubic feet of gas per day for a quarter century.

As Utah publicized its intentions, Pacific Lighting and Texas Eastern both showed interest in the project. Then in late 1971, a joint venture of Utah International, Pacific Coal Gasification Company, and Transwestern Coal Gasification Company conducted a feasibility study for a coal gasification plant in northwestern New Mexico. Utah would supply coal and water to the plant to produce a substitute natural gas—the first of its kind to go into operation on a commercial scale. Producing 250 million cubic feet of substitute natural gas per day, it would exceed the daily energy output of Hoover Dam by five times. Markets on the Pacific Coast and in the Midwest would receive gas from the project as the people of New Mexico and the Navajo Nation benefitted from steady jobs, tax revenues, and continued lease and royalty payments. The plant would represent an investment of $380 million, $40 million of which covered environmental protection equipment, with the possibility of three more plants under consideration.

The gasification process that the joint venture planned to employ, developed in West Germany by the Lurgi Company, required half as much coal as other methods. It also had the advantage of lower pollution levels; emissions of sulfur dioxide (the major pollutant from coal burning) totaled only one-sixth as much as from coal combustion. In addition, gas produced in the project would be completely interchangeable with natural gas. Although times changed and the project never materialized, its planning and potential represented the forward-looking perspective of the combine. To be located thirty miles southwest of Farmington, New Mexico, adjacent to the coal reserves, the pilot plant would have gone into operation in 1975. Utah mines would have yielded 25,000 tons of coal per day to create the planned daily output of substitute natural gas and to generate the large quantity of steam necessary to operate a plant of its size. Coal reserves were sufficient to feed such a plant for a hundred years, and basic pipeline facilities for the gas already existed. Texas Eastern planned to construct the only new line the system would need to move the gas from the plant to those existing pipes, some fifty miles south of the plant site.

With that exciting and futuristic prospect on the drawing board, the Utah adventure in Navajo country shone high on the list of the company's postwar accomplishments. The development of the Navajo Mine project, however, was not without its challenges and controversies. Calling itself a "Native American OPEC," the Council of Energy Resource Tribes (CERT) inaugurated a campaign in 1979 for greater control of natural resources on Indian lands. This movement hit close to the Navajo project, inasmuch as the national head of CERT was also Nakai's successor as chairman of the Navajo Tribal Council, Peter MacDonald. When the controversial MacDonald was indicted on seven counts of fraud and income-tax evasion, the trial resulted in a hung jury with all charges dropped, but not before the affair gave MacDonald a national forum for his views. Labeling it a case of political persecution, MacDonald claimed that the real target was the Navajos. "I am the symbol," he told *Time* magazine in the August 20, 1979, issue. "Put me away, get me out of office, and it will be a while before any tribal chairman insists that the state treat Indians fairly."

CERT attracted national media attention when MacDonald asserted to *Time* that no Native American tribes with energy resources on reservation lands had been represented at the Camp David talks on energy in 1979. CERT, which controlled one-third of western America's strippable coal, demonstrated its serious intentions by hiring Ahmed Kooros as its economics and finance director. Kooros had been Iran's deputy minister for economics and oil. CERT's stated aim was to avoid the traditional practice of having Indian leases negotiated solely by the Bureau of Indian Affairs (BIA), claiming that such leases had traditionally paid low royalties and had given Native Americans little control over their own land. MacDonald pointed to the lease with Utah International, which had been contracted at a royalty of 15 cents per ton and had been increased only to 25 cents in the intervening twenty-two years. But a mineral officer for the BIA argued that the original lease price was not unfair at the time. The problem came because the agreement contained no escalator clause. MacDonald, who had renegotiated many such leases in court, began to threaten a similar course for Utah. "We are going to break it or shut things down," he warned in the *Time* article.

The flamboyant chairman did neither before leaving office shortly thereafter, but such contentions raised numerous questions about the genuine effects of the mine and the power plants upon the Navajos. After examining the history of the Utah Construction–Navajo relationship, few would argue that the arrangement had not benefitted the people of the reservation enormously, as lease and royalty payments from the mine and the power plants funded public works projects, including improved health and education programs. In addition to its $400 million investment, the company built an annual payroll of $2.8 million, 60 percent of which went to Navajos, a figure that would likely rise to 80 percent as more tribal members received training in the skills necessary for the highly mechanized process of stripping coal.

Utah also contributed to community well-being directly through significant donations. When Navajo Community College, for example, was established as the first public college on an Indian reservation, the company contributed more than $21,000. Mine employees donated livestock to Navajo Missions Incorporated and also gave money for an athletic field, bleachers, and athletic equipment at a local Navajo boarding school.

Additionally Utah offered Navajos a unique opportunity to learn mine engineering and related technologies by hiring them to fill gaps in the skilled work force when employees took vacation time. Such practical exposure to the mining industry encouraged many students to pursue professional training. In a related effort, the company donated money to the New Mexico Institute of Mining and Technology and cosponsored with that organization the first Opportunity Conference on Materials Engineering and Energy Resources. More than ninety people attended, at least half of them Native American high school students with high aptitudes in mathematics and an inclination to study one of the sciences. Other conference participants included interested Native American alumni, tribal leaders, high school teachers and counselors, and mineral industry representatives from firms on or near reservations in New Mexico. Following the conference, Utah representatives recruited at schools with significant Native American enrollments, demonstrating again the company's genuine commitment toward using Navajo talent whenever possible.

By the 1970s, whatever else mining companies did bought little public goodwill if their reclamation efforts did not meet increasingly stringent standards. Although Utah promised from the beginning to reconstruct the desert topography, this constituted no small commitment. Reclamation costs might run as high as $500 per acre versus a sale price of $100. Utah's record in this area reflected well on the overall quality of its entire commitment at Navajo-Four Corners. Before the company turned a shovel of earth on the reservation, it began planning to reconstruct the desert topography to resemble that of neighboring undisturbed areas. This meant replicating the barren beauty of the arid landscape, its dry washes and arroyos, occasional sandstone escarpments, and fragile topsoil, thin and capable of supporting only sparse vegetation—grass, tumbleweeds, and small shrubs.

At Navajo as elsewhere, strip-mining processes involved leaving a layer of overburden in a "spoil pile" alongside the cut. To reach the coal beneath, miners moved the overburden into the strip left from the previous cut. Each cut, however, became deeper as the coal seams dipped, creating a visual image of despoliation that was an easy target of environmentalists. As early as 1966, four years after mining operations began at Navajo, Utah began an expensive regrading and leveling program. Studies showed that an undulating topography would resist water and wind erosion more effectively than a flat surface, so graders plowed fly-ash waste into artificial ridges. In the meantime, researchers established test plots in which they planted sixty types of seeds for study, including many plants native to the area. Their work produced fast-germinating, short-lived plants for immediate erosion control and others that showed winter hardiness as well as tolerance to drought and salt. Only one non-native plant proved itself suitable for the project.

Utah took considerable pride in its reclamation efforts in the Four Corners region, having brought the Navajo Mine full circle. Indeed, the costly effort was emblematic of the whole enterprise. The company had removed a coal product many thought unusable or inaccessible, provided low-cost energy to the growing Southwest, offered employment to many, gave the Navajo people financial return for the use of their land, and then returned the land as nearly as possible to nature and to future generations. In addition, Utah leaders took pride in their sensitivity toward archaeological ruins, their long negotiations and friendly relations with tribal leaders, their donations to promote education and training, and their efforts to improve community resources.

In addition to going after coal in the energy resources business, Utah also toyed with petroleum exploration. In 1953 Utah invested $100,000 in a joint venture group, Petroleum Development, Ltd., to search for oil and to drill exploratory wells. Within two years, however, the company had decided to stay with mining basic minerals, such as phosphate, uranium, and coking coal, the removal of which better fit Utah's earthmoving skills equipment. Still, the company maintained a modest interest in petroleum, particularly in oil shale development.

As early as 1957, Utah entered into a contract with the Union Oil Company to mine all of the oil shale at Union's experimental site. At a 1962 meeting of the American Institute of Chemical

Engineers in Denver, Utah's James C. Allen presented a paper entitled "Latest Developments in Oil Shale Mining Equipment," which illustrated a long-standing company principle: techniques learned in one industry could often solve related problems found in another.

Then, the oil crisis of the 1970s refocused the company's attention on petroleum as the United States sought to develop domestic supplies. In November 1974, Utah announced the acquisition of the Ladd Petroleum Corporation, a Denver-based company, in existence since 1968, which produced 9.7 billion cubic feet of gas and 705,000 barrels of crude oil shortly before Utah's acquisition. Ladd owned producing oil and gas properties in fourteen states and two Canadian provinces. To facilitate the acquisition, the oil company's president, J. B. Ladd, joined the board as a director of Utah International. Shortly after the addition of Ladd Petroleum, Utah announced a merger with Clarcan Petroleum Corporation, which had explored, developed, and operated oil and gas properties in the United States and Canada.

In the final analysis, Utah executives went far beyond governmental requirements and the demands of being a good corporate citizen in all of its coal and oil enterprises, and particularly at Navajo, where profound benefits came to the native people because of the company's activity among them. Navajo coal and a smaller involvement in the oil business, however, represented only a part of Utah's legacy in the energy-producing industry. World events and advancing technology would bring the firm into the middle of a new energy extraction industry that had the potential to change virtually everything.

*

In the late 1930s, as the Earth teetered on the brink of global war, President Franklin D. Roosevelt took the advice of Albert Einstein and commissioned a group of scientists under J. Robert Oppenheimer to attempt to create a powerful new weapon through nuclear fission. The Danish physicist Neils Bohr had argued for the use of the unstable isotope uranium-235, because it could sustain a chain reaction. While plutonium-239 also proved successful in the creation of the Manhattan Project's atomic bombs, it was uranium ore that drove the gold rush of the modern age as the nuclear arms race accelerated in the late 1940s and early 1950s. Dreams of virtually unlimited electrical power fueled with "yellow cake" also made the heavy element extremely valuable. Anyone who could find and deliver this prize to weapons producers and the growing nuclear power industry could count on a fortune from Uncle Sam.

It all began for Utah when director Marriner Browning placed a momentous call to Christensen on July 11, 1955. Inasmuch as Christensen was out of the office, Littlefield took that call. Browning's nephew-in-law, Salt Lake City attorney Seaton Prince, was representing Lucky Mc Corporation, which had started exploratory drilling on supposedly uranium-rich land in Wyoming. Following a discussion with Prince, Littlefield immediately went to Wes Bourret, Utah's mineral exploration specialist, and said, "I know you have these leads running out of your ears; but before you dismiss this one lightly, it comes to us from one of our directors and I want you to take a good look at it." Neither man could know that this put the company on the trail of one of the richest uranium ore deposits in the country.

The story Bourret heard as he looked into Lucky Mc immediately explained the curious name of the deposit and the company trying to exploit it. On September 13, 1953, a weekend prospector and machine shop owner named Neil McNeice had taken his wife on an excursion into the Gas Hills area, some fifty miles from their home in Riverton, Wyoming. As they ate their lunch on a small shaley knob (now known as Picnic Hill), McNeice noticed an outcropping of "oddly-colored sandstone." When the couple approached the area with their Geiger counter, its needle went off the scale. Lucky McNeice had chanced upon the only commercial exposure of high-grade uranium ore in the area. Eventually, his find would lead to a yield of between eleven and sixteen million tons of the prized ore.

Naturally excited, McNeice and two partners sank their own money, much of it from a mortgage on McNeice's business, into mining and milling the ore, but they did not have enough capital to make much headway at the mine. Worried that large mining companies and other weekend prospectors might discover similar outcroppings at Gas Hills, McNeice turned to W. H. (Harry) Cranmer of New Park Mining Company, which conducted

In 1959, General Manager Allen D. Christensen (front row left) signed one of several contracts with the Atomic Energy Commission.

extensive exploration efforts, even recovering some ore near the surface. In the words of Wes Bourret, "they found the project over their heads," needing funds and expertise beyond New Park's capabilities. "Cranmer had already taken the Lucky Mc deal to everybody in the business," added Bourret, "including Homestake and Anaconda, and they had all turned him down."

When Bourret originally analyzed the deposit, he found "the mine was not adequately drilled, the drilling being too shallow and in the wrong places." Comfortable that Utah could correct these problems and be in full-scale operation by June 30, 1957, less than two years later, Bourret reported his findings to Christensen. Board approval followed in September 1955, for the company to get into the uranium business. Utah offered the Lucky Mc Corporation an option to acquire 60 percent of the company. Based on Bourret's initial findings, Utah executives authorized a budget of $200,000 for preliminary drilling while management attempted to negotiate a contract with the Atomic Energy Commission. "After ten to eleven months of drilling and a tough winter with tent camps," Bourret recalled, "we found an ore vein which took us off the Lucky Mc claim and onto a bonanza deposit, which was later to contribute 65 percent of Utah's total uranium ore output. It turned out we had one of the great uranium deposits." Even better, it was one of relatively few deposits that could be exploited with open pit mining methods.

The timing could not have been better. The U. S. government was negotiating cost-plus contracts in 1955 for producing uranium oxide, meaning that if Utah, or any other company, discovered accessible uranium ore in adequate quantities, the Atomic Energy Commission (AEC) would not only buy the product but contract to cover all production costs, including overhead expenses, thus guaranteeing a tempting profit. As an incentive to move briskly, the AEC had announced that it would not purchase uranium oxide after June 30, 1962. Additionally, a favorable depletion allowance of 23.5 percent permitted a tax reduction on income from natural resources. In this particular case, Utah could recover its total investment in less than five years.

Although Utah had ventured into open pit and strip mining during the war, the acquisition of Lucky Mc Uranium brought a new era. Under Bourret's direction, early in October 1955, the company moved three rotary drills to Wyoming, set up a geologic field camp, and established an assay lab in Denver. In addition, the firm employed the research foundation at the Colorado School of Mines to recommend sampling techniques for radiometric evaluation of the ores. By the end of 1955, exploration in the greater Gas Hills area slowly gained momentum as personnel discovered a deposit wider than anyone originally had supposed. Many eminent geologists from large mining companies had come to the area, taken a look, and then left, concluding the area contained only isolated low-grade pods of uranium-bearing material, insufficient for a commercial operation. Commercial geologists commonly regarded only the sandstone of the Colorado Plateau as sufficiently continuous for feasible ore pockets. Slightly more positive because they were less concerned about profitability, even AEC geologists did little to dispel the old impression. Exploration and development work through shallow drilling and trenching seemed to support a pessimistic assessment.

A major breakthrough occurred, however, in late December 1955, when Utah geologists decided to abandon dry drilling (then a district practice) and begin drilling below the water table to test the body of ore. Heretofore, prospecting confined itself essentially to the shallower areas of the central and eastern Gas Hills, where the yellow oxide uranium minerals lay at depths of eighty-five feet or less. The extensive brownish-black coffinite-uraninite-type ores remained undiscovered. In January and February 1956, Wyoming experienced one of the coldest winters in its history, and wet drilling became almost impossible. As a result, Utah personnel formulated a new technique in league with the drilling contractor Sprague and Henwood. Using diesel oil instead of water as a circulating fluid not only permitted the drilling to continue despite bitter temperatures, but it also kept the sand cores frozen, greatly improving recovery. Project supervisors then discovered that dry ice could produce a super-cooled drilling fluid, yielding the advantages of frozen cores regardless of atmospheric temperatures.

As engineers carefully and continuously logged the holes, the true regional geologic picture began to unfold: Gas Hills had multiple and complex ore horizons. The overall pattern resembled a series of meandering channels, stacked one on top of the other. Thus the north end of the now famous Project 4 channel appeared. As new subsurface deposits became manifest, this ore developed into a more or less continuously braided zone of mineralization more than three miles long and one thousand or more feet wide.

Late spring 1956 saw a lively boom underway in the Gas Hills area, as other mining companies took a greater interest. By late summer, approximately thirty drills operated, as word spread that tremendous tonnages of deep ore underlay the disappointing surface of the twenty-square-mile Gas Hills district. Utah drilled more than 47,000 miles, with results convincing Bourret that Lucky Mc likely could promise a minimum content of one million tons of high-grade uranium ore.

In light of Bourret's glowing assessment, in early fall 1956, the board gave its full support to the venture. It approved $300,000 to acquire 60 percent (3,638,748 shares) of Lucky Mc's common stock at an average price of 8.25 cents per share. On October 31, 1956, after the offer, the market price for the stock stood at $1.44

bid. At that point, Utah was ready to negotiate with the AEC for long-term purchase contracts and for the construction of a 750-ton mill. Discussions with the AEC yielded a contract to produce one thousand pounds of "yellow cake" per processing mill per year, later increased to two million pounds. Yellow cake, an oxide of uranium (U^3O^8) produced after lengthy refining, is a raw material for fueling nuclear reactors.

Littlefield estimated a price tag of $10 million to get the venture into full operation, and had great confidence in the project; but as chief financial officer, he needed assurance that the costly venture would not become an overwhelming burden. Consequently, he moved the Lucky Mc's financing off Utah's balance sheet, because "by this time we were already beginning to become fairly heavy borrowers; and since we were only going to own 60 percent of it, I was trying to obtain the money on a basis that would not require Utah's guarantee." This arrangement shielded Utah financially in case the project turned sour. To find a likely investor, Littlefield contacted Gene Witter, a cofounder in 1924 of the investment firm

As Utah Construction erected administration and communal buildings at the Lucky Mc operation near Riverton, Wyoming, an increasing number of residential trailers gathered nearby.

Dean Witter. He located Investors Diversified Services (IDS), headquartered in Minneapolis. Inasmuch as Utah had already proven the reserves of the Lucky Mc deposit, an IDS representative analyzed the company's feasibility study in San Francisco and indicated interest. Soon afterward, Littlefield and Witter flew to Minneapolis to discuss the terms of the loan: in exchange for 10 percent of the equity, IDS would lend $10 million to Lucky Mc Uranium Corporation, to be repaid over five years.

When Littlefield and Witter arrived at the corporate offices of IDS, they expected a brief meeting with the company's president, Joseph M. Fitzsimmons, after which they would sign the papers. To their surprise, the IDS leader instead began to question the feasibility of the transaction. Littlefield could tell Fitzsimmons was saying, "No." Thinking Fitzsimmons did not have all of the project information, Witter immediately tried to sell the venture to him. Witter was so stubborn and determined to triumph that Littlefield later commented, "Witter has the hide of a black rhinoceros." Fitzsimmons said flatly that IDS could make a great deal more money on other opportunities. Irritated, Littlefield reminded Fitzsimmons, "We were invited here to discuss the final details of the deal proposed by your representative in San Francisco, and as far as I'm concerned, the promise was made that IDS would consummate this loan." At that point, the president backed down and assured the Utah official that "they could work something out."

Annoyed at such a vacillating answer, Littlefield called off the transaction and walked out, dragging Witter with him. "Ed," Witter argued, "don't be discouraged. We've got them lined up. They'll take $8 million, and New York Life will take $2 million." He then reminded Littlefield that they had already "been around the country and there are not very many people interested. We've been turned down even by Chase Manhattan." Littlefield would not change his mind, so Witter offered to withdraw from further participation. Littlefield replied, "That's fine with me ... I'll be responsible." He flew back to San Francisco and phoned another friend, Ransom Cook, a senior vice president of American Trust Company, which had merged with Wells Fargo Bank. Littlefield candidly described the IDS fiasco, then said, "If I'm going to be screwed, I want to get screwed by my friends." Cook, with the same candor, replied that he was not exactly "a three-ball artist" (a pawn broker) but would do what he could. He added that his firm would not seek the 10 percent equity kicker IDS had required.

Littlefield proposed that the American Trust Company, Crocker Bank, and Bank of America lend $7.5 million. George Eccles could arrange the additional $2.5 million through his contacts in New York banks. "The final consummation of the loan included $1.7 million from two New York banks, one of which was Bankers Trust, and $2.2 million dollars each from three San Francisco banks," summarized Littlefield with satisfaction. The new arrangement consisted of "a five-year loan with a 20 percent compensating balance required."

Crocker Bank promptly agreed to participate, but Littlefield expected reluctance from Bank of America. He arrived for the evaluation meeting armed with a flip-chart presentation and an independent geologist's report. Only three or four minutes into the presentation, Lloyd Mazzera, the bank's chief lending officer, interrupted with,"Ed, I only have one question. Do you—Ed Littlefield—think this is a good deal for the Bank of America?" Without hesitation, Littlefield replied, "Yes, Lloyd, I do." Mazzera said, "Then we're in." As a sweet antidote to the stinging memory of IDS's reluctance, Mazzera's confidence bore fruit three years later when the mine was so profitable that the note was retired.

With financing secured, company officials moved the mine swiftly toward full operational status. After groundbreaking in March 1957, the processing mill went "on stream," not quite a year later, on February 28, 1958. The rapid construction and the outstanding efficiency of the operation attracted national attention, and *Mining World* magazine awarded its 1958 open-pit-mine prize to Lucky. Two years later, Utah acquired the remaining 40 percent of Lucky Mc Uranium Corporation stock.

Processing the ore entailed a complicated operation involving crushing and liquefying it, then filtering out impurities. The uranium, precipitated as yellow cake, was then filtered, dried, packaged, and shipped. In summer 1961, the Lucky Mc division achieved a breakthrough by installing an X-ray emission spectrograph in its metallurgical and chemical laboratory to detect

Refined uranium oxide was known as yellow cake.

uranium and other materials rapidly. The spectrograph, purchased from General Electric, was the first to be used in a uranium plant laboratory in the United States. Use of the XRD-5 instrument virtually eliminated wet chemical methods for uranium analysis, making costly reagents unnecessary. The device's great speed reduced laboratory direct-labor costs by 40 percent.

Other successes came in response to vexing problems no one could have anticipated. In 1963, for example, flooding suspended mining at Western Nuclear's neighboring Frazier-Lamac Mine, the largest single open-pit mine in Wyoming (roughly twenty-five hundred by eleven hundred feet). The pit filled with water to a depth of about seventy feet, creating a lake holding approximately 350 million gallons. When Utah started to strip the overburden from

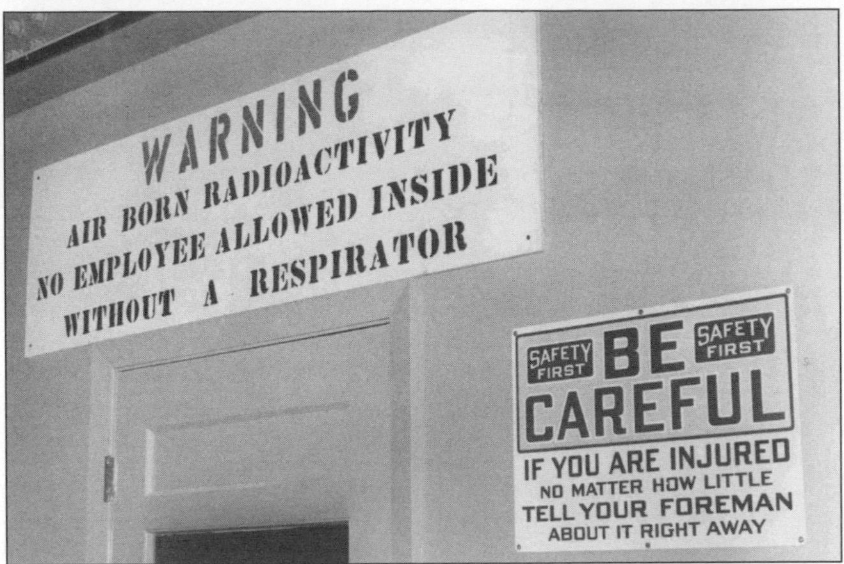

As company officials became aware of health hazards connected to radioactivity and mining, they increased safety precautions at the Lucky Mc operation.

Lucky Mc's adjoining Pit 5A, the danger of flooding prompted an attempt to pump down the adjoining lake. Thus the "Lucky Mc Navy" came into existence, headed by its flagship the *LMS* (Lucky Mc Ship) *Bowen,* actually a float built to support pumps from Utah's nearby Shirley Basin, where water was pumped from the basin's underground mining area. As it flowed into the existing creek beds, benefitting local livestock and game, discharge from these pumps successfully kept the water table below the working level of the mine.

In addition to such innovations, the Lucky Mc operation gained a reputation as a cost-cutting model, particularly through its use of specially designed hydraulic "wrist-action" buckets on the backhoe mining units, which lessened spillage during the swing-and-dump portion of the loading cycle. Developing this new method required close cooperation among Utah's production, maintenance, and engineering departments and produced profitable results. Another cost-effective program involved monitoring the milling process with closed-circuit television. Also, in summer 1964, a new solvent extraction section went into operation, reducing the cost of reagents used in processing the ore to obtain the uranium oxide. All told, Lucky Mc reached a unique milestone, in July 1964, when the ten millionth pound of yellow cake issued from the mill. At that point, Lucky Mc's production surpassed a total value of $80 million. Four years later, the flexibility of the mine's stripping operations increased dramatically when two unique push-pull scrapers went into operation. In the first-ever mining application of such machines, the mine's stripping capabilities increased by about 200,000 yards per month. When the Lucky Mc Mine celebrated its twentieth anniversary in 1973, it also marked its fifteenth year of milling operations.

Since stripping operations began modestly at Lucky Mc in the summer of 1954, more than 4.5 million tons of uranium ore had yielded in excess of twenty-six million pounds of uranium oxide. Until 1967 the Atomic Energy Commission was the sole buyer. In the mid-1960s, however, a commercial market began to develop and, by the early 1970s, all sales were to private customers. In 1976 Utah negotiated the sale of 9.25 million pounds of yellow cake for use after enrichment in the country's nuclear power plants. The federally owned Tennessee Valley Authority contracted for another 1.04 million pounds of yellow cake, then distributed the power it generated to consumers through 150 local electric power companies.

After Lucky Mc led Utah into the uranium business, the company acquired control of uranium-bearing properties in the nearby Shirley Basin area in 1957. The magnitude of the rich strike there attracted the attention of *Fortune* magazine, which highlighted the uranium boom in its March 1959 issue. The article included a glowing account of Utah Construction & Mining's early years and its successful mining ventures.

Under the direction of Superintendent John E. Reed, the first ore from Shirley Basin reached the surface in early 1960. The prevailing market and stripping costs indicated an underground operation, which continued until a sales cutback and unfavorable operating costs dictated a shift in strategy. The Wind River sediments, in which the ore lay, consisted of a poorly consolidated water-bearing sand, so loose that it took very little blasting to break it into moveable material. Unfortunately the costs associated with supporting the underground openings and keeping them drained more than offset the easy-blasting advantages.

Considering this development, Utah had been experimenting since 1961 with a new process called solution mining. Drillers would dig wells into the ore-bearing sands of the Wind River formation; then, using a Utah-patented technique, they leached the ore in place and brought the uranium-bearing solution to the surface. By means of a small mill located in the head frame and surface buildings of the old underground mine, they removed uranium from the solution in the form of uranium oxide slurry, which then went to Lucky Mc for further processing. This technique, which took several years to develop, owed its success to the research of the company's metallurgists and engineers. As a limited means of producing uranium oxide, it successfully sustained acceptable production at Shirley Basin beginning in 1963. After 1969, however, the open-pit method replaced it as increasing market demand justified large open pits there.

Consequently, in early 1968, an engineering group formed at Lucky Mc and Shirley Basin to block out the ore reserves and plan a coordinated open-pit operation in Wyoming. The Palo Alto engineering office began mill design studies later the same year. Actual stripping for the first pit at Shirley Basin began in late January 1969. The total volume of the field (known as Area 2) amounted to approximately 155 million yards in a fifty-foot-thick ore zone some thirty stories below the surface. The stripping and mining of this area eventually intersected the old underground workings and areas subjected to solution mining. But even after moving into the open-pit category, the Shirley Basin Mine remained one of a kind. By the beginning of the 1970s, construction crews had erected a 1,200-ton-per-day mill and related facilities at Shirley Basin, with an annual capacity of producing 2.2 million pounds of U^3O^8 in concentrate.

Utah's entry into this new area of energy development played a tremendous economic role, especially in central Wyoming. That area produced an estimated $500 million of minerals, equaling the value of Alaska's placer-gold output for the past one hundred years, and exceeding even the historic Mother Lode rush in California and the Cripple Creek strike in Colorado. Added to that figure were the substantial economic benefits represented by the creation of jobs and payroll distribution, purchases of supplies and services, and the payment of local, state, and federal taxes. So the company's sortie into the energy extraction business paid off, not just in profits but in economic benefits to widening communities around its facilities.

Section III

Utah International, Incorporated

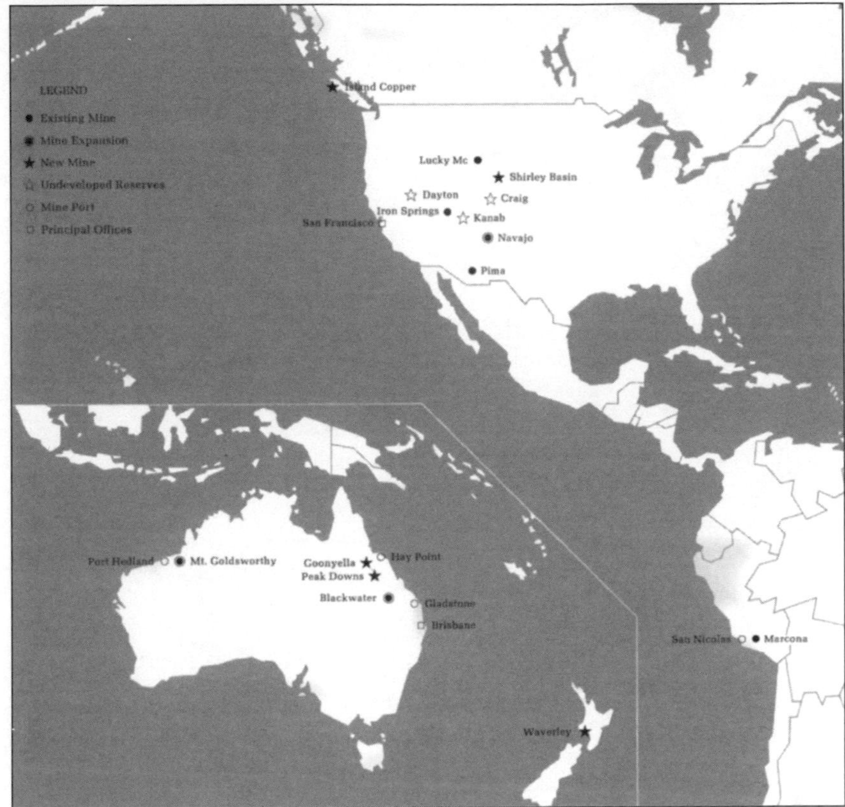

The *1970 Annual Report* used this map to highlight the company's multinational mining explorations and operations.

Chapter 11

Utah Down Under

For decades prior to Captain James Cook's voyage up the fertile east coast of Australia in 1770, European explorers told stories of a vast island between the Indian and South Pacific Oceans, filled with exotic plants and strange animals, fit only for wandering aborigines, and devoid of worth to the Western world. To the English, who established the first permanent white settlement at Port Jackson (later Sydney), the place seemed useful primarily as a dumping ground for criminals, bankrupts, and other dregs of the British Isles. By the middle of the nineteenth century, however, the massive agricultural and mineral potential of "the land down under" created the foundation for what became the united Commonwealth of Australia in 1901. Subsequently joining the modern family of nations with a strong and diversified economy, Australia emerged from World War II as one of the most highly industrialized exporting nations. Yet much of its huge store of mineral wealth was still undeveloped.

With the continent's strategic proximity to the burgeoning markets in eastern Asia, particularly Japan, the great potential of Australian mining attracted the attention of the bustling Utah Construction & Mining Company. By the late 1950s, when Utah moved forcefully into Australian mining, the firm already had done extensive construction work and strip mining on the huge continent-nation. The company's first major project there began in 1951 when the State of Victoria commissioned the Big Eildon Dam project, designed to increase by more than nine times the irrigation capacity of a former dam at the site. Most of the water from the resulting 2.75-million-acre-foot reservoir would flow into the arid Goulborn Valley some hundred miles away.

Reminiscent of the Hoover Dam project in scope and difficulty, Big Eildon required an excavation of more than six million cubic yards of rock, much of it from a 300-foot-deep cut for the spillway. When completed in late 1955, the dam crest—more than twenty-five stories high—stretched more than half a mile across the gorge, making Big Eildon the largest earth-filled dam in the southern hemisphere; the outlet tower, spillway, and powerhouse swallowed 350,000 yards of concrete, enough to build a fair-sized concrete dam. The original $24 million contract (Utah held 60 percent and J. H. Pomeroy and Company 40 percent) expanded to $38 million, including agreements to erect a power station, install power lines, and construct a major portion of the building site township. By the time Utah finished this massive project, the firm had a considerable backlog of other heavy construction work in Australia, including contracts for tunnels, an industrial plant, and more dams. As a result, the parent company incorporated under Nevada law as Utah Australia, Ltd. (UAL).

Utah's next major Australian job became the Cairn Curran Reservoir, also in Victoria. In less than a year, the firm compacted a 130-foot earth-filled dam to back up 240,000 acre-feet of water, installed a reinforced-concrete outlet tower, built a concrete spillway structure and road bridge, erected three 60-ton radial gates, and raised a 220-foot steel access bridge to the tower. In the meantime, UAL finished ahead of schedule a mile-long tunnel for the Hydro-Electric Commission of Tasmania, removing 80,000 cubic yards of rock and earth and placing enough concrete and steel reinforcing to pave New York City's Broadway from the Bronx to Broad Street at the tip of Manhattan.

At the same time, a vast water project commenced to the north in New South Wales that would dramatically increase the company's Australian opportunities. Between 1949–51, the government began to realize a dream of harnessing the water of the Snowy Mountains with an inland diversion project to bring irrigation water to hundreds of square miles of arid ground.

Located midway between Sydney and Melbourne, the Snowy Mountains Hydroelectric Scheme envisioned a billion-dollar complex of dams, tunnels, and powerhouses to channel Snowy River waters across the Great Dividing Range into the drier Murray-Murrumbidgee drainage. A central three-million-acre-foot reservoir at Lake Eucumbene would provide storage and regulation while the Snowy-Tumut Tunnel took water from the Eucumbene to the upper reaches of the Murrumbidgee tributary of the Tumut River, and the Snowy-Murray section delivered water to the upper Murray. Surveying the proposed project, the American Society of Engineers marveled at its scope and named it "one of the five future wonders of the world."

Utah's involvement in the Snowy Mountains project started near the decade's end in May 1958 when it sponsored a joint venture of UAL and Brown and Root Sudamerica, Ltd., to take a $16 million contract for the construction of Tantangara Dam and the Murrumbidgee-Eucumbene Tunnel. Working with speed and against adverse climatic conditions, the combine finished the fifteen-story mass gravity concrete dam six months ahead of schedule and the ten-mile tunnel five months early, in February 1961. Tunnel crews, driving in a horseshoe-shaped pattern from only two headings, established a world record of 590 feet in a six-day week. The Murrumbidgee-Eucumbene Tunnel equaled in length a highway from downtown San Francisco to San Mateo, California.

Along with the Snowy Mountain project, in 1959 UAL completed in less than a month a fourteen-acre sports ground for employees of General Motors–Holden in Victoria, preparing sites for a cricket pitch, a running track, a football field, five tennis and three basketball courts, and a bowling green. On a more technical project, UAL also finished that year a facility for the first commercial use in Australia of radioactive isotopes for sterilizing industrial raw materials. Also located in Victoria, the $225,000 project called for precision engineering in constructing a large building, an isotope block house with six-foot-thick walls and roof, a stainless steel, concrete-encased underground tank to house the isotope source tubes, and an intricate system of instrumentation and automatic controls.

In 1961 Utah Construction and Engineering Proprietary, Ltd., obtained a huge $47 million contract for a joint venture with Brown and Root to build another massive portion of the Snowy Mountains project. This venture involved building more than eighteen miles of horseshoe-section tunnel (twenty feet high and twenty-one feet wide), five shafts totaling nineteen hundred feet in length, one mile of ninety-six-inch aqueduct with two small dams, and the Island Bend Dam, a curved concrete gravity structure that would divert the Snowy River by tunnel into Lake Eucumbene. The men worked within sight of 7,314-foot Mount Kosciusko, Australia's highest peak, and unusually severe weather plagued the project much of the year. Despite this, hole-through on the Eucumbene-Snowy Tunnel was achieved in June 1964, after driving a record breaking 2,600 feet per month; and the hole-through on the Snowy-Geehi Tunnel to the Murray came by the year's end. The Australian Federation of Civil Engineering Contractors recognized these accomplishments with its 1964 Australian Construction Achievement Award.

In addition, the combine successfully bid on constructing the Jindabyne Dam, the Blowering Dam, and the $3.4 million

Utah joined two local construction firms in building the Manapouri Power Project for the New Zealand Ministry of Works. Here, Vice President Weston Bourret celebrates seven years' labor.

Blowering power station (with Morrison Knudsen). The Jindabyne and Blowering Dams both reached completion ahead of schedule, the former some four months early, in September 1967. In the late 1960s, UAL also completed the Mulwala Power Station in New South Wales and the Carrum Outfall on the Patterson River, with similar speed and profitability.

The most challenging and certainly the largest tunneling operation Utah ever undertook in the region occurred in New Zealand as part of the Manapouri Power Project. In July 1963 the company's wholly owned subsidiary Utah Construction and Engineering Pty., and two local firms, W. Williamson Construction Company, Ltd., and Burnetts Motors, Ltd., successfully bid for the initial phase of the project, winning a $26 million contract from the Ministry of Works. Calling for the excavation and removal of more than 1.3 million cubic yards of earth, the job included six miles of a thirty-foot concrete-lined tunnel, an outlet channel thirty-six hundred feet long, and fourteen miles of gravel-surfaced road across mountainous country to connect the tunnel portal to the powerhouse site. The tunnel provided the tailrace (flume) for the powerhouse built underground on the edge of Lake Manapouri, located in the southwest portion of South Island. The tailrace tunnel discharged into the Tasmania Sea via Deep Cove and Doubtful Sound, picturesque fjords on the island's west coast.

The Manapouri project took seven years to complete, which some characterized as seven years of bad luck. Plagued with unanticipated hazards and obstacles, Manapouri ended up costing $54 million more than the original bid. The combine had to import skilled labor, install steel supports in unstable ground, and pump and shore cracks in the quartzite tunnel. Nevertheless, Utah and its partners persevered, finishing in 1970. Hailed as the world's southernmost power plant, Manapouri could generate more than 700,000 kilowatts, boosting the country's total capacity by 25 percent.

To house comfortably the crews working on the Manapouri project, the company leased the 9,876-ton passenger liner *Wagenella* and anchored it near the site. This made sense since rainfall at Deep Cove averaged 250 inches a year, so the usual workers' camp would be costly and unstable if built on the waterlogged and hilly shore. Though housed on a ship, the crews contributed to the community, donating to the blind and buying playground equipment for orphans in nearby Invercargill. They also built a memorial at "Nick's Landing" to honor war hero Alan Nicholas, a Kiwi bush pilot who brought them mail and news until a plane crash in March 1965 took his life.

As Utah Construction moved steadily toward mining elsewhere in the world, it undertook mining projects in Australia, beginning in1959. Vice President Weston Bourret, then managing the exploration and development department, recruited American geologist Richard D. Ellett, who had recognized exciting opportunities in the largely unexplored reaches of Western Australia while working for the National Lead Company. Ellett also sampled the political climate and found it favorable for a possible multinational investment in iron ore extraction in the region. His report persuaded Utah's board of directors to authorize a subsidiary organization, the Utah Development Company (UDC), with $40,000, to initiate an exploratory operation. Although the board doubled the appropriation the following year, it insisted that any Australian mining operation must "raise itself by its bootstraps," an instruction consistent with the company's "project by project" philosophy. In other words, Ellett must find projects requiring low initial costs but with reserves large enough to accommodate expanded production as cash flows increased.

The company's interest in Australia's minerals related to its philosophy that feasible market demand must precede mining operations. Japan's ever-growing demand for iron ore and coking coal made Australia a natural choice under that principal. Among the first to recognize this geographic juxtaposition of the Japanese market and Australian sources, the firm's executives, geologists, and engineers sought the ideal combination: high-grade ores or coal, "exploitability" by open-cut mining, plus existing or potential seaports nearby. With these conditions in mind, Bourret made three trips to Japan, working through the coal procurement division of the Mitsubishi Shoji Kaisha trading company, to determine the types and quantity of coal the steel industry required.

Arriving in Western Australia in the fall of 1960, Ellet quickly examined "every known significant iron-ore deposit in the country" and decided to run a geologic-economic feasibility study on Mount Goldsworthy, a site on Australia's northwestern coast that had seen the fabulous gold-mining region of Pilbara develop. The young geologist was convinced that Pilbara, and especially Mount Goldsworthy, held large deposits, the area consisting of "Pre-Cambrian rocks ... in which banded iron formations (jaspilites) are particularly thick and extensive." Such deposits resulted from "prolonged downward percolation of surface water through permeable parts of the banded iron formation," thus leaching out the silica and depositing iron oxide in its place to form concentrations of iron ore. Ellett identified three main areas he believed would yield at least ten years of production if developed sequentially. He was wrong, but in a positive direction—his estimate was far too conservative.

Utah invited in its Marcona partner Cyprus Mines, as well as Gold Fields Mining and Industrial, Ltd., of London and New York. Known as the Mount Goldsworthy Mining Associates (MGMA), the consortium began preliminary negotiations with the Western Australian government, which, in December 1960, lifted its limited embargo on iron ore development within the state. Following Ellett's study, the partners inaugurated an extensive prospecting program in the area some six months later, hoping to locate more potential sites. Then, in September 1961, MGMA made a successful offer to the State of Western Australia to mine the Mount Goldsworthy deposits. The group announced early in 1962 its intention of beginning a $675,000, eighteen-month program to assess the potential of the ore field and the product's marketability as well as surveying for rail, road, harbor, and living facilities. Predicting an annual production of one (later two) million tons, MGMA anticipated at that point a seed investment of some $22 million, with production commencing within four years.

Next, Ellett and Bourret turned their attention to coal, in response to Allen D. Christensen's ongoing interest in exploitable coalfields on the Pacific Rim. After considering briefly an operation in the established New South Wales coalfields, they settled on a relatively undeveloped area in the northwestern state of Queensland. "One must admire their vision and optimism," wrote one Australian observer. "Few Australians in the early 1960s saw a future for their country in the large-scale export of coal, and little attention was focused on the coal-producing potential of Queensland." To help in these explorations, Ellett assembled a small team composed mostly of Australians, including a geologist named Don King, who entered the Bowen Basin of Queensland, some 550 air miles northwest of Brisbane, in the winter of 1960–61. Setting up shop some thirty-five miles south of known coal reserves at Kianga, King rapidly mapped the district and chose drilling sites, but test holes revealed "thick, rich" seams of coal suitable for steaming but with weak coking characteristics. Inasmuch as there was little market at the time for steaming coal, King continued to search, convinced that the "salt-and-pepper" sandstone, petrified logs, and fossilized leaves he observed in the area often accompanied large deposits of commercial-grade coal.

By October 1961, King had worked his way to Blackwater, an area of Queensland that had been mined between 1911–41. For some reason, however, all of that activity had been north of the existing railway even though government reports identified the area south as the more promising. Consequently he applied for prospecting rights and headed south. Using aerial photographs, he began a dogged reconnaissance about forty miles south of Blackwater township and surveyed northward. He sifted through the coal dumps of old mines, studied seismic shot-hole reports, catalogued virtually every natural feature, and interviewed "old-timers" who knew regional mining well, including one who had ridden a horse over every swale in the area and "knew the site of every bore hole." Eventually, King located three areas worthy of detailed testing.

He first selected an area around the Taurus Cattle Station, drilling the first holes on April 24, 1962. After three tries, the drill produced a large black cloud of soot, a sure indicator of coal that had perished under oxidation. The fourth hole broke into a seam of commercial-grade coal some twenty-five feet thick. Within two days, Ellett arrived from Melbourne and confirmed that the seam was thick enough to fulfill all his prior expectations, for field tests showed that the coal was ideal for coking. Utah had known for more than a year that the Japanese government was deciding to phase out the production of coking coal from some its own deep mines on Kyushu and would be looking for a replacement source. Obtaining financing for the Bowen Basin project depended on a sustained expansion of the steel industry in Japan and the cooperation of the Japanese government.

Consequently, within a day of the Taurus discovery, company President Edmund W. Littlefield flew to Japan for a series of meetings with business and government officials in Tokyo, accompanied by George S. Ishiyama, a business consultant who had assisted Bourret during his earlier visits. Littlefield came away impressed with the country's booming steel industry and with the

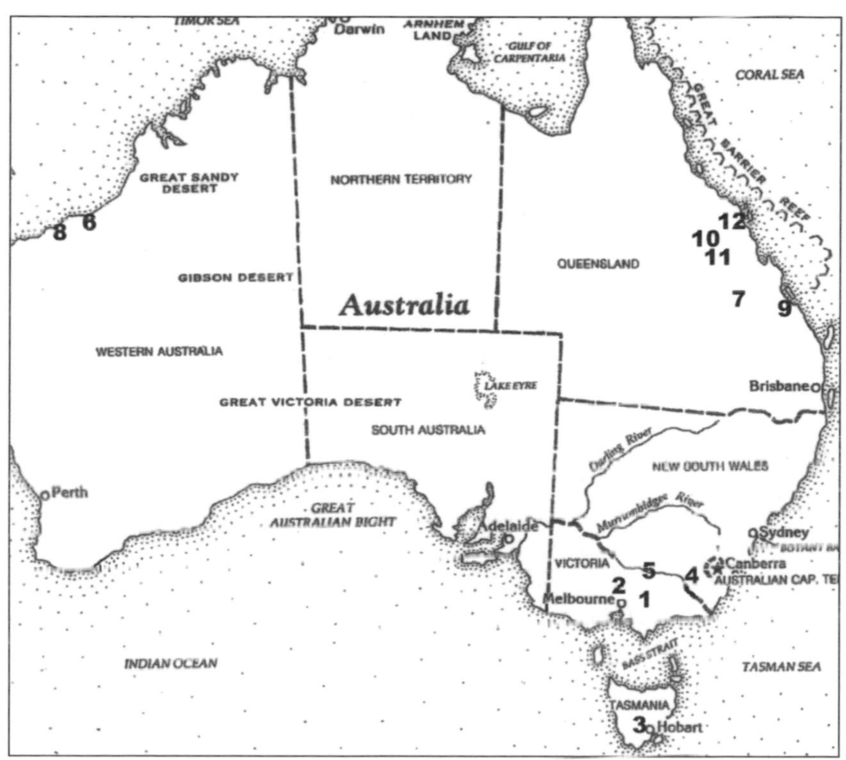

Utah Construction projects in Australia.
1. Big Eildon Dam, Victoria; 2. Cairn Curran Dam, Victoria; 3. Wayatinah Tunnel, Tasmania; 4. Tantangara Dam and Tunnel, Snowy Mtn. River Project, New South Wales; 5. Mulwala Power Station, Victoria; 6. Mt. Goldsworthy Mine, Western Australia; 7. Blackwater Mine, Queensland; 8. Port Hedland, Western Australia; 9. Gladstone Mine, Queensland; 10. Goonyella and Peak Downs Mines, Queensland; 11. Saraji and Norwich Park Mines, Queensland; 12. Hay Point Mine, Queensland.

encouraging reception he received. He had no doubts that the Japanese market was ready for Utah's Queensland coal.

The discovery at Taurus spurred further testing in adjacent areas. In October the team reported: "Upper Permian coal measures along the western limb of the Bowen syncline ... extend continuously as far north as Goonyella," which lay 135 air miles to the north of Blackwater township. Realizing the exploration in Queensland represented "the most significant discovery of metallurgical coal certainly in this century and is one of the really major discoveries of mineral deposits that has ever been made," Littlefield ordered the studies accelerated. Based on those results, company executives decided in 1964 to develop the Blackwater Mine fully, and they leased some 33,457 acres from the Queensland government. The contract called for mining rights lasting twenty-one years, with the option to renew. Six years later, a second lease increased the acreage under contract to 51,770 acres.

Ellett and his men worked arduously long hours, which they bore with good humor. In his first report to Utah's board, for instance, Ellett inserted a picture of three young people running into the Australian surf, calling them examples of "the country's natural resources." The field men also delighted during those early days in playing practical jokes on visiting officials from company headquarters. They housed one VIP in the Blackwater Pub in a one-window room over an old gas generator. "It was not that we did not like him," mused Ellett, "but ... [we] thought it would be helpful if those with 'cushy' jobs in San Francisco experienced some of the discomforts of the field men!"

Meanwhile, across the continent at Mount Goldsworthy, eight hundred air miles northeast of Perth, surface geological mapping and sampling, along with some geophysical test work, had begun in May 1962. Positioning their bits so that they would strike the main ore bodies at right angles, drillers sank twelve shafts totaling some four thousand feet combined. They also bored several other test holes to allow bulk sampling deep underground, in addition to more than two hundred percussion holes that reached a maximum depth of 220 feet from which geologists examined chips and dust. Four adits (an almost horizontal passageway into a mine) required twenty-three hundred feet of tunneling. To figure the extent of the deposit in probable tonnage available, investigators divided the ore bodies into a series of vertical sections at 100-foot intervals and by horizontal planes at 40-foot intervals, each plane showing a possible mining level. They then estimated possible tonnages by calculating the weight of the samples relative to the determined extent of the field. This process included establishing grades for each ore block with a determination of values for "phosphorus, the silica/alumina ratio, sulphur, copper, other metals and loss on ignition," a formula the geologists, at least, understood well enough to predict that sufficient ore of shipping quality existed to justify immediate development.

Estimated tonnages at Mount Goldsworthy alone ran in the neighborhood of forty to fifty million at about 64 percent iron, a very rich fraction. The team also investigated other sites, one of which eventually proved similar in size and quality to the original discovery. As part of the feasibility study, detailed metallurgical surveys provided information on the fundamental ore characteristics of "crushability, abradability (to rub off), and reducibility."

Meanwhile, MGMA was investigating overland transport and shipping. The coastline of northwest Australia had no natural deep harbors, and a suitable port would have to provide protection and deep draft for large bulk carriers. After considering three possible sites, planners selected Port Hedland, some seventy miles west of Mount Goldsworthy, a choice that also required constructing a railway to link Mount Goldsworthy and the ship-loading facilities on nearby Finucane Island.

Invariably, large multinational ventures encounter political complications. Prior to MGMA's preliminary investigations, Australia had enforced stringent curbs on exports to conserve known reserves for its domestic iron and steel industry. Recent explorations, however, had increased known reserves by more than twenty-fold. After gentle but persistent urgings from MGMA and others, in July 1963 the government announced relaxed restrictions, allowing the export of the entire proven reserves at Mount Goldsworthy—sixty-four million tons of hematite ore. This was very good news for the consortium, and MGMA made the final decision to push ahead. After investing $2 million of the estimated $42 million necessary to bring the mine to full production, the group announced on December 17 that it had obtained a license to export up to four million tons of iron ore per annum under the liberalized export policy.

Utah successfully concluded its five-year investigation in early 1964. The iron ore at Mount Goldsworthy in the west and the coal at Queensland to the east gave the company firm footings for two legs of its new mining complex. Following further discussions with Japan, it achieved the crucial third leg of marketing. Late in the year, MGMA announced an initial agreement with Japanese steel mills: it would supply 16.5 million tons of iron ore over a seven-year period commencing in 1966, promising an annual revenue of $23 million. The group now calculated that it would take $50 million to build the facilities necessary to produce 2.5 million tons annually. MGMA also negotiated a shipping contract with its San Juan Carriers affiliate to transport the raw ore to Japan.

A few months later, Utah Development also reached an agreement with Mitsubishi Shoji Kaisha, Ltd., covering sales of UDC's Queensland coking coal that would provide gross revenue of approximately $130 million over a ten-year period and increase Utah's total backlog of mineral sales to half a billion dollars. With deliveries scheduled to begin in 1968 under the contract, total sales would involve 13.5 million tons of coking coal at an opening rate of 500,000 tons annually, with a rapid increase to three times that amount. UDC estimated that $15–18 million would be required for the large strip-mining project at Blackwater. The coal mining venture in Queensland would resemble Utah's Navajo Mine with a large dragline operation, although the Australian coal would undergo both complex processing and lengthy transshipment—two hundred miles by rail to the port at Gladstone, then a 3,850-mile journey to Japan—while Navajo's coal moved only a few miles from mine to power plant.

Such huge start-up costs—$50 million at Goldsworthy and $15–18 million at Blackwater—naturally concerned Utah executives, but they realized the staggering profit potential and hedged their bets with escalation clauses to guard against inflation. "The boldness of Utah's strategy," wrote one Australian, "is reflected ... in the extent of the imaginative and detailed planning that preceded development." Computerized data from more than

15,000 test holes combined with a veritable library of geological information to give Utah engineers mining intelligence not previously available. Additional economic feasibility studies and satisfactory political negotiations ensured that the development would go forward. Utah then created an agile administration based on its commitment to people as its most valuable resource; and, as a Blackwater mine manager later put it, "They also purchased, organized and administered well."

By the end of 1965, both mining projects had built up a full head of steam. To get a 3,000-ton sample of Blackwater coal to Japan, Utah Construction and Engineering removed some 50,000 cubic yards of overburden and coal from the sample pit and mobilized virtually every available truck in Queensland to haul the raw coal fifteen miles to the railway siding for the trip to Gladstone, where a pilot plant washed the trial shipments at the rate of twenty tons per hour. As the first sample left Gladstone on October 23, bound for the Australian steel company, Broken Hill Proprietary Company, Ltd., in Newcastle, New South Wales, one reporter gleefully recorded the coincidence: "As the side-boarded cattle truck drove away from Auckland Point, the Utah team realized it was an historic moment; here was a truck of Utah's Blackwater coal headed for Newcastle"—literally "carrying coals to Newcastle."

An equally impressive surge of activity went on in Western Australia, particularly at Port Hedland where MGMA established a job site office in February, after ordering equipment and arranging prefabricated housing for a 128-man camp. In addition, preparations for the dredging operation began with the procurement of equipment, mostly in Perth, in anticipation of the arrival of Utah's dredge *Alameda,* then undergoing an overhaul at Yokohama, and the 50-ton derrick barge *San Bruno,* which MGMA had acquired in Portland, Oregon. The *Alameda* arrived and by year's end had completed dredging the mooring basin and portions of the inner channel. It was then moved outside the harbor to work on the outer approach channel. This work paralleled inland operations at the mine site and along the rail route, where crews worked overtime preparing for full production in 1966.

Not surprisingly, all this activity raised considerable interest at company headquarters. Speaking at the 1966 Stanford Business

School Conference, Alexander M. (Bud) Wilson, then senior vice president and manager of the firm's mining division, discussed the expanding opportunities in Australia along with the economic and political realities. Indicating that both agreeable and troubling conditions would greet foreign investors, particularly those interested in mineral exploitation, Wilson accurately predicted many of the problems Utah and others would face in the ensuing years. They included labor shortages, high income taxes, government involvement in labor relations, the cost of exploration and overland transportation facilities, and the expensive outlay for ports and ocean shipping. Still, he sounded optimistic, given the rich geologic environment.

Littlefield further demonstrated the company's heightened interest in the area with a trip to Australia and New Zealand during late March 1966. He inspected the company's many construction sites, surveyed the work at Port Hedland, visited the nearby iron mine site at Mount Goldsworthy, then flew east to Queensland for a look at the Blackwater coal project. In just fifteen days, he met with virtually every Utah staff member in Australia, but his trip's main focus was on talks with government officials, including Prime Minister Harold E. Holt, as well as the premiers of the states of Victoria, Queensland, and Western Australia. Littlefield returned to San Francisco convinced Australian officials understood Utah's aims and activities. He also announced that Utah Development and Mitsubishi Shoji Kaisha had agreed on the coal contract. With this news, the full-scale start-up of the Blackwater project began.

Meanwhile, work at Mount Goldsworthy proceeded at a feverish pace, despite the arrival on March 31 of Cyclone Shirley, whose effects could have been disastrous but did little harm, thanks to damage-control efforts and some good luck. The storm came up with short notice early in the morning. The main concern was for the *Alameda*'s safety. Moving the pipelines that would carry the mud from the bay to the land occupied most of the day, with two-inch tow ropes breaking more than a dozen times as tugs fought against high waves and strong currents. The next day passed without incident as the dredge rode out the swells from the security of two storm anchors. On April 2 the swing wires securing the *Alameda* to the anchor began to break under the strain, forcing crews to spend a rough afternoon weighing anchors and towing the vessel into the harbor. Fortunately only the ship's tree and considerable lengths of swing, quarter, and stern wires suffered heavy damage. There was so much water in the vessel, however, that the crew suspected a hole in the hull, but finding none after they pumped it out, they returned to work.

Hoping to have everything ready for a first shipment of iron ore ahead of schedule, crews raced the clock to complete port conveniences, the railroad, and the mining facilities. On May 31, 1966, the first shipment of iron ore left Port Hedland for Japan aboard the 31,000-ton *Harvey S. Mudd;* on June 28, representatives from the government, the owners, and the purchasers gathered on Finucane Island to dedicate the Port Hedland facilities. Wilson and financial vice president O. L. Dykstra headed the Utah delegation, but Ellett and other key company men also shared the scene with such dignitaries as the premier of Western Australia. Shortly afterwards, the directors of MGMA's Australian organization, Goldsworthy Mining Pty., Ltd., sent an exuberant letter to San Francisco acknowledging Utah's crucial role in the venture. "Without knowing the ruggedness of the North West," they wrote, leaders of the Utah Construction & Mining "gave without hesitation their services in progressing the large initial capital expenditure programme within a limited period," without which, they continued, "the first stage of a challenging adventure" could not have been possible.

During the next few months, production at Mount Goldsworthy steadily accelerated and by the middle of October 1966, workers completed essentially all construction and shipped 441,000 tons of ore in sixteen shipments to Japan. Ore trains between Mount Goldsworthy and Port Hedland, loaded at the rate of two thousand tons per hour, could haul between two and four thousand tons, depending on the locomotive. The seventy-mile route traversed essentially flat terrain, descending less than two hundred feet from the mine plant to the loading docks, with only two significant obstacles along the way, the DeGrey River and West Creek between the mainland and Finucane Island. To span the DeGrey, bridge builders erected a span the length of three football fields that would carry not only rail but motor traffic. They included a fourteen-foot clearance for occasional floods but also made allowances for the bridge to remain operable even during a rare deluge that might see more than half the region's annual rainfall come in one twenty-four-hour period. Worse than this happened, as a matter of fact, on January 26, 1967, when a low-pressure system dumped fifteen inches of rain in a single day on northwestern Australia, which usually gets only eleven inches in a whole year. Due to the area's aridity, the railroad also required (in addition to flatcars and boxcars) three 15,000-gallon tankers to carry water to Mount Goldsworthy and Finucane Island, inasmuch as the total freshwater supply for the mine and the port came from the DeGrey River bore-hole complex.

Upon arrival at a discharge point, the trains dumped their ore into 65-by-12-foot hoppers below the tracks for deposit either into a stockpile or directly onto a vessel. Stockpiles usually grew to the height of a five-story building with some 200,000 tons of ore, loadable at a rate of sixteen hundred tons an hour. Supported at the docks on trestles, the cyclone-resistant ship loader used a four-foot belt to move the product from the stockpile conveyers onto the vessels. One operator controlled not only the movement of the loader itself but also the flow of ore from the stockpiles.

More important than all of this activity were human considerations. The company gave priority not only to effective and safe work stations but also to comfortable living accommodations. MGMA constructed its workshops and executive/administrative centers at Mount Goldsworthy and located its main supply point on Finucane Island with a 280,000-gallon fuel storage tank to supply offshore office and residential needs. Power stations at Goldsworthy and Finucane provided electricity for both the project and townships. Comfortable housing went up, along with a social club, swimming pool, shop, medical center, and a small school for the primary grades. Older children attended the state high school at Port Hedland, where there was also a hospital and a Royal Flying Doctor service.

Because of harbor development delays, most of the 1966 shipping had to go out on relatively light-draft vessels; the average cargo taken out of Port Hedland that year weighed only 30,000 tons, causing a significant increase in MGMA's projected shipping costs. Late in the year, however, a decline in world market charter rates for carriers allowed the company to hire vessels on more favorable terms than spot market conditions would have permitted. While not completely offsetting the cost of using lighter-weight carriers, by year's end the consortium had marketed nearly one million tons of ore from the Mount Goldsworthy mine, almost fulfilling its first fiscal year contract before the end of the calendar year. Before-tax profits amounted to $187,350; after the commonwealth took its share, the consortium netted $97,422. Following a careful analysis of the 1966 financial results, MGMA decided to go ahead with plans to contract for an additional sale of 3.1 million tons over a period of six years to another group of Japanese steel mills. The Mount Goldsworthy operation responded immediately, and the first shipment of ore left Port Hedland simultaneous with the signing of the $22 million agreement in mid-February 1967. In August, another contract worth about $1 million further profited Goldsworthy's mining venture. This new commitment of 517,000 tons to Japan by 1969 raised total sales to more than three million tons per year.

On the other side of the continent, Utah's Blackwater coal project had also come to nearly full production. Littlefield and company director E. C. Arbuckle visited the mine in April 1967, while attending the Pacific Industrial Conference organized by the Stanford Research Institute. Pleased with what they saw, Littlefield announced an additional agreement with Mitsubishi Shoji Kaisha, Ltd., for another eight million tons of coking coal, a deal that brought potential revenues from Blackwater coal sales to approximately $210 million. At that point, Utah's total investment rapidly approached its projected ceiling of $30 million.

In July, the huge dragline went into operation at Blackwater after two weeks of training for the crews from an expert on loan from Utah's Navajo Mine in New Mexico. By August 1, the outfit's thirty-cubic-yard bucket worked almost nonstop on twenty shifts per week. Shortly thereafter at Gladstone, just south of Rockhampton, the *Toei Maru* took on board the first shipment of 23,181 long tons of Blackwater coal bound for Japan. When it arrived at Yawata Works on the island of Kyushu on January 26, 1968, Utah's representative George S. Ishiyama called it "only the beginning of Utah's development of the tremendous coking coal resources in the Bowen Basin." Ishiyama alluded to Utah and Mitsubishi's joint-venture exploration program in Queensland north of the original Blackwater site, predicting that the two companies would "be in a position to make a proposal to the Japanese steel industry for the development of additional high-grade coking coals" by the end of the year. This pronouncement proved accurate. A year later almost to the day, agreements were executed covering long-term contracts for the sale of up to eighty-five million tons of coking coal to a group of Japanese steel, gas, and chemical companies.

The Blackwater Mine was officially opened on May 11, 1968, by Marriner Eccles and Queensland Premier J. C. A. Pizzey. Utah Vice President Alexander M. (Bud) Wilson is at the left rear.

On May 11, 1968, Queensland Premier J. C. A. Pizzey, Marriner Eccles, and Bud Wilson officially opened the Blackwater Mine. In his speech, Eccles briefly recounted Utah Construction's history and observed, "Capital, natural resources, and markets are mutually interdependent, each upon the other. Great progress has been made [here] ... because of a climate of understanding and mutual respect in a favorable economic and political environment." Eccles then touched on what had become an increasingly sensitive topic in international business: "I realize that there is a growing feeling in Australia concerning the investment of foreign capital." Pointing to America's own early history of dependence upon foreign investment, he urged Australians to think positively and to envision a better world for everyone in a "rapidly growing interdependent world." He then concluded with a call for the cooperative development of the world's resources: "We cannot expect to live peaceably on islands of abundance with seas of poverty all around us."

As if to reinforce the Utah chairman's words, the Queensland venture rapidly expanded in the early weeks of 1969, with new contracts promising revenues of $1 billion, 85 percent of which would go to Utah. The contracts also boosted the company's overall backlog of mineral sales for future deliveries to approximately $2 billion. Preparations quickly began to open a second mine, the Goonyella, in Queensland, at the northern end of the venture's 1,333-square-mile exploration area.

Contract terms also called for the eventual opening of a third mine at nearby Peak Downs, with combined sales projected to reach a maximum of seven million tons yearly. UDC committed to build a new town to serve the mines, construct a port at Hay Point, and finance a railroad, complete with locomotives and railcars. Subsidiaries could also provide ocean transportation, should Utah decide to build large coal carriers in the 75,000- to 100,000-ton class. With these impressive developments, the Queensland venture became a colossal part of the company's mushrooming worldwide expansion.

All the activity in the Queensland mining area, however, was not strictly business. Not surprisingly, the Bowen Basin soon became a favorite haunt for Australian paleontologists, as Utah draglines excavated the strata. Responding to reports of fossils in the rocks taken from the Blackwater Mine, scientists discovered fish fossils estimated to be more than 230 million years old, similar to a freshwater type of the same age in South Africa, thus substantiating hypotheses of continental drift.

The boom town of Blackwater became something of a Utah showcase as the company cooperated with government agencies to ensure orderly and beneficial growth. Swelling almost overnight from its original ten houses, one-room school, and hotel, Blackwater soon boasted asphalt streets, modern homes, an ultra-modern school, a swimming pool, and "an overall civic pride which comes near to arrogance," according to one visitor. To the north, an entirely new community went up to serve the housing and trade needs of the new Goonyella and Peak Downs mines. UDC carefully planned this new town, Moranbah, from the ground up. Construction began in 1970, with 435 homes projected by April 1973. Based on a town square reminiscent of classic New England plats, Moranbah contained a civic center, shopping center, hotel/motel, sports oval, and recreation facilities, including an eighteen-hole golf course. Moranbah was, in the judges' terms, "a very easy win" for the "Queensland Tidy Town" award in 1973. They were particularly impressed with the preservation of native trees. By the end of 1974, Moranbah was a bustling little city of 3,100 people.

The company remained sensitive to Australian civic and national pride, including ever-increasing concerns that too much of the commonwealth's natural resources had fallen into the hands of foreign investors. "Utah's greatest bugbear was its public image," wrote Alan Trengrove, an Australian mining historian, "especially when the period of moderate profits ended." The company's triumphs had impressed its hosts, conceded Trengrove. "Its timing was immaculate. But it was too successful to be popular." While meticulously complying with commonwealth and state rules, Utah could not escape criticism that "it was an American multinational company making excessive gains by ripping out an irreplaceable Australian resource which it was selling at relatively cheap rates overseas."

Ironically, criticism heightened through the sale of stock to Australians only, in Utah Mining Australia, Ltd. (UMAL), formed

By 1970, ocean carriers moved coking coal from the Blackwater Mine in Queensland, Australia. That year the mine doubled its shipments and sharply increased its profits.

in early 1970 to acquire 10 percent of UDC stock. As shareholders, the country's financial community thus became privy to Utah's highly profitable Australian operations. UMAL held a tenth of Utah's one-third interest in the Mount Goldsworthy project, as well as a tenth of the firm's whole ownership of Blackwater, and its 85 percent share in Goonyella and Peak Downs, the total representing an investment of more than $200 million. While both U. S. and Australian restrictions on foreign investment necessitated this holding company, Utah Construction & Mining agreed to conduct all its Australian operations through UDC and to continue to provide technical and management services under contract.

In response to rising anti-Utah murmuring, when Littlefield spoke at the dedication of the Goonyella Mine and the port at Hay Point in late 1971, he reminded the Australians that their coal was "not the only coal in the world" and that it was "still on trial, for those who buy it have billions of dollars invested in steel plants dependent upon a continuing and certain flow of raw materials." He concluded his remarks suggesting that good sense prevail so that

Utah and Mitsubishi could maintain their "competitiveness with the rest of the world and ... the continued confidence of prospective buyers in reliability of supply." At the same event, Wilson predicted that the Central Queensland Coal Associates soon would produce as much as sixteen million tons annually, "if all goes well."

In mid-1972, Utah announced the opening of a fourth Queensland mine at Saraji some fifteen miles south of Peak Downs. When it became operational late in 1974, Saraji increased the Bowen Basin's output to an annual rate of about fourteen million tons with option-related tonnages and spot sales increasing the total volume. This announcement followed another sales agreement with Japanese and European steel companies for deliveries of Queensland coal to range from thirty-four to fifty-two million tons. The resulting revenues topped $1 billion. In addition, UDC's wholly owned operation at Blackwater increased production to such an extent that a new agreement had to be negotiated with the Queensland Railway Department so that UDC could almost double its maximum annual tonnage being hauled to Gladstone.

Despite these bright statistics, dark clouds began to cast ominous shadows on Utah's fortunes in Australia. First came a dash of bad news from the Japanese markets. In 1970 the Marcona Corporation offered MGMA a spot price of $8.45 per ton for 500,000 tons of ore at 61 percent iron. The price was so much higher than anything then under contract that the steel industry in Japan worried that such a deal between the two corporate cousins would trigger a chain reaction of spiraling higher prices. Since the Japanese had already determined to cut steel production by 10 percent, news of the Marcona offer sent a shock wave through the iron ore market. The Marcona deal and its aftershocks were just the beginning of problems for Utah in Australia during the 1970s. Most, however, related to the Australian public's inability to handle the overwhelming success of foreign mining companies. A new Labour Party government under Gough Whitlam, which took office on December 2, 1972, immediately tightened considerably the previously generous mining policies, including taxation, of the former Liberal government, which had prompted Utah, Gold Fields, and Cyprus Mines to go into Western Australia in the first place.

The new government seemed determined to redress what it saw as irresponsible laxity in government oversight of precious natural resources. In a confidential report to the federal committee in charge of "ownership, control and development of the Australian mineral resources," a government spokesman hammered the Liberals for a policy designed "to maximize short-term company profits at the expense of any national ideals or goals." He then stated the new government's horror at the discovery that "foreign ownership and control has [*sic*] reached the alarming figure of 62 percent for minerals.... We are not going to allow these figures to rise and will work to see them decline over all," the report vowed. "It is a wonder there is anything left of the quarry at all." True to its word, the Labour government imposed an immediate ceiling of 62 percent on the foreign ownership of mineral rights and stopped all "farm-in" agreements, whereby small companies would invite larger companies to work their leases. The government argued that because much of the exploration for new mineral reserves had proceeded without an "equity participation in the mineral wealth recovered," the discoveries came at the expense of the Australian people, who provided support through "Commonwealth subsidies and taxation concessions." The world energy crisis, of course, had aggravated the whole problem. Australia openly resented attempts by the United Nations Committee on Economic Cooperation and Development to pressure smaller nations holding surplus reserves "to make them available at prices to be dictated by the major powers."

Harsh rhetoric from their new leaders echoed the distress of many Australians over the lack of policy restricting foreign capital and/or operations in Australia. While Utah and its partners had taken advantage of this situation, they could argue honestly that they did so openly, lawfully, and without malice. As late as the fall of 1970, the Queensland mines minister had praised UDC for having "clearly demonstrated a genuine interest in development so planned as to provide the best possible benefits for Queensland and its people." Local citizens also seemed generally pleased. Operations in the Bowen Basin had brought beneficial changes to the desolate barrens of northeastern Australia; Moranbah and Blackwater appeared to be contented communities. Recalling the

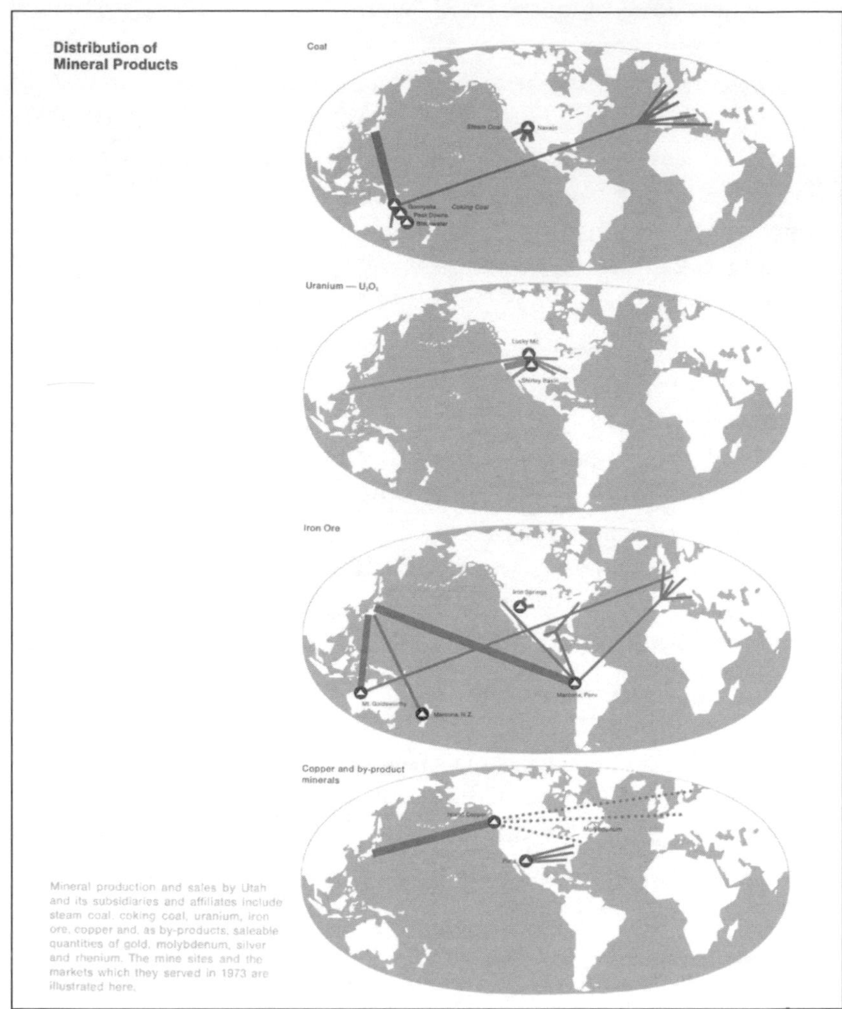

The *1973 Annual Report* used this chart to demonstrate shipping routes and mining markets.

rugged days of the country's early history, one newspaper called the rise of Moranbah "pioneering in the space age." Another praised UDC for teaching "an object lesson in large-scale planning and construction, the likes of which had never been seen before in this district." No one complained about hundreds of new jobs, a 125-mile railroad connecting Goonyella with a new deep-water port at Hay Point, or recurring signs of continuing prosperity through long-term contracts and expansions. In fact, negotiations with

Japanese steel companies yielded contracts in mid-1971 that pushed Queensland coal deliveries to nearly four million tons annually by 1973, at a price of $12.50 a ton beginning January 1, 1972, and with incremental rises each year.

With public opinion apparently split on the question of foreign investment in the country's mineral wealth, pressure mounted against the Labour government's stiffer policies when the cash flowing into Australian pockets slowed. At a bitter meeting between representatives of the mining firms and cabinet officers, tempers flared when a government official called the companies "hillbillies and mugs," making the government seem overly aggressive and unreasonable. To counter the impression that it had gone too far with ill-conceived and short-sighted policies, the minister of minerals and energy asserted that his government did not seek to reject foreign risk capital nor to "deny foreign companies (including those already in Australia and those yet to come) the opportunity to spend their money and get a reasonable return." He made it plain, however, that the Labourites would not "spend taxpayers' money in searching for oil, gas, and hard minerals." He also promised that the government would do all in its power both to protect Australia's national interests and to encourage "genuine Australian-owned companies" to stay in the oil and minerals business. Claiming harassment from both the press and the mining industry, he finished with a restatement of Labour's belief that its policies would not scare away foreign investors because Australia held all the important cards, namely the natural resources themselves.

Despite the government's claim that its tougher policies would not discourage foreign companies, Utah found itself in very difficult straits. First, it had to have an export license for each shipment; but before granting the license, the federal government must be satisfied on the terms of any sale to any customer. This naturally increased prices for the coking coal. Furthermore, the government dramatically increased the tax levy on coal exports to offset any gain to Utah from higher prices. "It also scared the hell out of the buyers," Littlefield said, "because they could not rely on a contract negotiated with one of the private parties." To defend themselves, buyers diversified their sources of supply to protect themselves from the whims of the Australian government. This provided an opportunity that was seized eagerly by competing coal and iron ore suppliers in the United States, Brazil, Canada, and South Africa. With Japan no longer locked into Australia because of lower prices, Utah lost part of its market share. Littlefield later observed that Australia thus became something of a no-win investment during the 1970s:

> It is true that we attempted to be in Australia as a low profile company. It was not only consistent with our tradition and our culture, but also we felt because we were a foreign company in Australia that we were not eager to be highly seen. That turned out to be impossible once we became one of the top corporations insofar as corporate earnings were concerned. The problem was compounded in part, in my view, by a sense of nationalism that cuts through Australia's financial grain. We have enjoyed consistently good relationships with the state governments in Queensland. That doesn't mean we've received everything we've asked for or that we always will, but basically it's been one where they had respect for us insofar as our integrity was concerned, our ability to perform, and our capability to deliver on our promises. We have had good relationships with the federal government with the exception of the time when the [Gough] Whitlam Labour government was in office.... I don't know that we have done badly in Australia outside of being foreign-owned and prosperous.

It did not take long before the Labour government's policies began to destabilize the iron ore industry. In a September 15, 1973, article in *Forbes* entitled "Too Much Too Soon," Littlefield openly suggested that by making "nationalistic noises about foreign domination of the country's natural resources," the government endangered the very objectives it hoped to protect. Bluntly questioning the wisdom of the Labour positions, Littlefield pointed to the continuing healthy growth of the Mount Goldsworthy operation and the economic benefits that had come to the Pilbara region. He also stated clearly the consortium's intentions to press ahead with further development and expansion, a promise the group made good in 1974 by opening new developments in the Opthalmia Range. This significant venture represented the first mine cut in the Marra Mamba iron ore formation, the richest and purest deposit then known in Western Australia. To support its activities in Opthalmia, MGMA constructed new facilities, including a company township at Shay Gap and a rail link to Port Hedland, some one hundred miles northwest of Shay.

Shay Gap, in design and function, contained every possible convenience despite its location in one of the most inhospitable places on the continent. Situated some forty miles from the coast with hot temperatures, dusty winds, and cyclones, Shay Gap required yeoman efforts to make it a pleasant place for miners and their families to live. The innovative designs and ingenious technologies included a centralized chilling unit to deliver cooled water underground to each building, a vacuum-method sewage system, an integrated system of medium-density housing linked by walkways, and construction techniques that ensured buildings could withstand heavy winds. Shay Gap won an award from the Western Australia government for the 1973–74 outstanding engineering project in the state, and it also won the 1974 Prince Phillip Design Award.

Another community, Dysart, rose from the bush to serve the needs of Central Queensland coal miners and their families working at the Saraji Mine. Because of the possibility of another cut at Norwich Park, Dysart was located between the two sites, approximately a hundred miles from the coast and about fifty miles south of Moranbah. Building a town from scratch in the middle of the Bowen Basin presented considerable challenges. Utah built transportation and communication facilities where virtually none existed before and piped culinary water from Moranbah. Completed well ahead of schedule, Dysart became a modern community by late 1975, with more than sixteen hundred residents spread over some two thousand well-groomed acres. Containing five different home styles made of natural timber, Dysart boasted a shopping center, an Olympic-size pool, a 400-meter track, and courts for tennis, volleyball, and squash. As in Moranbah, a sense of community rapidly emerged. To complete a municipal golf course, for example, residents organized weekend working bees. A certain excitement permeated the whole Dysart experience, much to the satisfaction of Utah, its associates, and the local government.

The national government, on the other hand, continued to grumble, but Utah and its partners pressed ahead, confident enough to contribute 11 percent interest to a new group looking into developing the "McCamey's Monster" deposit. But shortly thereafter, news came that Japanese steel companies sought an interest in the Opthalmia discovery, forcing MGMA into the awkward position of having to ignore its own customers to salve the feelings of the commonwealth government, which urged greater domestic investment. Unfortunately, Australian investors found it very difficult to raise enough capital to bring them into the venture in any meaningful way. Besides all of this, due to their worries over steeply rising production costs, which had more than doubled for both iron ore and coking coal, the Japanese refused to commit themselves to additional contracts with Goldsworthy Associates because of tenuous world market conditions and steeply rising production costs, which had more than doubled for both iron ore and coking coal. An article published in *Metal Bulletin* in October 1975 stated that the Japanese were increasingly wary of political conditions in Australia, finding it very "difficult to determine their likely iron ore requirements while they are uncertain about their future Australian coal supplies." Only four years after Littlefield's cautious remarks in 1971, mining Queensland coal became problematic indeed.

As if storms in terms of market and political forces were not enough, actual weather conditions also bedeviled the company's Australian adventure. During the early months of 1974, heavy rainfalls lashed the interior of Queensland, causing the Brisbane River to rise to a perilous twenty-one feet, which flooded much of the city. Although most of Utah's mining and transportation activities soon returned to normal, the flooding caused considerable losses and delays. On December 20, a freak storm something like a tornado struck the Peak Downs Mine, causing almost half a million dollars in damage, snapping trees in half, ripping roofs from buildings, and totally destroying the radial stacker. A few days later, Cyclone Tracey hit Darwin in perhaps the worst natural disaster in Australia's history. Thousands of people found themselves homeless on Christmas Day; UDC donated $100,000 to the Darwin Disaster Fund. Bowen Basin's coal production nevertheless increased that year, partly due to a new mine at Saraji beginning production and shipping its first railings from Hay Point ahead of schedule.

Weather and market conditions notwithstanding, the company's biggest problems remained political. When the Liberal-National coalition returned to power in December 1975, it vowed to reactivate the stagnant mining industry. But six months later, mining remained sluggish due to high costs. Inflation stood at 15–17 percent per year, and economists estimated it would cost roughly 30 percent more to open a business enterprise in Australia than it would in the United States. After several months, the new coalition had not eliminated many of the "taxation hangovers" from Labour government policy. Additionally, a bill in Parliament giving Aboriginal tribes the right to claim traditional or sacred lands left mining companies understandably jumpy.

The Hay Point port facility was designed to load simultaneously two ships of the 100,000 deadweight ton class. In June 1976, Hay Point set a record for the largest single coking coal shipment in history, with a delivery of 135,007 tons.

Despite the return to power of the Liberals, criticism of Utah International continued unabated, due to its multinational, big-business image. This was particularly disquieting to company officials, because its huge investment in Australian mining projects concentrated its risks. The situation worsened when Utah's positive relations with organized labor deteriorated when the company refused to hire Australian crews for its coal tankers because union prices were too high. (Wages among Australian labor unions had nearly doubled between 1970–75.) Labour leaders reacted by branding the corporation a "multinational rip-off," "arrogant," and "American." *Wall Street Journal* reporter Barry Newman wrote that the feeling among Australian labor unions could be summarized in an epigram: "The coal went to Japan; the profits went to America."

To improve its corporate image, the company created the Utah Foundation, which donated nearly $3 million to Australian charities and produced television commercials featuring Rod Taylor, an Australian turned Hollywood actor. Both the press and the public nevertheless turned against Utah when it announced a $174 million profit on $685 million in sales in 1977. As one Utah executive lamented, "The only thing worse than failure in Australia is success."

At that point, the company had no choice but to follow the approved model set out by Australia's federal government, allowing Australian interests to buy up significant blocks of its mining concerns. In July 1976, Utah reduced its holdings of Queensland coal from 89 percent ownership to 76 percent. Australian Mutual Provident Society, the nation's largest mutual life insurance company, assumed the balance with Mitsubishi Development Pty. In 1980, UDC moved its corporate headquarters to Sydney. Three years later, Broken Hill Proprietary of Melbourne purchased Utah's assets in Australia for $2.4 billion, and the company's nearly three decades in "the land down under" came to an end.

As an epilogue, Littlefield summed up Utah's Australian involvement in a retirement interview. From the first job Utah Construction & Mining undertook—the Big Eildon Dam—to its final involvement as part of the largest mining consortium in the country, the firm behaved ethically, he said. Although the corporation received some very bad press for being low profile, for hiring an actor to help its image, and for being prosperous, it nevertheless kept its standards high. "Utah had absolutely nothing that it had to hide," said Littlefield, "because one of the things we have done is to behave as a highly ethical institution, and we have avoided anything that would smack of improper business practices and unethical behavior. That's cost us something." Whatever the cost, the meeting of Utah International and Australia left both indisputably richer.

When George S. Eccles returned from Europe in the fall of 1950, he was greeted by his brother, Marriner S. Eccles, chairman of the Federal Reserve Board.

Chapter 12

The Multinational

When Britain suddenly left Ghana in West Africa in 1957, it triggered a massive scramble of colonial powers to get out of the empire business. The spirit of the Atlantic Charter and a rising tide of nationalism across the world had made the old imperialism passé and reactionary. Earlier grants of independence to India and Pakistan had presaged a new age of "nation building," until by the end of the twentieth century some two hundred countries, most of them former European colonies, would belong to the United Nations. Not only were these new countries hopefully and often naively trying to build stable governments, but they also yearned for the physical infrastructure that would allow them to join the modern family of prosperous nations. Consequently, opportunities for multinational companies such as Utah to move into the overseas arena multiplied dramatically as the decade of the sixties got underway.

Utah Construction entered this new era as no stranger to overseas enterprise. A last push in its climb toward the summit of leading multinational companies would take it to new levels of international expertise, with projects in sixteen countries on six continents. While devoting most of its energy elsewhere, Utah engaged in several major construction projects even as mining profits poured into the parent company. Company leaders saw many reasons for continuing to pursue Utah's historic role as a heavy construction outfit. For one thing, mining profits depended on too many variables. Lucky Mc's success, for example, relied on the Atomic Energy Commission's shopping list. Also, Utah's offshore involvement faced a rise in nationalism and the threat of expropriation, rumblings of which were echoing from Peru and even Australia. Additionally, general instability overseas unsettled company executives. Already Utah executives worried that their recent contract for a 40 percent interest in building the Troneras Dam in Colombia was a mistake. Beyond these anxieties were such uncertainties as the Alameda project and the overall investment in dredging. On the optimistic side of the ledger, Utah's opportunities were expanding around the Navajo Coal Mine, and the company had begun consulting for both Korean and United States government agencies to rehabilitate Korean mines and railroads, and explore new opportunities. Overall, however, as the decade of the fifties ended, business activity seemed in decline.

The Utah Construction & Mining Company nevertheless celebrated its growth and prosperity by completing its move to the Cahill Building at 550 California Street in San Francisco on November 11, 1960. The dredging headquarters remained at the Belair yard in San Francisco, and both the Design and Engineering Office and the Metallurgical Research Lab continued operations in Palo Alto, adjoining the Stanford University campus. Allen Christensen's name went up as president on the new corporate directory, but in 1961, he left the company to pursue personal business interests. In a cordial resolution, the board acknowledged Christensen's resignation and thanked him for "thirty years of service as employee, director, and officer of the company."

With Christensen's departure the working dynamics between Marriner S. Eccles, chairman of the board, and Edmund W. Littlefield, now president and general manager, became paramount. Inevitably Littlefield and Eccles locked horns on certain issues. In one particular instance, director Marriner A. Browning criticized Littlefield for "being overly generous in matters of compensation to members of the staff." The drift of the message was that Browning saw Littlefield as "more interested in rewarding the staff than necessarily [in] protecting the interests of the shareholders," although he did not personally convey this conviction to Littlefield. In transmitting the criticism to Littlefield,

Eccles may have shared Browning's view. In any case, Littlefield quickly realized that the real "bone of contention was our profit-sharing plan for retirement purposes."

The men discussed the matter literally for months without finding agreement. Finally Eccles took Littlefield aside and said, "Look, Ed, let's face it. You and I just can't agree on this." During their conversation about the subject, Eccles told Littlefield that he should present both Marriner's view and his own view to the board, and leave the outcome to the board. Littlefield agreed he could not "ask for a fairer shake than that." As it turned out, the majority of the board favored Littlefield's position. Eccles did not want the board to be split on important decisions, so he said, "I think our action should be unanimous, and I think we should be in support of Ed's view." The motion was passed unanimously in the affirmative, with Eccles supporting a position he had long opposed. "Now I submit," Littlefield related, "that's the mark of a big man!"

One amusing account relating to the Eccles tenure as board chairman involved Littlefield's efforts, during his stint as financial vice president, to obtain the prime rate for the company's working capital loans because of its credit worthiness, including the maintenance of modest compensating balances in its bank accounts. To achieve this goal, he believed it important for senior management to establish its own banking relationships and not rely solely on the traditional help of George Eccles. "When we had to borrow money, George took it over, and the First Security would keep what they could in regard to their legal limit, and then he would lay it off with different banks," Littlefield said. "I took some pains to get in control," by exploring prime rate possibilities with other banks without letting George Eccles know who the other banks were. Successful in his search, Littlefield notified Marriner Eccles of his actions, and Marriner endorsed them.

When Littlefield brought the topic before the board, "George [Eccles] went right through the roof and said, 'No construction company in history has ever had the prime rate.'" Marriner responded with equal heat, as Littlefield withdrew, thinking it best to let the two Eccles men fight it out. The conflict "got hotter and hotter" until Marriner slammed his fist on the table and said, "Damn it, George, if the First Security won't give us the prime rate, you know damned well the Bank of America will, and we'll take the business to them." Quite a discussion between the brothers ensued, prompting director Lawrence Dee to say, "This I'm thoroughly enjoying." According to Littlefield, "this was typical Marriner." Littlefield credited Marriner's knowledge, abilities, and extensive contacts in consistently aiding the company's progress, but it ran both ways. While effective and synergistic cooperation between board chairmen and top managers was not unusual in successful corporations in twentieth-century America, the Eccles-Littlefield relationship was arguably exceptional. The two men understood each other very well, and each recognized and admired the genius and skills of the other. There also existed an extraordinary trust between them, providing a seamlessly unified will at the top of management, strengthened by different perspectives.

As management was realigned, the commitment to persevere in heavy construction continued, partly due to beckoning building opportunities in California. In 1961, Utah linked up with sponsor Haas and Haynie Corporation to tackle a major joint-venture construction project for the City and County of San Francisco. This $3.4 million Civic Center Garage unfortunately became a nightmare of subcontractors' claims that dissipated all profits. The annual profit outlook, however, brightened with the completion of a meat processing plant in South San Francisco for Armour and Company, a two-year project that brought in more than $2.5 million. Late that year, Utah bid successfully for a contract from Alameda County to build a parking facility and heliport in Oakland, a profitable job that wrapped up in 1963. Also underway in Alameda County was the $3.5 million Barrows Hall, a nine-story, reinforced-concrete building that opened in March 1964 at the University of California in Berkeley. Utah held a 30 percent interest in a contract with Johnson and Mapes Construction Company to build the Philco Corporation plant near Palo Alto, completed in 1962. The year after, Utah completed a silica sand plant in Ione for International Pipe and Ceramic at a cost of $1.5 million. At mid-decade, a Utah crew built a small plant in California for the Hercules Powder Company to produce ammonium nitrate for use as commercial fertilizer or, when mixed with diesel oil, as an explosive that could be used instead of dynamite.

General Manager Edmund Littlefield confers with a general at Schilling Air Force Base near Topeka, Kansas, where the company built Atlas F missile enclosures and supporting equipment.

Just when it seemed that Utah's heavy construction workload in California might taper off, the firm joined a massive project to build a pair of huge earth-filled dams in Los Baños for the Bureau of Reclamation. Utah took a 25 percent interest in this $86 million joint venture with Morrison Knudsen (M-K) and Brown and Root. Work on this third-largest earthen dam complex in the world commenced in early 1963 and concluded in September 1967. The package included the San Luis Dam, the Forebay Dam, and related structures. A great army of men and heavy equipment slowly stacked the embankment of the San Luis Dam to a height of more than thirty stories, approximately three and one-half miles wide at the crest. The Forebay Dam stretched some two and one-half miles at the crest and rose to sixty-five feet. These structures swallowed more than eighty million cubic yards of material. Besides the two dams, the project included four penstocks and pump generating stations. The San Luis project represented a major addition to California's Central Valley Project, storing winter surplus water from the Sacramento-San Joaquin River delta, partly to irrigate the west side of the San Joaquin Valley and partly for urbanizing Southern California.

The firm's construction projects spread beyond California. As the Cold War deepened, Utah joined M-K in extensive missile site contracts. In 1962, the two firms received an $84 million contract to build two hundred Minuteman missiles silos with twenty launch control centers sprinkled across some eighty-three hundred square miles of Wyoming, Colorado, and Nebraska. Warren Air Force Base, Cheyenne, served as headquarters for the sprawling underground network that linked ten Minuteman-firing silos clustered around buried control centers—capsule-like chambers of fabricated steel and reinforced concrete.

A mild winter spurred the work forward, aided by Utah's revolutionary method of sinking shafts. Each missile silo consisted of a hole fourteen and one-half feet in diameter and sixty-two feet deep, to house a steel liner (or missile "barrel") twelve feet in diameter. Previous contractors required six to eight days to sink these shafts, but the sandstone formations led Utah's experienced engineers to suspect the shafts could be drilled like wells. They developed a huge drilling machine that could complete as many as ten shafts a week, setting a fast pace for the entire project. Personnel placed the steel liners and then encased them in concrete, built rooms for equipment and structural support, then backfilled the site to the original grade, and installed complicated electrical and mechanical equipment. The resulting launch control facilities, one for each ten missiles, lay forty-five feet underground.

In 1964, again in a joint venture with M-K, Utah gained a contract for $121.9 million to construct another 150 Minuteman underground launching complexes with fifteen control centers, this time near Grand Forks, North Dakota. The next year the two firms won a $46.5 million contract to construct fifty launch silos and five control centers dispersed over an area of about thirty-five hundred square miles in northern Montana near Great Falls. Utah also participated in building the North American Aerospace Defense Command (NORAD), an underground command headquarters facility. This project included several hundred Minuteman missile launching sites and generated exceptional earnings.

All of this varied work in North America reestablished Utah as one of America's leading heavy construction contractors, but the firm's international activities brought particular notice. As projects ranged from Mexico to Korea, from the construction of breakwaters in Tasmania to railroads in the Congo, from building whole cities in Peru to dams in Pakistan, Utah's reputation spread as a highly skilled firm that could build almost anything.

In 1964, the company installed an underground control center for Minuteman missile launching facilities near Grand Forks Air Force Base in North Dakota. Here, a silo liner is installed.

Already well-established south of the border from the halcyon days of Mexican railroad building, Utah completed several projects in the State of Chihuahua, Mexico, beginning in the 1950s. In 1956 the company finished the Chihuahua Dam Tunnel at a cost of $400,000. Then, between 1958–61, Cia. Utah, S. A., a wholly owned Mexican subsidiary, built the earth-filled Chihuahua Dam for irrigation and flood control at a cost of $4.7 million. Unfortunately, the state defaulted on notes the company held and, after a protracted contract dispute, Utah incurred a substantial loss. More profitable was building a $1.4 million zinc fuming plant, in 1952, for American Smelting and Refining Company in Chihuahua.

In Colombia, Utah undertook the building between 1950–53 of the Coello Irrigation Project on a tributary of the Magdalena River, providing irrigation water to more than 37,000 acres on the right bank of the river between Chicoral and Espinal. A public corporation, the Caja de Credito Agrario, Industrial, y Minero, contracted Utah and two firms headquartered in Bogota to build the $1.5 million complex as a joint venture. Then in the early 1960s, Utah again became involved in Colombia on the Troneras Project—another earth-filled dam on the Guadalupe River, a $5 million joint venture between Brown and Root, Inc., and Utah of the Americas (a subsidiary). Around the same time, the Tres Marias Dam on the San Francisco River in Minas Gerais, Brazil, part of the colossal Corinto Project, reached completion.

On the other side of the continent in Chile, Utah Construction joined a $50 million project to develop mine facilities for the El Teniente Mine, thirty miles south of Santiago at an elevation of seven thousand feet. This job included excavating a five-and-one-half-mile standard gauge railroad tunnel and the constructing railroad facilities through this new tunnel to the mine. With the historic name of Companía Constructora Utah, a wholly owned subsidiary of Utah Construction & Mining handled the contract for the Sociedad Minera el Teniente, S. A., a Chilean corporation. The project aimed to improve facilities to produce an additional 100,000 tons of copper per year.

Utah's lone European venture was the construction of the Serre Poncon Dam on the Durrance River in southeastern France, between 1955–60. A joint venture with Compagnie Industrielle de

Travaux Entreprises Schneider (CITES) and three other French contractors, Utah's role was providing technical assistance and personnel. In addition to recovering all costs, Utah received 6 percent of the net profit on the $27.5 million project. The dam was composed of alluvial material with an impervious core, stood four hundred feet high, and had a crest length of two thousand feet. More than eighteen million cubic yards of materials went into this dam. The Serre Poncon Reservoir held nine hundred million cubic meters of water to supply power, irrigation, and flood control.

Dam building in Tunisia and Liberia, railroad work in the Republic of the Congo, and construction projects in Nigeria brought the company into the developing continent of Africa. The completion of the Oued Nebaana Dam in March 1966, for example, marked a significant step in the development of Tunisia's economy. The earth- and rock-filled dam, fifteen hundred feet long with 80,000 acre-feet of storage, supplied irrigation water to some 15,000 acres planted in fruit orchards and vegetables. During almost four years of work in Tunisia, Utah's personnel contended with more than one flood that hampered their progress with unforeseeable delays. Despite a variety of such problems, the embankments for the main dam were completed by October 1965. Concrete work on the spillway, requiring 40,000 cubic yards, ended in February 1966.

South of the Sahara, Utah erected in 1964 the University Center in Lagos for the University of Nigeria at a cost of $862,000. Then, in the mid-1960s, it participated in the Mount Coffee Hydroelectric Project on the St. Paul River, some fifteen miles northeast of Monrovia, the capital of Liberia. This $18 million job included building a rock-filled dam, concrete spillways, and a powerhouse containing two 15,000-kilowatt generating units. Raymond International sponsored the joint venture, in which Utah had approximately a 35 percent interest. After a delay starting the project, due to the rainy season, and the need to relocate part of the dam and redesign part of the powerhouse, the job ended on schedule in September 1966.

Another international joint venture for Utah in Africa was a $26 million, 172-mile railroad in the Republic of the Congo (formerly French Equatorial Africa), finished in 1962. Working with the

British firm of Taylor-Woodrow Construction, Ltd., and the French firm Compagnie Industrielle de Travaux of Paris, company crews laid rails to transport manganese ore for a mining company owned by the United States Steel Corporation and several French interests. Rails went down the grade in a unique manner, for specifications required that rails be solid-welded throughout, and to foil white ants and termites, the contract also required using steel ties.

The African experience helped prepare Utah for its South Asian adventure—building the Kaptai Dam and powerhouse in East Pakistan (later Bangladesh) for East Pakistan Water and Power Development. The dam's completion in April 1962, two months ahead of schedule, climaxed five years of effort. Shortly after partition from India in 1947, the newly independent government of Muslim Pakistan began to explore the possibilities of developing the hydroelectric potential of the Karnafuli River. A tentative start in 1952 bogged down, resulting in a request for additional financial assistance from the International Cooperation Administration of the United States, which sent the International Engineering Company, of San Francisco, and Utah Construction & Mining, as contractors. The Karnafuli Dam became one of the company's largest and most challenging international construction ventures.

Utah moved first into East Pakistan in April 1957, with a scheduled completion date of June 1961. Soon afterwards, advance crews discovered that flooding during the previous monsoon season had caused extensive damage to a diversion channel and the dam foundation. Redesigning the foundation and spillway required considerably more construction, and the projected cost rose to $53 million, even as the completion date slipped to June 30, 1962. To Utah's credit, the company not only completed the project within cost estimates but also wrapped up two months ahead of schedule.

But it had not been easy. Construction on the colossal Kaptai project introduced Utah to some new and difficult problems. Extreme weather conditions and inadequate transportation led the list of obstacles, for a five-month monsoon season halted work completely, and virtually all supplies came upriver thirty-five miles by barge from the port of Chittagong. Utah maintained a fleet of five tugs and a dozen barges, including an oil barge, just to keep its supply lines flowing. Aggregate for the 320,000 cubic yards of

Over time, the company trained around forty-five hundred Pakistanis in construction skills to build the Karnafuli Dam, a much-needed source of hydroelectric power.

concrete poured into the job came from the foothills of the Himalayas, three hundred miles distant. Collected in small boats on river tributaries and then moved by larger boats to a railhead, the cargo traveled to Chittagong, where company crews laboriously transferred it back to barges.

To compound such difficulties, engineers had to plant part of the dam foundation underwater and consolidate it by blasting after dewatering. Compacted earth fill in the dam and saddle dams amounted to some five million cubic yards, enough to bury New York's Central Park under a layer of dirt and rock a foot deep. The powerhouse installation consisted of two 40,000-kilowatt generators.

The project's uncertainties also included a cyclone of major proportions. The dam was completed in time to save Chittagong and the surrounding area from a catastrophic flood, but a staggering amount of water fell during the storm. Project manager Stuart Bartholomew recorded 15.5 inches of rainfall in a twenty-four-hour period, and the maximum inflow into the reservoir behind the dam (averaged over an eight-hour period) amounted to about 360,000 cubic feet per second, 50 percent higher than the greatest flood previously recorded. The lake rose 10.2 feet in a five-day period, as the stored water increased by 803,000 acre-feet. "There would have been no Chittagong," a government official observed, "and nothing would have been left of the adjoining villages if there was no dam at Kaptai."

The maximum number of American employees on the job at any one time was eighty-three, nine of whom remained after completion to train the Pakistanis in operating and maintaining the generators. Throughout much of the job, members of the government labor force cooperated only minimally, showing their resentment at having the project taken away from them. This made training much tougher for the Utah men who stayed behind. The plan called for company operators to be in charge in the powerhouse during the first half of the training period. As soon as the local personnel took over, animosities erupted openly and American advice was generally disregarded. As a result, the Pakistan project concluded on a discordant note, although Utah had accomplished much in what would become the troubled nation of Bangladesh.

Utah also joined other companies, principally Reed and Martin, on projects within the Kingdom of Thailand. The Yanhee Multipurpose Project, a dam and power plant on the Ping River some 250 miles north of Bangkok, became one of the first. Brown and Root, S. A., in which Utah held a 40 percent interest, built the concrete arch structure, rising fifty stories above the river bed, with a crest length of more than five football fields and a base thickness of 171 feet at the widest section. The powerhouse of reinforced concrete housed eight 70,000-kilowatt generating units and featured a service bay that included a control room, machine shop, and handling facilities. The project's mammoth scope made it the largest in Southeast Asia. Besides the dam and power plant, it required the construction of a 250-mile transmission line to Bangkok. The project not only improved the extensive river navigation on the Ping and Chao Phya rivers but also provided large quantities of water for irrigation. The joint-venture contract for construction of the dam, powerhouse, and related facilities amounted to $35 million.

At the peak of all these exciting adventures in the jungles and deserts of the world, Utah mourned the loss of Lester S. Corey, who died on October 26, 1964. Utah executives correctly realized that his passing marked the end of an era in the history of the Utah Construction & Mining Company. Joining the company as a timekeeper just months after it was organized in 1900, Les Corey had risen through the ranks to the presidency in 1940. After fifty-three years of continuous employment at Utah, he had retired in 1954 and continued to serve on the board of directors until his death. Littlefield held Corey in high esteem and eulogized him as "a man of wisdom and great integrity." The last image of the rugged little construction outfit from the American frontier had departed; in its place stood a company that was becoming a multinational giant.

Another significant milestone came just a few months before Corey's death when in June 1964, Littlefield was elected to the board of directors of General Electric, a tribute not only to his capabilities but also to his company's reputation. As for Utah, the diversified operations that now fed the company's earning power boded well for its future. "These programs," Littlefield said, "administered by an organization of experienced, competent people, give us pride in our accomplishments to date, and optimism for the prospect of the new year."

Despite wide-ranging activities in construction, the mining division had taken center stage, with iron ore production, both domestic and foreign, responding to increasing levels of steel production in the United States and abroad. Earnings of the company's mining operations in the state of Utah and those of its Peruvian affiliate were well in excess of those of the previous year. At Marcona, progress on the political front had brought negotiations with Peru's Santa Corporation to a satisfactory (though temporary) agreement about the ownership of Marcona. The capacity of Marcona's pellet plant had been sold out and additional long-term contracts for direct sinter ore were in negotiation with Fuji and Nippon. (Sinter ore is produced by heating metal particles to form a larger mass.) The sinter sales were especially significant, providing long-term income from a product that could be used by steel mills with sintering plants with only a modest investment from Marcona in mining and hauling equipment.

New sales contracts heralded the best news at mid-decade. "These will lead to the expansion of Utah's present mining program," management reported to stockholders, "and are expected to have a substantial and sustained impact on the level and dependability of future earnings." As an illustration, Utah would supply coal from the Navajo Mine for a 1.5 million-kilowatt-generating facility adjacent to the Arizona Public Service Company's power plant and Utah's mine in the Four Corners area. If negotiations were successful, projected annual production would make Navajo the largest coal mine in the United States.

In 1965, changes in management reflected this growth in mining activities when John S. Anderson and Edwin C. DeMoss were appointed vice presidents of iron ore and uranium operations, respectively, to reinforce the Mining Division under Senior Vice President Alexander M. (Bud) Wilson. Charles T. Travers was also named vice president of commercial construction and development at the December meeting of the board of directors. Travers had been employed in the company's land development division since 1953 and had been instrumental in developing major land reclamation projects at South Shore. Littlefield believed such men key to the success of the company at that critical juncture. "At no time during my association with the company," he said, "has the management staff functioned more effectively or with greater devotion to duty despite the personal inconveniences and hardships involved."

Meanwhile, the growing Vietnam War was creating burdensome monetary conditions domestically and new challenges for the corporate world, given the uncertainties of demand and the availability of money. Eager to blame administrators of financial institutions for their problems, most Americans accused bankers of creating the "tight money situation" and further charged them with benefitting from the high interest rates of the period. In a speech before the Commonwealth Club in San Francisco on August 26, 1966, Marriner Eccles expressed doubts "that monetary policy alone can hold down prices in the present booming economy, increasingly stimulated by war and other huge government expenditures, without increasing taxes." Increasingly, he worried

Edwin C. DeMoss served as vice president for iron and coal operations.

that the escalation of the war would lead to price controls, wage controls, and rationing. In retrospect, the view of Utah's chairman was sensible. "Instead of being resented, feared, and distrusted," he said, "we have the strength, we have the power, we have the capacity, if directed in our own enlightened self-interest, to win acceptance as the world leader for good." It was enlightened advice, but it fell largely on deaf ears.

Despite such uncertainties, Utah's $1 billion backlog at the end of 1965 was encouraging. It included a contract with the WEST group of six companies to furnish coal for thirty-five years from the company's Navajo Mine for fueling the expanded generating plant at the Four Corners site. In addition, Utah signed three contracts with Swiss and Swedish interests to deliver 3.2 million pounds of uranium oxide during 1967 and 1970. The backlog figure did not include forward sales by the company's mining affiliates, Marcona and Pima. Impressively, the backlog of mineral sales had expanded from only $220 million to $1 billion in just three years.

Senior management changes continued to reflect corporate expansion with Littlefield's recommendation of W. Drew Leonard to the board at its December 1966 meeting for approval as a vice president. An eighteen-year veteran with the company, he continued his duties as corporate controller, a post he had held since 1962. During that meeting the board also paused to mourn the loss of one of its oldest members, Marriner A. Browning, a director since 1944, who died in Ogden in September. To fill Browning's chair, Marriner Eccles announced on December 15 that the deceased's kinsman, Val A. Browning, had been elected a director of the company. A son of inventor John Mose Browning, Val Browning was an inventor in his own right, holding forty-five patents for sporting firearms.

(At the close of 1967, the board consisted of Chairman Marriner S. Eccles; Edmund W. Littlefield; Ernest C. Arbuckle; Alf E. Brandin; Val A. Browning; Lawrence T. Dee; George S. Eccles; William R. Kimball Jr.; Shepard Mitchell; and Paul L. Wattis. Littlefield was president and general manager, with Albert L. Reeves as senior vice president and Frank M. Keller as secretary. Charles E. McGraw and Alexander M. Wilson were also named senior vice presidents; Orville L. Dykstra served as financial vice president and treasurer; and there were nine vice presidents: Joseph K. Allen; John S. Anderson; Weston Bourret; Wayne S. Byrne; William E. Chamberlain; Jr., Edwin DeMoss; W. Drew Leonard; Guy V. Sperry; and Charles T. Travers. The executive committee consisted of Eccles, Littlefield, and Reeves.)

During 1967, the expansion of the Pima Copper Mine would bring its capacity to 30,000 processed tons. There were also significant other contracts, including one with Southern California Edison, the Arizona Public Service Company, and others to furnish 6.5 million tons of coal annually for thirty-five years to fuel two 750,000-kilowatt generating units under construction on the Navajo reservation. Marcona's iron ore shipments exceeded those of the prior year. Lucky Mc and Shirley Basin uranium production increased substantially with new contracts, as did the output of the Navajo coal mine. Domestic mining operations generated revenues 15 percent above 1966 levels.

A principal reason for the surge in earnings from the mining operations was the continuing maturation of the billion-dollar-plus backlog of mineral sales, including uranium oxide. During 1967 two of Utah's top officials delivered speeches that discussed the underlying strategy then driving company interests in the uranium industry. In May, Wilson addressed an international symposium held in Frankfurt, Germany, on the subject of "the United States uranium mining industry." Later in the year Littlefield spoke to the

In 1967 the board of directors was pictured in the *Annual Report.* Seated left to right are William R. Kimball, Jr.; Alf E. Brandin; Paul L. Wattis; Shepard Mitchell; and standing, Albert L. Reeves; Edmund W. Littlefield; Ernest C. Arbuckle; Lawrence T. Dee; Val A. Browning; George S. Eccles; and Marriner S. Eccles.

Investment Bankers Association about "uranium and electric power." Both Utah leaders outlined the rocketing worldwide demand for electricity and argued strongly in favor of using uranium oxide in specialized power plants as a fresh approach to this challenging issue. They forecast bright prospects for the future of the industry with rapid nuclear technology developments, while describing the impact of uranium on the electric industry, the quantity of uranium reserves, economic incentives, and supply-and-demand considerations.

In the midst of this present success and cautious optimism about the future, company executives were warily observing the deepening American involvement in the Vietnam War and its effects on the economy, further complicated by the social woes arising out of the conflict. Experienced in public affairs, Marriner Eccles was among the first corporate leaders in the nation to become concerned that Washington policy makers were making a serious mistake. In a forthright address before the Commonwealth Club in San Francisco in 1967, he saw only one possible good in the quagmire: "The horrible Vietnam debacle, tragic as it is, may yet be a blessing in disguise if it forces us to recognize our staggering failures at home. Runaway crime, delinquency, the riots in our cities, loss of respect for law and order, and the rebellion of frustrated youth—all spring from this." Eccles underscored his foreboding with some shocking figures: "The Vietnam War is responsible for the huge federal deficit which, without a tax increase, could run to more than $25 billion.... We are by far the world's largest short-term debtor.... In 1966, we were spending in excess of $6 billion per year for veterans' benefits, and the Korean War alone is costing more than $700 million a year." In conclusion, Eccles pleaded for America's withdrawal from the war: "History does not show that a nation that liquidates a bad venture suffers from loss of prestige." Instead, "nations have gained stature by doing so." Eccles could see what so many others of the era could not—that the war and all the problems it had created were crippling America. For businesses to run, for people to work, and for individual security and contentment, the government would have to forsake its excessive involvement in the affairs of other countries, whatever the justification. Once again, his plea fell on deaf ears.

Facing the problematic future squarely, management candidly reported on the dangers that could develop down the road in its annual report for 1967:

> In the year ahead our operations may be adversely affected by conditions beyond our control. The fiscal situation in this country may well cause a decrease in federal spending for public works and foreign aid, as well as decreasing the amount of mortgage money available. This would hurt our construction and land activities, and the proposed increase in taxes would penalize all our earnings. Compulsory controls over foreign investments may deny us the opportunities we have for promising new mining projects for our own account and construction contracts for others. Bad as the fiscal situation is in the U. S., in Peru it is relatively worse. This could have a severe impact on Marcona in the long run, although the present legislation by the Peruvian Government does not necessarily hit reportable profits since it is primarily in the form of an involuntary loan to the Government through compulsory prepayment of taxes. The devaluation of the British pound may hurt the Japanese economy. We cannot now evaluate the possible impact of all these forces, but we cannot ignore them.

Facing such imponderables, Utah began the new year of 1968 by realigning top management to meet its need for seasoned leadership in its broadening worldwide endeavors. The current form of organization had been adopted in 1958 and remained virtually unchanged while the size and the complexity of the firm had increased substantially: gross revenues from operations had more than doubled, net income had increased from $4.7 million to $16.5 million, total assets had more than doubled, and the consolidated surplus had increased from $33 million to more than $84 million.

Growth of this magnitude called for significant change to cope with present activities and prepare for those ahead. On February 13, 1968, Littlefield announced Wilson's appointment as executive vice president in charge of company operations, reporting directly to the president and general manager. The managers of the three operating divisions—construction, land development and special ventures, and mining—would report to Wilson. The two other senior officers, Albert Reeves and Orville Dykstra, continued to report to Littlefield. Wilson, elected to the board of directors a month later, became a member of the executive committee. A metallurgical engineer, he had been with the firm in various positions since 1954, most recently as head of the mining division; he also served on the boards of the Utah Development Company and the Pima Mining Company.

That same year, the board of directors approved Charles K. McArthur, Hollis G. Peacock, and Keith G. Wallace to occupy key positions in the company's mining organization. McArthur, a twenty-year veteran of the mining business and formerly a manager of technical services, became a vice president and manager for the Island Copper Mine. Peacock, with thirty years of experience in mining, had been Utah's chief geologist and assistant exploration manager. He would serve as manager of western hemisphere mineral development from his new post as a vice president. Wallace, a graduate of Stanford University's mining engineering program, had managed Utah's Australian mining operations prior to his appointment as vice president.

Another development in 1968 was Utah's acquisition of a 50 percent interest in the Haas and Haynie Corporation of San Francisco. Utah's partner on a project in the early 1960s, Haas and Haynie specialized in building high-rise office and apartment buildings, hotels, resorts, and airport/aviation facilities, as well as engaging in several urban redevelopments, including shopping centers and other commercial and light industrial projects. The financial arrangement gave President Robert M. Haynie a half interest and doubled Haas and Haynie's financial capability for construction projects, then at an annual level of $50–60 million. In addition to its equity interest, Utah advanced funds to maintain an appropriate level of working capital and bonding capacity for Haas and Haynie, which would continue to operate under Haynie's leadership.

Utah's management also engaged in another round of strategic planning for mining that year, outlining ways to expand existing ventures and begin new ones. Over the next five years, this growth likely would require new investments in the $180 million range. "These funds will be provided in part out of cash generated from internal sources," said Littlefield, "but must also be obtained from new financing, the first phase of which we are already arranging." Utah found new backing primarily from European sources and from U. S. banks controlling Euro-dollar credits, as required by government regulations on direct foreign investment.

Reports from around the company demonstrated a prosperity and exuberance unimaginable just a few years before. Lucky Mc was selling approximately two million pounds of uranium oxide annually from the Gas Hills area, and it now planned a comparable operation on the Shirley Basin properties, which would double the output of Utah's uranium mines. Inasmuch as government forecasts indicated a mushrooming demand for "yellow cake," Littlefield wanted to be sure Utah was in a prime position to capitalize on it. In addition to the company's copper mine in Arizona, Utah's exploration team investigated the feasibility of another such project on the "Bay" claims in British Columbia. Although an initial outlay of $38.5 million would be required to get the Bay properties into production, the possibility of some 20,000 tons of copper ore per year inspired active contingency planning.

The Navajo coal project gave nothing but rosy forecasts. Its 1.1-billion-ton deposit of steam coal, the largest in America, promised ample reserves for Utah to meet its contract to deliver 2.5 million tons each year for thirty-five years to Arizona Public Service Company for its power-generating plants. Under construction were two more 750,000-kilowatt generating units, owned jointly by the Southern California Edison Company, Arizona Public Service Company, and four other utility companies. Utah had signed contracts to furnish an additional 6.5 million tons of coal annually for thirty-five years to fuel them. By 1970, coal deliveries were expected to rise to 8.5 million tons each year.

At the end of the thirty-five-year period, 325 million tons would be consumed, but an estimated 450 million tons would remain. The water required for steam generation—44,000 acre-feet annually—flowed from the Navajo Reservoir by contract with the United States Department of the Interior, effective in 1972. The Four

In 1969 New York Stock Exchange president Robert W. Haack (left) and stock specialist John V. Seskis (right) welcomed Utah Construction & Mining president Edmund W. Littlefield.

Corners generators could supply an additional 2.4 million kilowatts of electricity. Given tremendous growth in the West, Utah executives believed that it was hitching its wagon to a star that would only continue to rise. As Littlefield put it:

> With this far-ranging program we believe that Utah Construction & Mining Company will enter its period of greatest and most vigorous growth. It is a period of special significance for the company and its future, both because it will enlarge our role as a factor in the natural resources industry and because our endeavors, if successful, will add both to the substance and to the continuity of our earnings and increased returns on our shareholders' investment in the future of their company.

To critics outside the company who branded this ambitious program "foolhardy," Littlefield said, "We've expanded even farther than the original expansion, but that was the decision that really moved Utah from modest earnings to where it became ultimately the most profitable of all U. S.-headquartered mining companies." This achievement had "involved borrowing more money than our entire net worth."

Despite numerous difficulties, including a copper strike and tense labor negotiations in the steel industry, Utah's fortunes continued to rise as the decade neared its end. As a result, late in 1968 the board authorized a two-for-one stock split, with two additional shares to be distributed on February 14, 1969, for each share outstanding. Furthermore, it declared a regular quarterly dividend of 35 cents with the split. After the split, there were 12,912,711 shares outstanding. In a repeat performance, 1969 also produced record results. "On the earnings side," the annual report declared, "the 1969 profit was approximately equal to the total income earned by the enterprise in the first fifty years of its existence." In addition to this incredible statistic, the report reminded stockholders that booming company profits represented an earnings record for the fifth consecutive year.

At this veritable peak in Utah's long history, the company was admitted to the New York Stock Exchange, on April 2, 1969, with a listing of 14,500,629 shares of common stock. The firm's newly assigned ticker symbol—UC—flashed above the stock exchange floor when the opening bell sounded that morning. The sale of one hundred shares of Utah stock to Littlefield became the morning's first transaction. Robert W. Haack, exchange president, marked the historic occasion in a greeting to Utah officials. After fourteen years of moving toward that goal, Utah finally stopped trading over the counter. Littlefield subsequently savored the success:

> We have continued to be well received by the investing public. The dividend rate was increased for the 19th consecutive year. Our stock was listed on the New York Stock Exchange and the price of the shares has performed remarkably well in the face of an adverse market. Our two [convertible] debenture issues are selling at a considerable premium and our company seems to be held in increasing regard by the financial institutions with whom we do business or who view us as potential clients.

That same month, Utah capped another long change in its identity by selling its construction business to Fluor Utah Engineers and Constructors, Inc., effective April 30, for $14 million plus a percentage of sales over three years. Not included in the transaction were dredging assets, sand and gravel, certain joint ventures, and Utah's interest in the Haas and Haynie Corporation. The company gain of $1.8 million helped boost total corporate net income to a new record of $28.7 million. Although this development seemed counter to its own historic raison d'être, Utah had sound reasons for the sale, among them shrinking construction profits in the face of a colossal expansion in mining. "It was critically important that we sell the construction division when we were headed into this really heavy expansion program of our mining assets," Littlefield explained, "because we couldn't afford the risk to our cash flow that was inherent in the unpredictability of the construction business." Thoughts of selling Utah's construction assets first arose in the early forties when many of the shareholders were understandably disgruntled with the lackluster progress of the company. When the transaction materialized twenty-five years later, it followed the opposite logic—the company had become astoundingly successful, although along a different path. Quite simply, heavy construction had become an albatross about the neck of mineral development.

Over the years, Littlefield had increased construction profits by gradually changing the kinds of construction projects the company would and would not undertake. He believed that part of the problem was that "construction people love to build big, challenging jobs. They don't care whether they make money, but they love to build." Management's job, on the other hand, was "to concentrate on making money." Littlefield noted in the late 1960s that the company had not made any money on building dams in more than ten years "even though we thought we were the greatest dam builders around." Astutely, Littlefield recommended selling the construction side of the company only after it reached its highest level of profitability. The board held mixed views. While Littlefield's figures were uncontested, an intangible weighed significantly—pride that the company had been in heavy construction since the early 1900s. Furthermore, the construction division accounted for more than 60 percent of Utah's gross revenues, 48 percent of its salaried employees, and 69 percent of the company's total payroll. Despite this dominance it was clear that for mining to achieve its potential, Utah would have to get out of the construction business.

In searching for a purchaser, Littlefield contacted Paul Davies, who represented Lehman Brothers of New York City and was also a retired chief executive officer of Food Machinery Corporation. Littlefield and Davies finally approached Fluor Corporation of Newport Beach, California, and the two companies moved swiftly through the usual preliminaries. The dredges were part of the original deal with Fluor, but it backed away, for dredging seemed irrelevant to the conventional construction business. Articles in such business publications as the *Wall Street Journal, Business Week,* and *Fortune* congratulated Utah on its sense of timing. Selling the construction division would allow the mining program to expand on every front, assuring future earnings for the company through its sizeable backlog of mineral sales. And fortunately, Littlefield related, "all of the people in our construction business either were able to go with the buyer of that business or to stay with Utah, so no one lost their job."

In the *Utah Report,* Littlefield described the year's significance, not only due to record earnings and the sale of its construction division, but also because Utah had increased its mineral backlog. "The amount of new business put on the books," he said, "was the greatest in our history and underwrites our future prosperity for many years to come." Highlights of the year included the sale of additional uranium totaling approximately $26 million, the negotiations for the output of 90 percent of the Island Copper production on a favorable basis, and the extension of the Colorado Fuel and Iron (CF&I) contract. As the year ended, the mineral sales backlog stood at $1.1 billion, virtually all of it protected by price-escalation agreements. Despite some inevitable worries in the market sector, Utah management in its 1969 year-end summary dropped its traditional inhibitions to state without reservation: "We are truly taking giant strides forward to become one of the major mining companies in the United States and indeed the world."

In light of this bold prognosis, Littlefield raised an interesting question to the board in 1969:

> Let me put the problem in perspective as I see it. It took us 58 years before we earned over $5 million annually. It took another 8 years to earn over $10 million annually. It took 4 more years to exceed $20 million annually. With a little luck and reasonably good general business conditions, we could exceed a $40 million level by 1972, just three years from now. So, the problem is—what are we going to do for an encore?

The company would have to make its curtain call during perhaps the most difficult time in the postwar history of the United States. As America retreated from Vietnam, something called "stagflation" hit the economy, higher inflation rates bedeviled credit, the Arabs mounted an oil embargo, and President Richard M. Nixon resigned over the Watergate scandal. Marriner Eccles, who had an early foreboding of such events, retired from the board chairmanship in February 1971 with the firm in excellent condition in terms of mining capabilities, back orders, and profits. Littlefield candidly appraised his colleague's crucial role in an address to the shareholders at the annual meeting on October 7, 1971.

When Eccles had joined the board in early 1921, the company was operating at a loss and had a net worth of only $4 million. More than half of its assets were represented by ranch lands, cattle, sheep, hogs, horses, and feed. Its principal construction project then underway was the O'Shaughnessy Dam for the Hetch Hetchy water system serving San Francisco. Ten years later, in 1931, Eccles was elected president of the company and, in 1940, was elevated to the position of chairman of the board. "His was a critical role in the trying days of the Depression and the Second World War," Littlefield said. "His record as a public servant has earned him admiration and respect throughout the world." Eccles had returned to private life in 1951, never lessening his multinational interests, and resuming a more active role as Utah's chairman of the board. During his distinguished career, the company had "undergone a transformation in the nature of its business and is now engaged principally in mining and has enjoyed remarkable growth and success, especially during the last 10 years." Littlefield also commented on the company's sound program of expansion, a favorable earnings trend, and the commitment of "a very talented, hard-working and dedicated staff," whose contributions to the firm had been invaluable.

In gratitude for a half-century of devotion to the company, the shareholders approved a resolution on the spot that expressed "their appreciation for his record of accomplishment, their esteem and respect for his high personal qualities of leadership and integrity." In a speech some years later, Littlefield again honored Eccles:

> Marriner Eccles served the company very capably for over 50 years and was as wise as mortal men come. He was my mentor and my esteemed friend. He is entitled to great credit for his contribution to Utah's success.... He was the constant watchdog of the shareholders' interest and the toughest, highest hurdle we in management had to clear in getting approval for the revolutionary things we proposed and did.

Littlefield became the new chairman of the board and chief executive officer in 1971. Eccles acknowledged in the *Utah Report* that the bulk of the credit for the company's significant changes and progress over the last twenty years rightfully belonged to Littlefield: "The company was more fortunate than we realized when Mr. Littlefield was persuaded to come into the Utah organization over 20 years ago. He has served the company brilliantly for that time and has been general manager for the past 13 years and its president for the last 10 years, the decade of its greatest progress." At the same meeting, Bud Wilson succeeded Littlefield as president. In keeping with the practice of most large corporations, Littlefield had been both president and chief executive officer, handling all of the managerial and policy implementation responsibilities of both.

In yet another move indicative of Utah's continued transition, the company assumed the title of Utah International, Inc., with shareholders' approval on June 30, 1971, "to identify more accurately the present geographic scope of Utah's ... operations and the international character of its business." Just a few months prior to the name change, both *Fortune* and *Forbes* saluted the company's excellent record in their annual ratings of American business corporations. "Good news about profits was relatively scarce for the companies on the [second 500] list," the *Fortune* editors observed. "Perhaps the most profitable company was Utah Construction & Mining Company ... that ranked first in return on sales, with a margin of 33.3 percent, and also had the highest income, $30 million."

The firm took a long stride forward in the early 1970s by acquiring Ladd Petroleum Company in November 1974. As J. B. Ladd noted in an address to Ladd shareholders in June 1974, "Natural gas and crude oil are in particularly short supply," and this acquisition reinforced Utah's profit. Only a few months later in 1975, Utah brought Clarcan Petroleum and LVO Corporation into its family of subsidiaries. These developments brought Utah to a higher level in a company-maintained ranking of the twenty-five top mining firms in the United States. In 1968, Utah ranked seventeenth; in 1972, eighth; and in early 1976, third.

It was soon to be number one. During this period the price of coking coal shot through the roof, due to a worldwide shortage that was expected to last well into the eighties. These windfalls increased company profits by $27 million in 1974 and $52 million in 1975. "This would be fourteen times the earning level of ten years ago," reported management, with earnings of $100 million or $3.30 a share possible. Utah International reported a net profit of $96,941,000 in 1974, which exceeded the entire earnings in the first sixty-four years of Utah's history. The gain of more than $41 million was greater than the entire earnings of any single year in Utah's history except 1973. Littlefield remembered when the price of coking coal was a meager $11 to $15 per ton. Then "all of a sudden it was $50 a ton and these mines became much more profitable than we anticipated."

The jumbled background of ever-changing prices created an erratic picture of 1975 earnings from Utah International's various subsidiaries and joint ventures, complicated by uncontrollable foreign waves of anti-U.S./big business sentiment. For multinationals, the phrase, "Yankee, Go Home! (But leave your assets here)," echoed painfully in their ears. Utah, however, could not go home, inasmuch as the majority of its earnings—some 95 percent—now emanated from one commodity, coking coal, and from one country, Australia. In the understatement of the year, Littlefield portrayed the current situation as "an uncomfortable concentration of our fortunes in one area." Management further stressed the irony: "Impressive as this performance appears, it bears some resemblance to the performance of Babe Ruth, when in the same year he broke both the record for home runs and for striking out." Ed Littlefield summed up Utah's stance, "We painted ourselves into a corner. We were a victim of our own success."

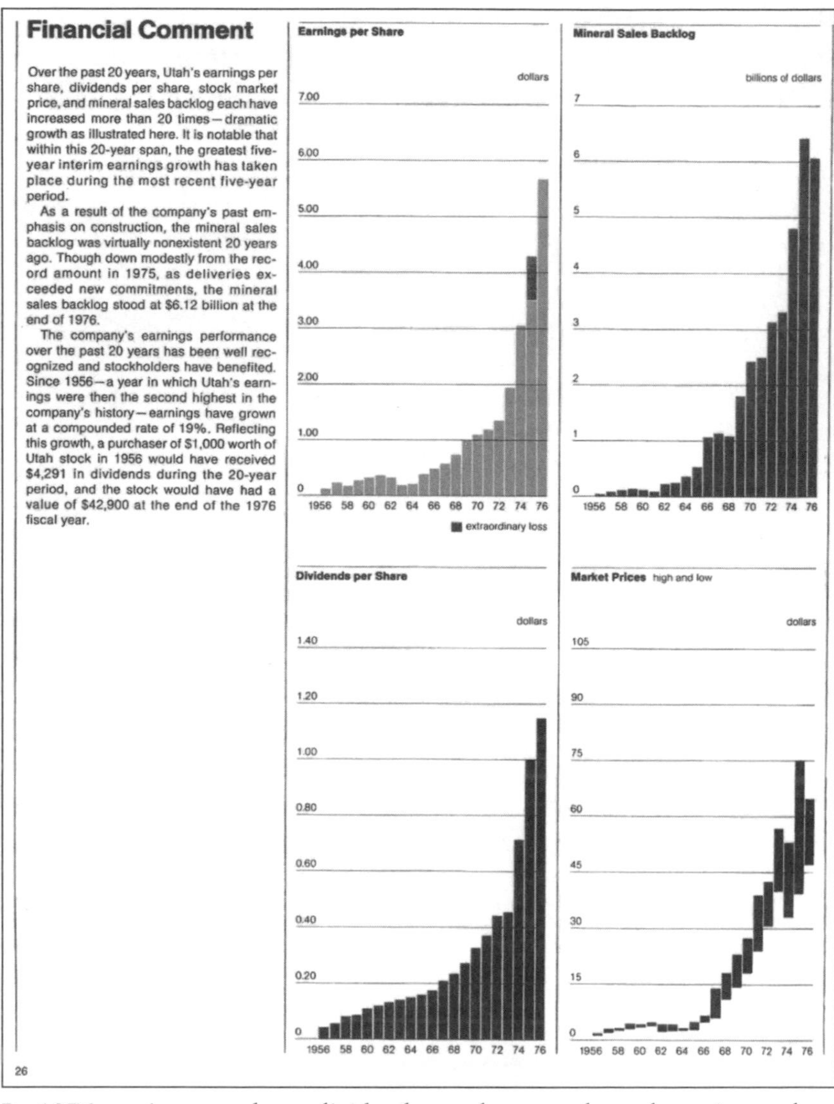

Financial Comment

Over the past 20 years, Utah's earnings per share, dividends per share, stock market price, and mineral sales backlog each have increased more than 20 times—dramatic growth as illustrated here. It is notable that within this 20-year span, the greatest five-year interim earnings growth has taken place during the most recent five-year period.

As a result of the company's past emphasis on construction, the mineral sales backlog was virtually nonexistent 20 years ago. Though down modestly from the record amount in 1975, as deliveries exceeded new commitments, the mineral sales backlog stood at $6.12 billion at the end of 1976.

The company's earnings performance over the past 20 years has been well recognized and stockholders have benefited. Since 1956—a year in which Utah's earnings were then the second highest in the company's history—earnings have grown at a compounded rate of 19%. Reflecting this growth, a purchaser of $1,000 worth of Utah stock in 1956 would have received $4,291 in dividends during the 20-year period, and the stock would have had a value of $42,900 at the end of the 1976 fiscal year.

26

By 1976 earnings per share, dividends per share, stock market price, and mineral sales backlog each increased more than twenty times, as shown in Utah International's final *Annual Report*.

Chapter 13

Merger

The year 1975 was not a good one for Utah International, Inc. After a decade as an outstanding performer in the market, the company's common stock declined sharply—from 75 points in the early summer to 45 in September. Several factors combined to create this slide in market value. First, investors had watched Utah's stock skyrocket in the early 1970s in anticipation of major profits from Australian coal, due partly to much higher coal prices after the 1973–74 oil embargo. By late spring, however, jittery stockholders worried that Utah's phenomenal growth might be over. Then in June 1975, the Peruvian government expropriated Marcona Mining Company, of which Utah International owned 46 percent, resulting in a catastrophic after-tax loss of almost $20 million. Two months later, the Australian government imposed a heavy export duty on coking coal at the same time labor unrest forced a suspension of operations for three weeks. After three-quarters of a century in business, Utah found itself in a tight corner with few possibilities.

Having recognized the coming crisis for some time, Edmund W. Littlefield nevertheless determined to find a profitable way out for the company's stockholders. Despite all his efforts to cushion the company through diversification, inexorable forces had boxed Utah into the untenable position of having the bulk of its profits coming from two commodities—iron ore and coking coal—both located in one foreign country, Australia. By the fall of 1975, as alternatives dwindled, senior management assessed the firm's options.

One alternative was for the original family members to sell their large blocks of stock with handsome profits, but they would then face large capital gains taxes. This was not a feasible solution, because many of them had a cost basis on Utah stock of a few pennies a share. If such sales were to be consummated, the 1975 taxes on capital gains could be as much as 70 percent. Additionally, the initial unloading of large blocks of shares would depress stock prices considerably, disadvantaging the newer shareholders, who had a right to insist that share prices remain attractive with the prospect of gaining in value. Erosion of the stock's price/earnings ratio seemed inevitable, however, given the industry and the times. This was true even if Australia's leanings toward taking adverse political action against the ownership of Utah's holdings could be averted, and even if an exorbitant levy on foreign shipments could be avoided. "I calculated that if we doubled our earnings I could see the same stock price," mused Littlefield later. "I wasn't far wrong. Strategically, I felt that we should diversify into other natural resources."

To acquire a natural resources firm, however, posed many challenges. While there were a few promising candidates, the time required to consummate the deal would take too long, given Utah's immediate problems. Also, according to Littlefield,

> it would have required arranging about $1.5 billion to acquire a firm that had an earning power comparable to ours. I thought that was a very high-risk venture—to buy that much that fast—and this was bound to take us beyond the field of our expertise in natural resources and raw materials. We didn't have the breadth of management to manage a lot of different things far removed from the kinds of skills that we are obviously good at. And if we [did] that, we [were] going to end up somewhere along the line making a bad mistake, and we'[d] pay for it.

Besides all this, the acquisition of an available competitor would surely draw the attention of the Federal Trade Commission and the Justice Department on the basis of anti-trust measures.

A more promising alternative was to diversify by merging with an already diversified company large enough to digest a $2 billion bite, which was Utah's market value as determined by share price, times the number of shares outstanding. This condition narrowed the field considerably. "I came out with four companies that I thought were probables—and that's all," said Littlefield. At the head of the list was General Electric Company, which, Littlefield said, "appeared by all odds the most attractive merger partner that we could seek."

As Utah's executives pondered a possible alliance with GE, Littlefield was not sure how the "old line shareholders" would respond, "because one of the things about Utah, there has always been a sentimental feeling about the company, and nowhere has it been as bad as in my family." Littlefield was particularly concerned about how Marriner S. Eccles and George S. Eccles would react to his plan, since they were part of the original shareholder families. He need not have worried. "Both George and Marriner thought this was a stroke of genius," Littlefield related. "I think everybody recognized that, from a standpoint of all those concerned, this was a great idea." He was convinced that "the only people that had any real opposition to it ... would be the brokers and others, who didn't like the idea of an independent vehicle disappearing."

As word of the initiative got around, some key employees and a few shareholders resisted the idea of a merger, but Utah director Ernest Arbuckle grasped the point immediately and exemplified the more common reaction: "The merger was important in the defense of family interests." Even more importantly, he described the attitude of General Electric officials as "most remarkable in regard to leaving in place an existing company organization: you run your own business." From its perspective, GE found Utah a most attractive suitor. Out of the fifteen hundred companies listed on the New York Stock Exchange, it was one of only eighty-three enjoying a decade of uninterrupted earnings growth. Standard and Poor's *Outlook* declared 1975 "an especially rough year for U.S. corporations, with overall after-tax profits declining about 17 percent.... In contrast, Utah's 1975 earnings rose 14 percent."

Naturally, this rate had not been steady over Utah's history, although earnings had improved as Utah phased out of construction and into mining. The stock market did not typically favor construction firms, nor was it particularly fond of mining. Utah's top management, however, succeeded in persuading influential Wall Street analysts to accept the company as different because its earnings were relatively predictable, based on a large backlog of orders with price escalation clauses. When other mining companies were selling at five or six times earnings, Utah sold even as high as twenty times earnings. As a result, Utah had become a hot stock on the New York Exchange.

This success represented a radical change from earlier days when, by 1920, there remained few railroads to be built, which forced Utah to seek other pursuits. While rarely losing money, its profits were less than spectacular from 1919–46 and later. During these years, the name Utah Construction Company, alone or in joint ventures, was associated with many of the landmark structures transforming the West and Southwest. Not least among its achievements were huge dams such as Hoover, Grand Coulee, Davis, and Bonneville. Other major projects included construction of the Geneva Steel plant at Orem, Utah; the Alcan Highway; vast earth-moving projects both domestically and abroad; the building of thousands of miles of railroads and tunnels; and the construction of large industrial plants, underground missile systems, and the San Francisco Bay Bridge. During World War II, the company had participated in building ships, marine engines, storage facilities, and Pacific military bases, simultaneously providing magnesium for incendiary bombs. Surprisingly, all this effort, including the ranching operations, produced annual profits averaging a meager $321,000.

Naturally discouraged with these results, shareholders seriously considered liquidating the firm in the early 1940s. The 1945 sale of the ranches justified a partial liquidation in 1946, when 25 percent of the shares were retired for $2 million. Then, Utah began its ascent by increasing its traditional construction activities, launching its first projects in international construction work, and entering into commercial and industrial building. Most importantly, the company took its first small steps into mining. In 1946, Utah opened an iron ore mine near Cedar City, Utah, and a coal mine in Arkansas in 1950. Other mining operations followed and then, toward the decade's end, senior management became aware of a vast Japanese market for Utah's minerals.

At that time, Utah had only 150 shareholders, most of whom were members of the Browning, Christensen, Dee, Eccles, and Wattis families, with the E. O. Wattis family being the largest shareholder. Representatives from these families also constituted the board of directors. Subsequently, no genuine market existed for the available shares, although the newspapers carried bid and ask prices that were usually below book value.

Significant managerial changes became as important to the company's future as diversification when, in 1951, Allen Christensen took the general manager's chair and Littlefield came aboard as financial vice president and treasurer. The company then pushed forward at a terrific pace over the next twenty-five years. For example, through the Marcona Corporation and Mount Goldsworthy, Utah became a major iron ore producer, with operations in Peru, New Zealand, Brazil, and Australia. In Queensland, Utah Construction's mineral experts made perhaps the most significant discovery of metallurgical coal ever, and the company consequently became the world's largest exporter of coking coal. Because it used ships owned by its Marcona joint venture or by its own charters, Utah became a substantial player in the ocean transport of bulk commodities. The firm also became a major uranium producer for the United States, with two mines and mills in Wyoming.

Utah's major achievements included the development of huge western reserves of steam coal in New Mexico and Colorado to serve mine-mouth power plants. The company's Navajo Coal Mine in the Four Corners area became the nation's largest when it opened in 1963. Utah also acquired a 25 percent interest in the Pima Copper Mine near Tucson, Arizona, when Cyprus Mines hired it to construct the operational facilities. The firm also discovered and developed a major copper deposit on Vancouver Island, British Columbia. In 1969, the company sold the assets of its construction division to Fluor Corporation, increasing the pace at which its intensive mineral explorations began to pay off.

"I guess it's fair to say I am the chief proponent of the idea that if you're going to be a mining company," said Littlefield, "you'd better explore, and if you're going to explore ... you [have] to keep at it." When he first began working for the company, he had to go to the board for every appropriation to explore possible projects. Convinced this was inefficient, he worked on the executive committee with Eccles for an annual exploration budget, which they soon produced. "This is an activity where it pays to be lucky," observed Littlefield, "but the good guys also make some of their own luck. If we got more bang for the buck out of our exploration, it was because we were ever-ready to fund an ever-larger exploration budget. [We] never cut back on the exploration effort to improve the appearances of current profits, an error often committed by our competition." Utah enjoyed unusual success in its mineral exploration and development efforts. Its mines were low-cost producers, which gave the firm a real advantage in the market place.

By 1968 the firm's experience with land development had virtually run its course. Most of the land Utah owned had been sold to the benefit of mining ventures. When the high price of coking coal sent profits to unexpected levels, it brought with it "a degree of prosperity that was far greater than previous times, but it also changed the nature of our diversification and our risks," Littlefield explained. At the time Utah was not a big company but "a very well diversified mining company.... The company was not dependent on a single source for the lion's share of earnings, and not at risk in the political fortunes of any particular country. We could have been damaged if something should happen, but it wouldn't be a death blow." This changed with the exceptional demand for coking coal, which generated extraordinary net earnings and a very difficult political situation in Australia.

All this business activity turned out "reasonably well," Littlefield understated. Earnings per share in 1976 were fifty-four times the 1951 level. Dividends increased every year for twenty-six years. Share prices increased from 50 cents in 1949 to a high of $74 in 1975, then retreated somewhat when the stock market became queasy over threatening political developments in Peru and Australia. Finally, in 1976, among all mining companies headquartered in the United States, Utah International "ranked *first* in earnings and *first* in the total market value of its shares,"

Littlefield said. "None of the other companies on the list rivaled Utah's record for uninterrupted growth or exceeded Utah's rate of growth."

The reasons Utah International outperformed its competitors are many. To begin with, Utah sold its construction assets when the division achieved the highest profitability in its history. At the time of the sale, the construction division accounted for the majority of the company's staff. Utah's executives decided this traditional business had to be sold because its earnings and cash flow were frequently uncertain, making a construction-dominated company less desirable in the stock market. Second, Utah's administrators also displayed the ability to recognize opportunity and "to get in its way," as Littlefield put it. For example, the iron ore deposits near Cedar City, Utah, drew Mormon settlers there on an "iron mission" in 1851, but it took the construction of the Geneva Steel plant in Orem, Utah, during World War II to make the ore valuable. Utah officials also realized that established steel centers could no longer be served by nearby sources of iron ore and coking coal and would depend on faraway sources, including imports. They foresaw moving these raw materials from mine to market on a bridge of ships currently too small and inefficient. "Marcona led the way in pioneering bigger and bigger ships, ordering 32,000 ton carriers when the standard was 10,500 tons," Littlefield pointed out, "and now ships of 150,000 tons are not uncommon."

When opportunity knocked, Utah responded. "Once Bethlehem Steel was Marcona's biggest customer, but some years before, when Bethlehem's geologists were in Lima, they could not be bothered to take an extra day to look at the undeveloped Marcona deposits." In contrast, Utah management sent a representative to Lima the day after hearing of the potential iron ore deposits. As a final illustration of aggressive and discerning management, Lucky Mc's owners offered their holdings to many major mining companies before Utah recognized its potential. In a class almost by itself, Utah successfully shifted its major line of business—construction—to a dominant position in mining. Director Arjay Miller praised this transition: "I certainly know of no other company that has reallocated all of its assets out of one industry into another, from construction to mining, and done it so well. This achievement was due primarily to competence in strategy formulation including a precise execution of plans."

Persistence also characterized top management's style. For instance, in 1953, United States Steel Company officials told Utah management of plans to build an integrated steel facility in Pittsburgh, California. Immediately, company executives positioned the firm to provide U.S. Steel with iron ore and coking coal, finding iron ore near Carson City, Nevada. The quest for coal took Utah to Canada, Mexico, and South America, ending in Queensland, Australia, where it found its most valuable mineral discovery. Given an impending shortage of natural gas in the West, Utah searched for large, strippable deposits of coal. "This was not too hard to do because no one else was looking for such undefined deposits," Littlefield explained. "The black rock the Navajo Indian picked up off the ground to burn in his hogan was the clue to a billion-ton reserve." Ironically, it turned out initially to be easier to find coal than customers for the coal.

When Utah made mistakes, the company was quick to recognize and correct them. For example, dredging, manufacturing land, and land development were anything but blue-ribbon winners. "Our biggest loss ever," he said ruefully, "started from a modest investment in a golf course at Pauma Valley, California. Never did I have more management help from the board of directors. Each was a self-appointed expert on how to run a golf club."

The end point of all these business activities was to enhance shareholder value, as Littlefield described:

> First, we put our major efforts on the minerals that were more stable in price like iron ore and coal and put less emphasis on those minerals like copper, lead and zinc that are volatile in price. Second, we positioned ourselves to take advantage of markets that were growing rapidly: alternate energy forms to petroleum [and] international trade in raw materials for the steel industry. Finally, we made a virtue out of a necessity and built up a mineral sales backlog of $6 billion in long-term contracts with [price] escalation protection, giving us an assurance of margins and volume

that the investor found very appealing. These factors found their way into our price/earnings ratio.

Indeed they did. The original $24,000 investment in shares had a value in 1951 of "perhaps $7.2 million if they could have been sold at book value," Littlefield estimated. In late 1976, they represented 43 percent of the total Utah shares, valued at $926 million.

"I found it a very exciting adventure," Littlefield reminisced in 1978, "to come into top management as I did and ... be one of the participants and one of the architects in taking the firm from one of earning $4–4.5 million a year to one that was approaching profit levels of $200 million." He most enjoyed the post of chief executive officer "because it offers the most challenges, has the widest range of problems to solve, and if, you get the job done well, it has to be the most satisfying."

Along these lines, Littlefield demonstrated his awareness of the constant need to groom executives for top management succession. In his own retirement plan, he reported, "I started being concerned about the transition of authority some long time before I made any overt motions ... but I identified [Bud] Wilson as the one whom I felt had the potential for the job." As soon as the opportunity presented itself, Littlefield positioned Wilson as executive vice president, then as president and chief operating officer when Littlefield became chairman and chief executive officer. Wilson began his managerial career at Utah in charge of its uranium operations. Following Tony Mecia's death, Wilson took over Mecia's responsibilities as a temporary assignment. Although Littlefield searched outside the company for someone to fill Mecia's position permanently, he decided Wilson was best qualified.

Littlefield told his executive compensation committee he would not work beyond the age of sixty-five. When it came time for him to hand over complete control of the company to Wilson as chairman and chief executive officer, he would do as the board suggested, including resigning, to accomplish a smooth transition. The board agreed that the appropriate approach was for Littlefield to turn over increasing authority to Wilson so that when the time finally came, the transition of authority and power could be accomplished without any abrupt change. These plans went into effect in the early

Board of Directors

Edmund W. Littlefield
Chairman

Marriner S. Eccles
Honorary Chairman

Ernest C. Arbuckle
Chairman of the Board,
Wells Fargo & Company

Fred J. Borch
Retired Chairman of the Board,
General Electric Company

Alf E. Brandin
Senior Vice President

Val A. Browning
Chairman of the Board,
Browning

James T. Curry
Financial Vice President and Treasurer

Thomas D. Dee II
Vice President and Manager, Ogden,
First Security Bank of Utah, N.A.

George S. Eccles
Chairman and Chief Executive Officer,
First Security Corporation

William R. Hewlett
President and Chief Executive Officer,
Hewlett-Packard Company

Reginald H. Jones
Chairman of the Board and Chief Executive Officer,
General Electric Company

William R. Kimball
President,
Kimball & Company

J. Bertram Ladd
President,
Ladd Petroleum Corporation,
a subsidiary of the Company

Arjay Miller
Dean, Graduate School of Business,
Stanford University

Jack S. Parker
Vice Chairman of the Board and Executive Officer,
General Electric Company

Paul L. Wattis, Jr.
President,
Wattis Construction Co., Inc.

Alva O. Way
Vice President—Finance,
General Electric Company

Alexander M. Wilson
President

Committees of the Board:
Audit Committee
Executive Committee
Executive Compensation Committee

Edmund W. Littlefield — Marriner S. Eccles — Ernest C. Arbuckle

Fred J. Borch — Alf E. Brandin — Val A. Browning

James T. Curry — Thomas D. Dee II — George S. Eccles

William R. Hewlett — Reginald H. Jones — William R. Kimball

J. Bertram Ladd — Arjay Miller — Jack S. Parker

Paul L. Wattis, Jr. — Alva O. Way — Alexander M. Wilson

In 1976 the board of directors consisted of Edmund W. Littlefield, chairman; Marriner S. Eccles, honorary chairman; Ernest C. Arbuckle, board chairman, Wells Fargo & Company; Fred J. Borch, retired board chairman, General Electric Company; Alf E. Brandin, senior vice president; Val A. Browning, board chairman of Browning; James T. Curry, financial vice president and treasurer; Thomas D. Dee II, vice president and manager, Ogden, First Security Bank of Utah, N.A.; George S. Eccles, chairman and chief executive officer, First Security Corporation; William R. Hewlett, president and chief executive officer, Hewlett-Packard Company; Reginald H. Jones, board chairman and *(continued on next page, beneath photos)*

Officers

Edmund W. Littlefield
Chairman of the Board and Chief Executive Officer

Alexander M. Wilson
President and Chief Operating Officer

Alf E. Brandin
Senior Vice President

James T. Curry
Financial Vice President and Treasurer

Edwin C. DeMoss*
Senior Vice President

Ralph J. Long
Senior Vice President

Charles K. McArthur
Senior Vice President

Keith G. Wallace
Senior Vice President

John S. Anderson
Vice President

W. Drew Leonard
Vice President

Boyd C. Paulson
Vice President

M. Ian Ritchie*
Vice President

George W. Tarleton
Vice President

Robert O. Wheaton
Vice President

Bruce T. Mitchell
Secretary

J. Boyd Nielsen
Controller

Edwin C. DeMoss — Ralph J. Long — Charles K. McArthur

Keith G. Wallace — John S. Anderson — W. Drew Leonard

Boyd C. Paulson — M. Ian Ritchie — George W. Tarleton

Robert O. Wheaton — Bruce T. Mitchell — J. Boyd Nielsen

chief executive officer, General Electric Company; William R. Kimball, president, Kimball & Company; J. Bertram Ladd, president, Ladd-Petroleum Corporation; Arjay Miller, dean of the Graduate School of Business, Stanford University; Jack S. Parker, board vice chairman and executive officer, General Electric Company; Paul L. Wattis, Jr., president, Wattis Construction Co., Inc.; Alva O. Way, vice president of finance, General Electric Company; Alexander M. Wilson, president, Utah International, Inc.

Company officers in 1976 included Edwin C. DeMoss, senior vice president; Ralph J. Long, senior vice president; Charles K. McArthur, senior vice president; Keith G. Wallace, senior vice president; John S. Anderson, vice president; W. Drew Leonard, vice president; Boyd C. Paulson, vice president; M. Ian Ritchie, vice president; George W. Tarleton, vice president; Robert O. Wheaton, vice president; Bruce T. Mitchell, secretary; J. Boyd Nielsen, controller.

1970s. Littlefield learned early on the importance of putting the right people in the right places to test their management capabilities. Additionally, he encouraged risk acceptance. "One of the things that I have looked for in executives in Utah are those who are willing to risk making mistakes. I have never wanted anybody working at a high level reporting to me who hasn't made some mistakes, because if they haven't made mistakes, they haven't taken any chances."

Executives had to be principled and exemplary because Utah was the kind of company that simply did not participate in inappropriate conduct, such as "improper payments and that sort of thing." Littlefield believed that all Utah employees could take pride in the firm's corporate ethics. He acknowledged that this kind of integrity "cost us something, but the rewards have been most satisfying."

Due to all of these characteristics, GE found Utah attractive indeed, and after detail work that lasted through much of 1976, the two giant corporations merged in December of that year. The union enhanced dramatically Utah International's already legendary achievements in the mining and heavy construction industries, as innumerable shares of GE stock now made many a millionaire, built many a university building, and endowed many a foundation. For instance, in the state of Utah, the Eccles foundations benefitted substantially from the Utah International/General Electric merger. GE stock "remains the largest single source of the Eccles family wealth," according to a *Salt Lake Tribune* article (June 27, 1999). Similarly, GE reigned supreme in most of the industries it occupied, providing similar financial rewards for its shareholders. The two firms were well matched in terms of accomplishments and reputations.

For precisely these reasons, the United States Justice Department's anti-trust division prepared to scrutinize the merger petitions, arriving after the boards of both companies approved action to negotiate an agreement in simultaneous meetings on December 15, 1975. Within the month, business commentators began to speculate. An article in the *San Francisco Chronicle* on January 11, 1976, focused on the economic and federal jurisdictional issues which shadowed the intended merger. In essence, the Justice Department could block the alliance if, in the government's opinion, "it substantially lessened competition," by the provisions of the Clayton Act (1914). To prove such a circumstance, the government would argue against two types of mergers. The first was horizontal—a company acquiring its supplier. (In this case, GE would acquire Utah's uranium output.) To defend it against such a charge, Reginald Jones, then GE's president, told a group of Wall Street analysts in early 1976 that Utah held only a modest share in the uranium production market, and that uranium was but a small part of Utah's overall business revenue. The second type of merger on which the Justice Department frowned was one where the two consolidating firms would "manufacture or distribute functionally related products," which was not the case for this proposal.

After seven months of negotiating legal and accounting matters in a relatively routine way, the Justice Department mysteriously clammed up, refusing to indicate whether it would challenge the merger. The *Wall Street Journal,* on July 26, 1976, reported Assistant Attorney General Thomas Kaupe as saying, "Advance clearance for the proposed combination could not be given because of its probable anti-competitive impact, particularly in the nuclear steam-supply systems market." In summary, Utah's uranium and GE's nuclear fuel systems, when combined, could provide unfair competition. *Business Week* writers picked up Kaupe's comments in the September 13, 1976, issue: "The stock market apparently has strong doubts that the $2 billion merger between General Electric Corporation and Utah International, Inc., will ever be completed."

GE and Utah met the Justice Department's stated concerns by agreeing that, upon merger, GE would transfer all of Utah's uranium operations to a separate company (Lucky Mc). GE would own the equity, and the company would be managed by an independent board of trustees. GE also agreed to obtain its uranium from some other source until the year 2000. These concessions solved the Justice Department's concerns, and it announced on October 4, 1976, that it would not contest the proposed merger.

Now the stockholders took their turn. On December 15, 1976, on a typical winter day in San Francisco with bright blue skies and a mild temperature of 60 degrees, the elevators in the city's Wells Fargo Bank building lifted first-time visitors to the penthouse board room for a final meeting of Utah's shareholders. Descendants of the founding families and other shareholders filled the chambers, including cousins, friends, and long-time neighbors. Reminiscent of a sedate family reunion, the assemblage waited with whispered greetings, embraces, and quiet conversations. Among observers at the meeting was Sterling D. Sessions, then dean of the School of Business at Weber State College (now University) in Ogden, Utah, the town where it all began seventy-six years before.

Littlefield called the meeting to order promptly at ten, introduced the company's officers, and briefly saluted Marriner Eccles for his fifty-six years of service on the firm's board. He then confirmed the receipt of a majority of the proxy cards and identified the purpose of the meeting—to ratify a proposed merger of Utah International with General Electric Company. Bruce T. Mitchell, secretary and senior counsel, read the resolution officially declaring the intention of the companies to merge. Retired Utah Vice President Charles Travers seconded the resolution.

The merger was approved by a majority of shares held, due in part to the proxy statements mailed earlier to 23,000 Utah shareholders representing 31,540,032 shares, and a similar package sent to 529,000 GE shareholders who held 184,748,732 shares of common stock. "If the statements had been piled one on top of another," Littlefield told the crowd, "the last statement would be 3.5 miles above the earth, or if the pages had been placed end to end, the distance covered would be three and three quarters times across the United States." He reported a similar action that took place earlier in the day in Stamford, Connecticut, as GE shareholders also approved the merger with ballots representing 86 percent of shares.

Littlefield described Utah's merger with General Electric as necessary due to a business concentration in one area—Australian iron ore and coking coal. He then discussed Utah's options: either spending more than $1 billion in acquisitions that might take Utah out of its fields of expertise, or finding a very large, diversified, multinational company that could accommodate the purchase of a $2 billion company without financial strain. The meeting continued in a jovial mood with continued introductions of company officers past and present. Charlie Travers even spent some time at the microphone, detailing his competitiveness with Littlefield:

> I had read one of Horatio Alger's novels, I think it was *Ragged Dick,* and I learned that the way to get ahead was to

> beat the boss to work. On my first day of work, I arrived at 8:15 and Ed said hello as I passed his office. The next day I arrived at 8:10 and Ed said hello. Finally on Friday, after coming earlier each day, I arrived at 7:30, confident that no hello would be heard from Ed. At 8:15, I looked into his office and he wasn't there. I asked another man where Littlefield was, and he said, "He's not here. He took the 7:00 plane to Chicago."

Travers finished by describing the company's profit-sharing plan and how that opportunity had financially benefitted him. When Littlefield returned to the microphone he said, "Thank you, Mr. Travers. You always speak well, but you don't always speak briefly." Amid roars of laughter, he continued, "Perhaps your long speeches come from attending too many meetings of the Alameda Town Council," a wry allusion to a hot spot for Utah's land development activities in the 1950s.

The meeting adjourned at 10:47. As the shareholders began to rise, chatting and expressing satisfaction about the merger, a woman later identified as Emily Marie Kass, a friend of "a cousin," stood and insisted on being recognized by the chair. She proclaimed, "I would like to move that we extend appreciation to all those who have made the company what it is, and I propose a moment of silence in honor of E. O. Wattis, the founder of the company, and all those who have died in pursuit of company business." This gesture symbolically set the fabulous success and growth the company had achieved by 1976 against the early rivalries of the W. H. and E. O. Wattis families. Both family members and employees knew about the brothers' closeness, for they shared a most uncommon and intimate bond. Yet their deaths initiated frequent disagreements between their families about whose grandfather had contributed more or whose family should run the show at Utah headquarters.

Without missing a beat, Littlefield responded, "If you'll amend that proposal to include all the founders of the company, the chair will recognize that motion." No one contested his suggestion. The motion was seconded and passed, ending with an appropriate moment of silent respect and contemplation for Utah's leaders.

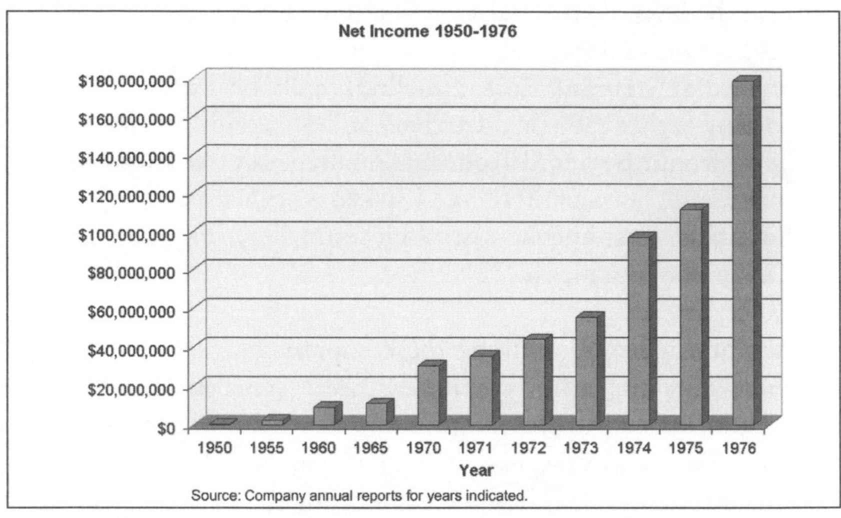

Chart showing Utah International's net income from 1950 through 1976.

With that action, an invisible gavel came down to conclude the final meeting of Utah's shareholders.

At the beginning of that momentous meeting, forty shares of Utah stock, purchased in 1900 for $4,000, had multiplied through stock splits and stock dividends to equal 1,289,360 shares. After the merger vote, at $68.25 each, those same forty shares were worth $87,998,820. Calculated a different way, a dollar invested in the Utah Construction Company in 1900 had grown to almost $22,000 by the end of 1976. This, of course, did not include cash dividends paid to investors during more than three-quarters of a century of busy, turbulent, and prosperous years of the company's operation. However, there was even much more growth to come.

In October 1991, when Littlefield dedicated the David Eccles School of Business at the University of Utah, he pointed out that the total value of all the General Electric shares received by Utah shareholders from the merger was "$11.5 billion today and the dividends received amount to $335 million annually. This alone is 89 percent more than our highest earnings before the merger." Littlefield himself (as of 1984) owned or served as trustee over 2,736,738 shares of General Electric stock. Contemplating all this paper wealth, Littlefield added, "It sure beats working."

Note on Sources

The single most important resource the authors mined while researching this history is the voluminous archival record of Utah Construction/Utah International. During the major period of research, the company archives, containing more than three hundred boxes of documents and a half million photographs, were housed at corporate headquarters at 550 California Street in San Francisco. They are now open for scholarly research in the Special Collections Department of the Stewart Library at Weber State University in Ogden, Utah. Copies of the register and index can be accessed electronically at http://library.weber.edu/ucc. Unless otherwise noted, all references in this essay to corporate documents, both primary and secondary, are references to materials now located at the Stewart Library.

The present study also drew upon a considerable number of other primary resources related to Utah's history that reside at the Stewart Library, including the David Eccles Papers and the Dee Family Papers. Additionally, the Marriott Library at the University of Utah houses important holdings relating to the company's principals, most significantly collections of papers of David Eccles and the extensive Marriner S. Eccles Collection. Other primary sources the authors consulted in their research are housed at the Utah State Historical Society, the Lee Library at Brigham Young University, and the Merrill Library at Utah State University.

Beyond materials in the company archives, the history of the founding of the company and antecedent events derives largely from secondary studies (listed here and in the Selected Bibliography) and from private collections of reminiscences and unpublished personal and family histories. Of particular help in this last regard were personal collections of photos, clippings, letters, and memorabilia of Dorothy Bowman Hetzel, Patricia McNamara, Helen Jarman, Mattie Wattis Harris, Marguerite Louise Heydt, Sharon Ruth Hite Lewis, James William Hite, Marilyn Harris Hite, Henry Harris Hite, and Earl Corey. Obituaries and newspaper articles from the archives of the Ogden *Standard-Examiner* were likewise invaluable as were Weber County probate records and abstracts of titles, and various editions of the *Ogden City Directory*. W. Dee Halverson, *The Wattis Family History (1710–1934)* (Salt Lake City: Heritage Associates, Ltd., 1994), and Leland Cutler, *Early Life of E.O. Wattis* (privately published, ca. 1930), provided wonderful data on two of the company's founders, while Harold R. Schindler, *Orrin Porter Rockwell: Man of God, Son of Thunder* (Salt Lake City: University of Utah Press,1966; second edition, 1983), glimpsed the arrival in Utah of their pioneer father. Information on the company's major founding investors came principally from the Dee Family History, in private circulation through Thomas D. Dee III, and Leonard J. Arrington, *David Eccles: Pioneer Western Industrialist* (Logan: Utah State University Press, 1975).

After the founding of the company in 1900, minutes of various company meetings, in particular Minutes of Meetings of the Board of Directors and Minutes of Shareholders Meetings (housed in the Broken Hill Proprietary offices in Houston), along with internal communications and annual and quarterly reports, formed the essential core of research materials. Additionally crucial to understanding the first several decades of the Utah story were two in-house studies of company history: E.R. Lubbers, "An Indexed History of Utah Construction & Mining Co.," 1962–64 (5 volumes), and John McInerney, "Memoranda on Company History," 1974 (7 volumes). Reminiscences, letters, and clippings in the possession of Paul Wattis, Sr., Patricia McNamara (the Lawler letters), Edna Wattis Fretwell, Edna Wattis Dumke, and Barbara Wattis Kimball Browning served as invaluable references to much of the story during the first half of the twentieth century. Typescripts of "The Reminiscences of Lester S. Corey" (ca. 1954) and "Family Recollections of Edna Wattis Dumke" (ca. 1977) shed much light on behind-the-scenes activities during the halcyon days. Always useful throughout, but particularly for the early years, were local newspapers such as the *Daily Astorian* (Oregon), *The Salt Lake Tribune, Deseret News*, and the Ogden *Standard-Examiner*. Among secondary materials that offered excellent insight were the many volumes available on western railroad building (see Selected Bibliography). David F. Myrick's collection of books and his incredible knowledge of railroad building, particularly in Nevada, filled a number of holes. Alfred E. Perlman, *Western Pacific Railroad, "The Feather River Route"* (New York: The Newcomen Society of North America, 1975), provided an excellent narrative of that adventure.

Much has been written on the Hoover Dam project. Among the most informative was William H. Gates, *Hoover Dam, Including the Story of the Turbulent Colorado River* (Las Vegas: Hoover Dam Scenic Corporation, 1982). The Utah Construction/Utah International Collection includes records of Six Companies, particularly the Minutes of the Executive Committee of Six Companies, which reveal the inner workings of the joint venture. Extensive interviews with Johnny Horrigan and Irma Hogan brought color into the account and were of great value, as were insightful memoranda and letters of reminiscence, written by such company insiders as Marriner S. Eccles. Industry periodicals, such as *The Constructor, Western Construction News, Roads and Streets, The Earth Mover*, and *Electrical West* ran numerous articles on the engineering marvel and its impact on the West. Clippings from newspapers all over the country, found in the company archives, lent important contemporary viewpoints and commentary on the project. Also important to the Hoover Dam chapter were corporate histories and other materials relating to Utah's partners in the venture, including Morrison Knudsen, Kaiser, and Bechtel corporations. Of less importance but containing useful data were the publications on the dam produced by the Bureau of Reclamation.

After the 1930s, a company newsletter entitled *Utah Reports* became increasingly valuable, providing almost a chronological history of the company. Combined with the Lubbers and McInerney histories, a comprehensive outline of events and a compendium of data readily came forth to elaborate the story of the company's growth into the heady 1950s and '60s. At that point in the narrative, the letters, oral interviews, and speeches of Edmund W. Littlefield gathered by the authors became the central resource for comprehending the remarkable evolution of the company into a multinational giant. These Littlefield materials are extensive, well-referenced, and eventually will be available for research in the WSU Stewart Library Special Collections Department.

Each of the topical chapters relied heavily on oral interviews with company principals, such as Charles Travers on dredging and land development, but it was also necessary to resort to contemporary publications. The exploration of Utah's move into the international mining business, and the Peruvian adventure, benefitted greatly from such periodicals as the *Peruvian Times, The Tex Report, Iron Age, Metal Bulletin, American Metal Market, The Japan Commerce Daily, Skillings Mining Review*, the DuPont Research Department's *Investment Values for Today*, and *The Wall Street Journal*. In addition, Sterling Sessions was dean of the Stanford-administered Escuela de Administración de Negocios, a graduate school of business in Lima, Peru, from 1966–68, and became personally familiar with Utah's operations and personnel in that country. Such company publications as the Marcona Corporation Progress Reports (1967–72), *Twenty Years of Growth Through Innovation* (San Francisco: Marcona Corporation, 1972), and *Nationalization of Marcona Mining Company Peruvian Branch by the Revolutionary Military Government of Peru* (San Francisco: Marcona Corporation, 1975) were invaluable. W. D. Leonard, "Marcona Mining Company History," *Utah Construction Company Mining and Metallurgical Operations* (Confidential Memorandum, 30 April 1958), served as an excellent preliminary guide to composing the Marcona chapter.

The Annual Reports of the Lucky Mc Uranium Corporation (1955–59), as well as the Prospectus of the Lucky Mc Uranium Corporation (January 5, 1960), enriched the account of Utah's domestic mining scene, as did various publications of the Cyprus Mines Corporation and Pima Copper. Numerous articles in *Business Week* were particularly valuable in chronicling this portion of the company's postwar diversification. David Lavender, *The Story of Cyprus Mines Corporation* (San Marino, CA: The Huntington Library, 1962) thoroughly covered that ground. In addition to sources already listed in this essay, the Farmington (NM) *Daily Times, Utah International Resource Review* (General Electric, 1978), and *Coal Gasification: A New Alternative in Clean Energy Production* (Farmington, NM: Western Gasification Company, ca. 1977), added significantly to the Navajo Mine chapter.

The account of Utah's early ventures into Australia drew heavily on Chapter 2 of Alan Tensgrove, *Discovery: Stories of Modern Mineral Exploration* (Victoria, Queensland: Stockwell Press, 1979). R.I.J. Agnew, "Mount Goldsworthy Iron Ore," *Mining Magazine* (Dec. 1966), 433–437, provided excellent information on that project, as did the pamphlet *Goldsworthy Mining Limited* (Victoria, Queensland: Frank Daniels Pty. Ltd., n.d.). Periodicals such as *Mining Review, The Japanese Echo, Forbes*, and *Metals Bulletin* supplemented primary materials in the corporate archives to flesh out the story of Utah's iron and coal mining activities in the Land Down Under.

The historic merger of the company with General Electric created a climactic and culminating event for the story better than any fiction writer could have imagined. In addition to Sterling Sessions's firsthand observation of the shareholders' meeting in which the union was consummated, a two-volume study in the Collection, and articles in the *San Francisco Chronicle* and *The Wall Street Journal* complemented the recollections of other participants in the merger to make the final chapter of the present study come to life.

Bibliography

Adams, John A. *Damming the Colorado: The Rise of the Lower Colorado River Authority, 1933–1939*. College Station: Texas A&M University Press, 1990.

Adams, Stephen B. *Mr. Kaiser Goes to Washington: The Rise of a Government Entrepreneur*. Chapel Hill: University of North Carolina Press, 1997.

Ahmad, Nafis. *An Economic Geography of East Pakistan*. 2nd ed. New York: Oxford University Press, 1968.

Aitkin, Don. *Stability and Change in Australian Politics*. New York: St. Martin's Press, 1977.

Akinsanya, Adeoye A. *The Expropriation of Multinational Property in the Third World*. New York: Praeger, 1980.

Arrington, Leonard J. "David Eccles: A Man for His Time." *Journal of Mormon History* 1999 25(2): 1–10.

———. *David Eccles: Pioneer Western Industrialist*. Logan: Utah State University Press, 1975.

———. *The Richest Hole on Earth: A History of the Bingham Copper Mine*. Logan: Utah State University Press, 1963.

———, and Barrett, Gwynn. "Stopping a Run on a Bank: First Security Bank and the Great Depression of the 1930's." *Idaho Yesterdays* 1970/71 14(4): 2–11.

Bain, David H. *Empire Express: Building the First Transcontinental Railroad*. New York: Viking, 1999.

Barber, Phyllis. *And the Desert Shall Blossom*. Salt Lake City: University of Utah Press, 1991.

Barrett, Glen. "Reclamation's New Deal for Heavy Construction: M-K in the Great Depression." *Idaho Yesterdays* 1978 22(3): 21–27.

Berglund, Abraham. *The United States Steel Corporation: A Study of the Growth and Influence of Combination in the Iron and Steel Industry*. New York: AMS Press, 1968.

Bergsten, C. Fred. *American Multinationals and American Interests*. Washington: Brookings Institution, 1978.

Berlow, Lawrence H. *Famous Engineering Landmarks of the World*. Phoenix: Oryx Press, 1998.

Bonny, J. B. *Morrison Knudsen Company, Inc.: "Fifty Years of Construction Progress."* New York: Newcomen Society in North America, 1962.

Borth, Christy. *Mankind on the Move: The Story of Highways*. Washington: Automotive Safety Foundation, 1969.

Bowman, Nora Linjer. *Only the Mountains Remain*. Caldwell, ID: Caxton, 1958.

Brandenburg, Frank Ralph. *The Making of Modern Mexico*. Englewood Cliffs, NJ: Prentice-Hall, 1964.

Brash, Donald T. *American Investment in Australian Industry*. Cambridge: Harvard University Press, 1966.

Brookings Institution. Institute for Government Research. *The U.S. Reclamation Service: Its History, Activities, and Organization*. New York: AMS Press, 1974.

Buckley, Peter J., and Ghauri, Pervez N. *The Global Challenge for Multinational Enterprises: Managing Increasing Interdependence*. New York: Pergamon, 1999.

Cahill, Marie, and Paide, Lynne. *The History of the Union Pacific: America's Great Transcontinental Railroad*. New York: Crescent Books, 1989.

Carman, Gary. "The Evolution of Compensatory Fiscal Policy During the Depression Era." *Essays in Economic and Business History* 1991 9: 128–140.

Clements, Kendrick A. "Engineers and Conservationists in the Progressive Era." *California History* 1979–80 58(4): 282–303.

Coates, Kenneth S., ed. *The Alaska Highway, Papers of the 40th Anniversary Symposium*. Vancouver: University of British Columbia Press, 1985.

———, and Morrison, W. R. *The Alaska Highway in World War II: The U.S. Army of Occupation in Canada's Northwest*. Norman: University of Oklahoma Press, 1992.

Cooke, Alistair. *America*. New York: Alfred A. Knopf, 1973.

Crowley, Francis Keble. *A New History of Australia*. New York: Heinemann, 1974.

Cutler, Leland. *Early Life of E.O. Wattis*. Privately Published, ca. 1930.

Denfeld, D. Colt. "How World War II Bases Were Built Fast—and Good!" *Journal of the Council on America's Military Past* 1991 18(1): 24–31.

Dias, Ric A. "'Built to Serve the Growing West': Kaiser Steel Corporation, the Federal Government, and Regional Development." *Journal of the West* 1999 38(4): 57–64.

Ditzel, Paul. "A Dam Site: Better Than an Unleashed River." *Westways* 1976 68(11): 50–53, 82–83.

Dunar, Andrew J. and McBride, Dennis. *Building Hoover Dam: An Oral History of the Great Depression*. New York: Twayne, 1993.

Eccles, George S. *First Security Corporation: The First Fifty Years, 1928–78*. New York: Newcomen Society in North America, 1978.

Eccles, Marriner Stoddard. *Beckoning Frontiers: Public and Personal Recollections*. New York: Knopf, 1951.

———. *Economic Balance and a Balanced Budget: Public Papers of Marriner S. Eccles*. New York: Harper & Brothers, 1940.

Eccles, Stewart B. *The Eccles Family of Utah*. Salt Lake City: Eccles Family Organization, 1975.

Edwards, John. *Australia's Economic Revolution*. Sydney: University of New South Wales Press, 2000.

Espeland, Wendy Nelson. *The Struggle for Water: Politics, Rationality, and Identity in the American Southwest*. Chicago: University of Chicago Press, 1998.

Ferrell, Mallory Hope. *Rails, Sagebrush and Pine: A Garland of Railroad and Logging Days in Oregon's Sumpter Valley*. San Marino, CA: Golden West, 1967.

Fitzgerald, Roosevelt. "Blacks and the Boulder Dam Project." *Nevada Historical Society Quarterly* 1981 24(3): 255–260.

Fleming, Thomas. "The Race to Promontory." *American History Illustrated* 1971 6(3): 10–25.

Foster, Mark S. "Five Decades of Development: Henry J. Kaiser and the Western Environment, 1917–1967." *Journal of the West* 1987 26(3): 59–67.

———. "Giant of the West: Henry J. Kaiser and Regional Industrialization, 1930–1950." *Business History Review* 1985 59(1): 1–23.

———. *Henry J. Kaiser: Builder in the Modern American West.* Austin: University of Texas Press, 1989.

Gates, William H. *Hoover Dam, Including the Story of the Turbulent Colorado River.* Las Vegas: Hoover Dam Scenic Corporation, 1982.

Gilpin, Laura. *The Enduring Navaho.* Austin: University of Texas Press, 1968.

Girvan, Norman. *Corporate Imperialism: Conflict and Expropriation: Transnational Corporations and Economic Nationalism in the Third World.* White Plains, NY: M.E. Sharpe, 1976.

Goldsworthy, Harry E. "ICBM Site Activation." *Aerospace Historian* 1982 29(3): 154–161.

Goodrich, H. C. "Boulder Dam: A Talk Given by Mr. H. C. Goodrich Before a Meeting of the Utah Society of Engineers, March 18, 1931." Typescript, Western Americana Collection, Marriott Library, University of Utah.

Grey, Alan H. "Roads, Railways, and Mountains: Getting Around in the West." *Journal of the West* 1994 33(3): 35–44.

Grey, Zane. *Boulder Dam.* New York: Harper & Row, 1963.

Griswold, Wesley S. *A Work of Giants: Building the First Transcontinental Railroad.* New York: McGraw-Hill, 1962.

Hainsworth, Brad. "Utah State Elections, 1916–1924." Unpublished dissertation, University of Utah, 1968.

Halverson, W. Dee. *The Wattis Family History, 1710–1934.* Salt Lake City: Heritage Associates, Ltd., 1994.

Harley, C. Knick. "Oligopoly Agreement and the Timing of American Railroad Construction." *Journal of Economic History* 1982 42(4): 797–823.

Heiner, Albert P. *Henry J. Kaiser—American Empire Builder: An Insider's View.* New York: Lang, 1989.

Hundley, Norris, Jr. *Water and the West: The Colorado River Compact and the Politics of Water in the American West.* Berkeley: University of California, 1975.

Hunter, Milton R. *Beneath Ben Lomond's Peak: A History of*

Weber County, 1824–1900. 5th Ed. Salt Lake City: Quality Press, 1995.

Hyman, Sidney. *Challenge and Response: The First Security Corporation, The First Fifty Years, 1928–78.* Salt Lake City: University of Utah Graduate School of Business, 1978.

———. *Marriner S. Eccles: Private Entrepreneur and Public Servant.* Stanford, CA: Stanford University Graduate School of Business, 1976.

Ingersoll-Rand Company. *The Story of the Hoover Dam.* Las Vegas: Nevada Publications, 1985.

Israelsen, L. Dwight. "Marriner S. Eccles, Chairman of the Federal Reserve Board." *American Economic Review* 1985 75(2): 357–362.

Iverson, Peter. "Hohokam, Hoover Dam, Hayden: Indians, Water and Power in the West." *American Indian Quarterly* 1988 12(4): 329–332.

Kelly, James E., Park, William R., and Lake, Herbert E. *The Dam Builders.* Reading, MA: Addison-Wesley, 1977.

Kendell, Timothy. *A Brief History of Uintah, Weber County, Utah, 1850–1934.* Uintah: n.p., 1934.

Krakauer, John. "Ice, Mosquitoes and Muskeg: Building the Road to Alaska. *Smithsonian* 1992 23(4): 102–111.

Lanks, Herbert Charles. *Highway to Alaska.* New York: D. Appleton-Century, 1944.

Larson, Gustive O. "Bulwark of the Kingdom: Utah's Iron and Steel Industry." *Utah Historical Quarterly* 1963 31(3): 248–261.

Lavender, David. *The Story of Cyprus Mines Corporation.* San Marino, CA: The Huntington Library, 1962.

Lear, Linda J. "Boulder Dam: A Crossroads in Natural Resource Policy." *Journal of the West* 1985 24(4): 82–94.

Levy, Jerrold E. "Who Benefits from Energy Resource Development: The Special Case of Navajo Indians." *Social Science Journal* 1980 17(1): 1–17.

Littlefield, Edmund Wattis. *As I Remember.* Indian Wells, CA: privately printed, 1997.

Lowitt, Richard. "More Power to You: Columbia River Development in the 1930s." *Columbia* 1998–99 12(4): 4–10.

McCartney, Laton. *Friends in High Places: The Bechtel Story, the*

Most Secret Corporation and How It Engineered the World. New York: Simon & Schuster, 1988.

Macintyre, Stuart. *A Concise History of Australia*. New York: Cambridge University Press, 1999.

Magaziner, Henry J. "The Rebirth of an Engineering Landmark." *APT Bulletin* [Canada] 1986 18(4): 52–64.

May, Dean Lowe. "New Deal to New Economics: The Response of Henry Morgenthau, Jr. and Marriner S. Eccles to the Recession of 1937." Unpublished dissertation, Brown University, 1974.

Menzel, Donald C. and Edgmon, Terry D. "The Struggle to Implement a National Surface Mining Policy." *Publius* 1980 10(1): 81–91.

Moler, Eleanor S. *Building a Dynasty: The Story of the Thomas D. Dee Family*. Ogden: n.p., 1987.

Morrell, Elaine. "Before They Drove the Golden Spike." *Journal of the West* 1991 30(4): 78–81.

Myrick, David. *Railroads of Nevada and Eastern California: The Northern Railroads*. Reno: University of Nevada Press

Ogden First National Bank. *First National Bank and First Savings Bank: Fifty-two Years of Leadership, 1875–1927*. Salt Lake City: Stevens and Wallis, 1927.

Perlman, Alfred E. *Western Pacific Railroad, "The Feather River Route."* New York: The Newcomen Society of North America, 1975.

Peterson, F. Ross, and Parson, Robert E. *Ogden City: Its Governmental Legacy, A Sesquicentennial History*. Ogden: Chapelle, 2001.

Peterson, Otis. "The Story of a Bureau." *Journal of the West* 1968 7(1): 84–95.

Pike, Fredrick B. *The Modern History of Peru*. New York: Praeger, 1967.

Pope, C. L. *Switchback to the Timber: A History of the Mt. Hood Railroad and the Oregon Lumber Company*. Hood River, OR: Old Forester Publisher, 1992.

Remley, David A. *Crooked Road: The Story of the Alaska Highway*. American Trails Series. A.B. Guthrie, Jr., ed. New York: McGraw-Hill, 1976.

Rhodes, Benjamin D. "From Cooksville to Chungking: The Dam-Designing Career of John L. Savage." *Wisconsin Magazine of History* 1989 72(4): 243–272.

Ringholz, Raye Carleson. *Uranium Frenzy: Boom and Bust on the Colorado Plateau.* Albuquerque: University of New Mexico Press, 1991.

Robbins, William G. "Franklin D. Roosevelt and the Emergence of the Modern West." *Journal of the West* 1995 34(2): 43–48.

Roberts, Richard C., and Sadler, Richard W. *Ogden: Junction City.* Northridge, CA: Windsor Publications in cooperation with the Ogden Area Chamber of Commerce, 1985.

Robinson, Guy M. *Australia and New Zealand : Economy, Society and Environment.* New York: Oxford University Press, 2000.

Rocha, Guy Louis. "The IWW and the Boulder Canyon Project: The Final Death Throes of American Syndicalism." *Nevada Historical Society Quarterly* 1978 21(2): 3–24.

Rohe, Randall. "Man and the Land: Mining's Impact in the Far West." *Arizona and the West* 1986 28(4): 299–338.

Ronda, James P. *Astoria and Empire.* Lincoln: University of Nebraska Press, 1990.

Rugman, Alan M. *Inside the Multinationals: The Economics of Internal Markets.* New York: Columbia University Press, 1981.

Sadler, Richard W., and Roberts, Richard C. *A History of Weber County.* Salt Lake City: Utah Historical Society, 1997.

———. *Weber County's History.* Ogden: Weber County Commission, 2000.

Schindler, Harold R. *Orrin Porter Rockwell: Man of God, Son of Thunder.* Salt Lake City: University of Utah Press, 1966.

Sigmund, Paul E. *Multinationals in Latin America: The Politics of Nationalization.* Madison: University of Wisconsin Press, 1980.

Sill, Van Rensselaer. *American Miracle: The Story of War Construction Around the World.* New York: Odyssey Press, 1947.

Slater, Robert I. *Jack Welch and the GE Way.* New York: McGraw-Hill, 1999.

———. *The New GE: How Jack Welch Revived an American Institution.* Homewood, IL: Business One Irwin, 1993.

Smith, Edward Ellis, and Riggs, Durward S., eds. *Land Use, Open Space, and the Government Process: The San Francisco Bay Area Experience, A Study*. New York: Praeger, 1974.

Sobel, Robert. *N.Y.S.E.: A History of the New York Stock Exchange, 1935–1975*. New York: Weybright and Talley, 1975.

Starr, Kevin. "Watering the Land: The Colorado River Project." *Southern California Quarterly* 1993 75(3–4): 303–332.

Stevens, Joseph E. "Building a Dream: Hoover Dam: The West's Biggest Adventure."*American West* 1984 21(4): 16–27.

———. *Hoover Dam: An American Adventure*. Norman: University of Oklahoma Press, 1988.

Stone, Peter Bennet. *Japan Surges Ahead: The Story of an Economic Miracle*. New York: Praeger, 1969.

Sutton, Imre. "Geographical Aspects of Construction Planning: Hoover Dam Revisited." *Journal of the West* 1968 7(3): 301–344.

Swain, Donald C. "The Bureau of Reclamation and the New Deal, 1933–1940." *Pacific Northwest Quarterly* 1970 61(3): 137–146.

Taylor, Raymond W. *Uranium Fever: Or, No Talk Under $1 Million*. New York: Macmillan, 1970.

Tensgrove, Alan. *Discovery: Stories of Modern Mineral Exploration*. Victoria, Queensland: Stockwell Press, 1979.

Thomas, Myrelle Eccles. *Our Eccles Family*. Salt Lake City: n.p., 1996.

Thompson, David. *Nevada: A History of Changes*. Reno: Grace Dangberg Foundation, 1986.

Tugendhat, Christopher. *The Multinationals*. London: Eyre and Spottiswoode, 1971.

Twichell, Heath. *Northwest Epic: The Building of the Alaska Highway*. New York: St. Martin's, 1992.

Warne, William E. *The Bureau of Reclamation*. Praeger Library of U.S. Government Departments and Agencies, no. 34. New York: Praeger, 1973.

Wattis, Phyllis C. *The Life Cycle of a Personal Foundation, 1958–88*. Berkeley: Bancroft Library Regional Oral History Program, 1991.

———. *An Oral History Interview with Phyllis C. Wattis.* Ogden: Stewart Library, Weber State University, 2002.

Weeks, John. *Limits to Capitalist Development: The Industrialization in Peru, 1950–1980.* Boulder, CO: Westview Press, 1985.

Welch, Jack, with Byrne, John A. *Jack: Straight From the Gut.* New York: Warner Business Books, 2001.

White, Jean Bickmore. "The Right to Be Different: Ogden and Weber County Politics, 1850–1924." *Utah Historical Quarterly* 1979 47(3): 254–272.

Williams, Griffith H. "Alaska's Connection: The Alcan Highway." *Pacific Northwest Quarterly.* 1985 76(2): 61–68.

Williams, John Hoyt. *A Great and Shining Road: The Epic Story of the Transcontinental Railroad.* Lincoln: University of Nebraska Press, 1996.

Willingham, William F. *Water Power in the "Wilderness": The History of Bonneville Lock and Dam.* Portland, OR: U.S. Army Corps of Engineers, 1987.

Wilson, Alexander M. *Leading a Changing Utah Construction and Mining Company, Utah International, GE–Utah, and BHP–Utah, 1954–87.* Berkeley: Bancroft Library Regional Oral History Program, 2000.

Wilson, Neill C., and Taylor, Frank J. *The Earth Changers.* Garden City, NY: Doubleday, 1957.

Wilson, Richard Guy. "Machine-Age Iconograph in the American West: The Design of Hoover Dam." *Pacific Historical Review* 1985 54(4): 463–493.

Wolf, Donald E. *Big Dams and Other Dreams: The Six Companies Story.* Norman: University of Oklahoma Press, 1996.

Woodcock, James Thorpe, and Radmanovich, M. *Broken Hill Mines.* Melbourne: Australasian Institute of Mining and Metallurgy, 1968.

Yamazawa, Ippei. *Economic Development and International Trade: The Japanese Model.* Honolulu: Resource Systems Institute, East-West Center, 1990.

Index

(Photographs are italicized)

This book
is
Number

____

of a
Commemorative Edition
of six hundred copies
published by
Weber State University
and the
Stewart Library

October 9, 2002.

UTAH CONSTRUCTION
& MINING CO.